Europeanizing Montenegro

Europeanizing Montenegro

The European Union, the Rule of Law, and Regional Cooperation

Vladimir Vučković

LEXINGTON BOOKS
Lanham • Boulder • New York • London

Published by Lexington Books
An imprint of The Rowman & Littlefield Publishing Group, Inc.
4501 Forbes Boulevard, Suite 200, Lanham, Maryland 20706
www.rowman.com

86-90 Paul Street, London EC2A 4NE, United Kingdom

British Library Cataloguing in Publication Information Available

Library of Congress Cataloging-in-Publication Data Is Available

ISBN: 978-1-7936-0775-1 (cloth)
ISBN: 978-1-7936-0776-8 (electronic)

To My Son Bodin

Contents

List of Tables

List of Abbreviations

AACI	Agency for Anti-Corruption Initiative
AII	Adriatic and Ionian Initiative
BIH	Bosnia and Herzegovina
CAACI	Commission and Agency for Anti-Corruption Initiative
CCCC	China Communications Construction Company
CEE	Central and Eastern Europe
CEFTA	Central European Free Trade Agreement
CEI	Central European Initiative
CEPEJ	European Commission for the Efficiency of Justice
CIETAC	China International Economic and Trade Arbitration Commission
CoE	Council of Europe
CPC	Criminal Procedure Code
CPCI	Commission for the Prevention of Conflict of Interest
CRBS	China Road and Bridge Cooperation
CSOs	Civil society organizations
CVM	Cooperation and Verification Mechanism
DACI	Directorate for Anti-Corruption Initiative
DF	Democratic Front
DPS	Democratic Party of Socialists
EU	European Union
FYROM	Former Yugoslav Republic of Macedonia
ICJ	International Court of Justice
ICTY	International Criminal Tribunal for the Former Yugoslavia
IMF	International Monetary Fund
IPA	Instruments for Pre-accession Assistance
JTC	Judicial Training Centre

MARRI	Migration, Asylum, Refugees Regional Initiatives
MED	Mediterranean program
MTMAM	Ministry of Transport and Maritime Affairs of Montenegro
NGOs	Nongovernmental organizations
NPI	National Program for Integration
OBOR	One Belt, One Road initiative
OSCE	Organization for Security and Co-operation in Europe
PRIS	Judicial Information System
RACVIAC	Centre for Security Cooperation
RCBS	Regional and Cross-Border Cooperation
RCC	Regional Cooperation Council
RoL	Rule of Law
RYCO	Regional Youth Cooperation Office
SAI	State Auditing Institution
SAP	Stabilization and Association Process
SEC	State Election Commission
SECI	South-East European Cooperation Initiative
SEECP	South-East European Cooperation Process
SEES	South-East European Space
SIT	Special Investigation Team
SAA	Stabilization and Association Agreement
TCE	Treaty establishing a Constitution for Europe
TOBB	Union of Turkish Business and Chambers of Commerce
UNDP	United Nation Development Program
WB6	Western Balkan Six
WBCIF	Western Balkans Chambers Investment Forum
WBF	Western Balkans Funds

Acknowledgments

I express my sincere appreciation to many colleagues and friends that unconditionally supported me throughout the entire journey. Primarily, I owe my deep gratitude to my supervisor Professor Vít Hloušek for his endless assistance, brilliant supervision, creative ideas, and quick feedback. This book is a product of fruitful cooperation with Professor Hloušek during doctoral studies, and I cannot be more than thankful to him and his commitment, patience, and encouragement to complete this volume in a timely manner. I emphasize my gratefulness to Associate Professor Hans Agné from the University of Stockholm with whom I closely worked during my study period abroad supported by the Swedish Institute (SI). His priceless ideas and remarkable comments represent an important contribution to the completion of the judicial reform chapter.

I demonstrate my special thanks to colleagues Professor Branislav Radeljić and Lecturer Marko Stojić for being excellent reviewers. Their professionalism together with a number of valuable remarks and insightful suggestions made my book substantially better. I am very grateful for all your efforts. Also, I express my deep affection to anonymous reviewers for their quality comments used to finalize the work.

And finally, I am deeply thankful to my wife Mirjana, and my mother and father Vera and Zoran, and my sister Ana for all these years believing me and being supportive from the beginning to the very end in writing and completing the book. None of this would have been possible without your support.

Vladimir Vučković, Brno, September 2020

Chapter 1

Introduction

Like all Western Balkan countries, Montenegro has defined integration into the European Union (EU) as its main strategic and foreign policy priority (Skupština Crne Gore 2013; Keil and Stahl 2014, 180). Shortly after the dissolution of the State Union of Serbia and Montenegro in 2006 and up to current times, Montenegro has made evident progress in addressing the Copenhagen criteria and complying with the acquis communautaire (acquis). As a result, Montenegro has positioned itself as the regional frontrunner among all Western Balkan states in the EU integration process. As of June 30, 2020, thirty three negotiating chapters have been opened. These include Chapter 23—Judiciary and fundamental rights, and Chapter 24—Justice, freedom and security, both on the rule of law. Out of the 33, three chapters (25—Science and research, 26—Education and culture, and 30—External relations) have been provisionally closed (Delegation of the European Union to Montenegro 2020a).

The rapid advancement of Montenegro in the accession process has been continuously monitored and supported by high-ranking EU officials. Oft-heard statements by the former EU Ambassador to Montenegro, Leopold Maurer, as well as the European Parliament Rapporteur on Montenegro, Charles Tannock, highlighting that the country remained the "regional EU integration leader," a "good news story," and a "success European story through overall progress in the negotiations, and more importantly, through reforms in the areas of rule of law and the fight against corruption and organised crime" have remained a testament to Montenegrin success (Maurer 2008; Tannock 2013; European Conservatives and Reformist Group—ECRG 2017). Similar claims to the state's progress was emphasized, for instance, by Federica Mogherini, high representative/vice president, in her speech addressing the Parliament of Montenegro in March 2017, stating that during the past decade Montenegro has made incredible progress. Additionally, Jean-Claude

Juncker, European Commission president, during his visit in February 2018, highlighted the country's substantial efforts in the field of European integration, noting that it had progressed faster than other countries of the region thanks to the serious reform that had been implemented (EU External Action 2017; Delegation of the European Union to Montenegro 2018b).

From gaining its independence to the present, Montenegro has made rapid progress in the European integration process as a result of two lucky factors: the status of the country, which is not contested either externally or internally, and the unanimous consensus of all political parties on the EU membership issue (Keil 2013, 350). Still, Montenegrin advancement in the accession process does not seem to depend on the capacity of domestic actors to induce governmental structural changes. Rather, it is a completely driven project in which the EU has positioned itself as a major actor of domestic change (Keil and Arkan 2015, 83). In line with the definition of Europeanization of candidate countries as an EU politically driven process in which EU policymaking processes, institutions, and legal systems impact domestic rules and laws, policies, institutional mechanisms, and actor behavior in non-EU member states, scholars within Europeanization and EU studies have been united in the common belief that the EU-externally driven pressure imposed by the conditional policy has overall resulted in a limited impact on domestic changes in Montenegro (Kmezić 2017, 5). By using the external incentive models as a tool of transformative power, the EU has adversely affected the process of democratization and consolidation of statehood in Montenegro, and slightly empowered institutional capacities to comply with the EU norms and rules. The EU transformative power has already been seen in only two instances regarding Montenegro: the visa liberalization process, so far the strongest conditionality mechanism toward the Western Balkans, and recommendations stipulated in the EU's Opinion of Montenegro's preparedness for EU membership (Keil and Arkan 2015, 96; Radeljić 2013, 125). However, the Montenegrin political elite have often used EU initiatives (policies and institutions) to ensure the survival of the current governing elites, to promote their own party programs, and to satisfy voters to get enough votes to remain in power. The extent to which the EU and domestic initiatives have influenced each other largely depends on the salience of certain EU policies (judicial reform, rule of law, corruption and organized crime, etc.) for voters. In the absence of public interest in certain EU policies, norms, and rules, the EU is expected to have limited impact on domestic institutional and policy change in Montenegro (Börzel and Risse 2012, 200; Keil and Arkan 2015, 9).

Unlike the praise of EU officials of Montenegro as "champions of EU integration," and also theoretical claims of limited effects on Europeanization of the candidate country, I argue that the EU has essentially failed to exercise pressure over Montenegro to comply with the political conditions in the accession process. Correspondingly, this study is based on the argument that EU transformative power produced negatively reinforcing effects in key accession criteria in the candidate country during the first decade of its integration process, specifically in the period between 2007 and 2017. I claim that the given deficiency of fulfillment of political conditions in Montenegro is, on the one hand, primarily the result of an inconsistent and inefficient EU conditional policy, and unfavorable domestic factors (lack of political will above all) to appropriately conduct reform activities, thus resulting in a generally weak and mitigating reform progress (Börzel and Risse 2012; Börzel 2011; Elbasani 2013; Sedelmeier 2011; Frayburg and Richter 2010; Noutcheva 2009; Noutcheva and Aydin-Düzgit 2012). In this respect, I hold the view that the EU foreign policy, in the form of the enlargement process, more likely contains characteristics of farce in the process of European integration of Montenegro. This particular point may be witnessed not only when the case of Montenegro is taken into consideration, but also when the rest of the Balkans is, in terms of the EU enlargement policy that is, analyzed.

The overall conditions under which the EU has imposed its pressure in Montenegro to address political criteria may thus be seen as an essentially faulty and uneven approach of the Union to the integration process. Arguably, this long-lasting and faulty approach of the Union toward Montenegro for more than a decade now is primarily the product of corelations between the EU and domestic factors significantly mitigating the process of effective implementation and enforcement of the EU rules and norms. On the one hand, Montenegro has been externally challenged with far more complicated, demanding, and strict accession criteria, newly proclaimed principles of EU conditionality (consolidation, conditionality, communication, integration capacity, concrete results, common values, etc.), ineffectiveness of the EU as a state-building actor, and enlargement fatigue. As a result, the EU has defined the accession process as an "open-ended process," being reluctant to provide any commitment toward a precise timetable for the accession of the country into the Union (Beiber 2011, 1785, 93; Đurović 2012, 334; Keil 2013, 349; Gateva 2015, 141–44). On the other hand, a certain set of internal problems, such as various limited statehood issues and the strong influence of autocrats and/or other veto players, have substantially restrained the EU transformative power on domestic political changes. Therefore, the combination of an enlargement process without a goal and an accession without a credible membership plan, along with the state's insufficient fulfillment of conditions due to the strong influence of veto players, is the definition of an EU charade in the EU integration process of Montenegro (Elbasani 2013, 11–14; Börzel 2011, 11; Keil and Arkan 2015, 16; Lavrič and Bieber 2020, 1–9; Samaradžić 2016, 333–34).

This sort of EU charade toward Montenegro in the accession process is particularly visible in the Union's inconsistency and ineffectiveness to impose its conditional pressure over the candidate country to effectively align with the EU requirements.[1] Following the EU's insufficient conditional policy approach, one might observe the integration tendencies of Montenegro continuing to advance in the accession process but demonstrating the political unwillingness of its ruling elites to actually fulfill the Copenhagen political criteria. Hence, the EU-externally driven pressure has applied a strategy of permissiveness during the whole integration phase by allowing the candidate country to select and tackle certain political criteria based on which the country can advance in the given integration process. Consequently, Montenegro has essentially been given the chance to selectively fulfill certain conditions by addressing easier political demands rather than harder ones (Vučković and Đorđević 2019, 177–79).

Although holding the status of regional frontrunner in the EU integration process, Montenegro is still not a system with a consolidated democracy. Rather, it can be defined as a hybrid regime with developed authoritarian mechanisms (Democracy Index 2019; Freedom House 2020, 12). As a semi-authoritarian system—which formally operates within a democratic system, according to its principles and standards, while misusing its governmental prerogatives in undermining the independent functioning of democratic institutions—it nominally commits to the EU accession process (Ottaway 2003, 3–27; Levisky and Way 2010, 5; Dolonec 2013; Ahram and Goode 2016, 834–49; Lavrič and Bieber 2020, 1–9; Kmezić 2020, 183–98, Pavlović 2019, 671–97). This semi-authoritarian rule of governance in Montenegro is primarily characterized by state capture by the ruling party, a weak and politicized judiciary and anti-corruption preventive bodies, misuse of public funds for party purposes, as well as institutionally rooted corruption, clientelism, and organized crime (Džankić 2018, 83–106; Radeljić and Đordević 2020; IA and CGO and CRNVO and CeMI 2018, 2). In fact, the thirty-year rule of the Democratic Party of Socialists of Montenegro (DPS), and its leader Milo Đukanović, has been used as a model for regional decline into semi-authoritarianism. The party has shown its ability to modify its politics to current foreign policy circumstances and, when necessary, to change its ideological position. This new type of autocratic rule of governance has created a new form of populism in the Western Balkans commonly known as "state-sponsored populism," being not populism per se, but using various populist mechanisms to preserve dominance over internal political processes and changes in society (Džankić and Keil 2017, 409–13). Đukanović has built a stable autocratic regime thanks to his infallible political instincts, smoothly adapting to new political circumstances, and carefully building its profile as a pragmatic reformist whose involvement is needed in achieving sociopolitical reforms.

The so-called stabilitocracy has been supported by the EU, allowing the semi-autocratic leader to combine both nondemocratic mechanisms with formal support for EU accession, therefore providing legitimacy to the constraint of democracy. As was the case with many autocrats in Balkans, the president of Montenegro, Milo Đukanović, has used various mechanisms to consolidate its power. These range from spreading panic to the creation of internal political crises among Montenegrin citizens. This approach has brought about many benefits for himself and his party for more than three decades, strongly relying on the well-tested recipe of sewing internal conflicts between the two most prominent ethnic groups, the Montenegrins and the Serbs, based on statehood and national identity issues, and on his ruthlessness in encouraging institutionally entrenched corruption and clientelism. However, none of the democratic backsliding in Montenegro would have been possible if the semi-authoritarian regime had not developed such effective mechanisms of rule, namely the fomenting of political crises, securing external legitimacy, capturing state and weak institutions, the spread of nationalism, control of the media, and the president's charismatic personality (Bieber 2020; BiEPAG 2017; Džankić and Keil 2017). The artificial emergence of political crises orchestrated from ruling circles aims primarily to further legitimize and strengthen its power, consequently paralyzing internal politics and processes. Once power has been consolidated through the introduction of a forced state of emergency and fear has been entrenched, efforts in locating enemies and culprits, both internal and external, who are "responsible for the endangerment of state sovereignty" become permanent. Following the case of Montenegro, the political crisis appears in the form of "overthrow of the current Government and the Constitutional order," where the creation of conditions for further polarization within society opens the opportunity for the detection of internal traitors, mostly opposition parties and critically oriented NGO's, and external enemies (Keil 2018, 59–82; Donno 2013, 703–16; Morrison 2018, 151–66; Džankić 2018, 83–100; Komar and Živković 2016, 785–99). The state of political crisis unequivocally leads to the monopolization of power and politics in the hands of the ruling party elite, thus eroding the ability of democratic safeguards (i.e., independent democratic institutions and media, etc.) to limit autocratic power.[2]

The importance of a case study of Montenegro has also become even more relevant after the introduction of the February 2018 European Commission strategy for "a credible membership perspective for and enhanced EU engagement with the Western Balkans" (European Commission 2018a). Undoubtedly, the geopolitical significance of the region for the EU has increased substantially after the growing involvement of other powers and their respective use of soft and hard power influence in the area, namely by Russia and China. For those semi-authoritarian elites from the Western

Balkans, the involvement of other regional powers and their investments is more than welcome. When viewed from the elites' perspective, policies of alternatives, unlike the "open-ended process" of the EU's conditional enlargement policy, bring more benefits because they do not call into question the political legitimacy of domestic autocrats nor do they interfere into internal politics, as was the case with the EU's asymmetrical imposition of power (Bechev 2017; Vangeli 2018). Therefore, as a result of current international political developments in the Balkans, the EU has finally decided to provide a credible membership perspective for Montenegro (as well as Serbia) by introducing a clear opportunity to join the Union by 2025, given the existence of strong political will to deliver real and sustained reforms, especially in the field of rule of law, and the resolution of open bilateral disputes with the neighboring countries.

However, although one might be certain about the Union's deficient reinforcing effects over the state's alignment with the given EU requirements, the question warranting interest and attention here is why the EU has actually created the given charade over its conditional approach toward Montenegro during the entire integration phase. An equally important question is why the Union hasn't sufficiently focused on this process in Montenegro, but in the entire Western Balkans region as well.

This study provides several assumptions which might be tested and therefore used as valuable explanations for the overall problematic process of Europeanization of Montenegro as conducted by the EU.

First, the EU has aimed to preserve legitimacy of the integration process in Montenegro and the Western Balkan states. In particular, to maintain regional political stability, the EU has been involved in the externally driven conditionality process by compliance in the Western Balkans by using a wide range of mechanisms, notably implementation of the EU-related legislation framework (alignment with the acquis), technical and financial support through the TAIEX and TWINNING projects aiming to enhance capacity-building measures, Instruments for Pre-accession Assistance (IPA), and socialization through political dialog and technical cooperation (Schimmelfennig and Sedelmeier 2005, 2; Börzel and Risse 2012, 195). However, although the EU has introduced various technical and financial assistance mechanisms to accelerate the candidate country's advancement in the accession process, its reluctance to enact a credible membership perspective, establish and specify initial and interim benchmarks, or introduce disequilibrium clauses has been reflected in the candidate country's reconsiderations of its own geopolitical and foreign policy interests. It is not rare for semi-authoritarian leaders in the Western Balkans to largely use the logic of bargaining by choosing policies of alternatives instead of opportunities, consequently opting for certain international actors who provide greater benefits than others. For instance, in the case of Serbia, the EU has established a "disequilibrium case" that can potentially postpone progress in the accession process if the normalization of relations between Belgrade and Priština becomes compromised (Gateva 2015, 124–50). As a result, Serbia, as the main regional actor, has changed its geopolitical and foreign policy position, consequently strengthening cooperation with Russia by signing a number of economic, security, and military agreements, and thus at the same time sending a clear message to the EU that its game is not the only game in town.

Second, it is quite clear the Union has kept the pretense of enlargement at the top of its foreign policy agenda due to the strong involvement of other international factors, such as Russia, in the Western Balkans region. Without any doubt, the strong historical, cultural, political, and economic influence of Russia in the Balkans, as its traditional sphere of influence, substantially raises serious concerns within the EU and its proclaimed foreign policy activities toward maintaining regional peace and stability. Given Mearsheimer's (2001) theory of neorealism as based on the concept of "offensive realism," it seems as if the EU and Russia are continuously trying to maximize their respective powers in the region by looking for opportunities at the expense of other rivals (Mearsheimer 2001, 2018; Burchill 2005; Little 2007). In other words, the Union is seeking to reduce and weaken Russian impact in the region by providing a wide range of accession advancement rewards (i.e., potential membership, signing of the Stabilization and Association Agreement [SAA] and entering it into force, granting candidate status and opening accession negotiations) and financial rewards (i.e., IPA), while on the other hand, Russia uses various soft and hard power means to destabilize the region and therefore destabilize the Union itself. Nevertheless, potential membership in the EU remained a solid leverage for the Western Balkans, especially for Montenegro and Serbia, because it has kept them under the Union umbrella of influence, mostly because Russia has been reluctant to provide the region with an alternative for achieving stability and prosperity when compared to the EU integration process. The advantage is obviously on the EU's side, since the EU external positive incentives, given the fact that Russia does not have any long-term strategy for development of its relations with the Western Balkans, are very powerful and tempting (Bechev 2017; Galeotti 2018; Mujanović 2018).

The third and final reason for maintaining the EU conditional policy is based on the claim that the Union has recognized Montenegro as an important regional factor of reconciliation as well as a reliable actor in the development of good bilateral relations with the enlargement countries and the EU member states. Indeed, these are essential conditions for moving forward in the accession process. Based on the introduced range of external incentives (rewards and threats), the EU has relied substantially on the principle of carrot instead of stick, thus aiming to improve conditions for strengthening fragile regional cooperation in the Western Balkans (Vučković and Đorđević 2019). Therefore, due to Montenegrin commitment to the development of regional cooperation and maintaining good neighborly relations, the Union has started to present Montenegro as a reliable factor of regional stability and a positive example of European integration, hence a sort of a role model in an already quite problematic region.

With all this in mind, the main aim of this study is to examine the Europeanization of Montenegro through the EU's impact on domestic governmental changes by focusing on three EU political membership conditions: judicial reform, fight against corruption, and strengthening regional cooperation and the development of good neighborly relations. This particularly means whether the EU's externally driven pressure has influenced domestic institutional and policy changes and if and under what conditions adoption of the EU rules and norms has actually resulted in domestic structural alterations. For the sake of argument, the research will scrutinize the three most prominent political conditions of the EU, all of which are stipulated in the SAA and in the new accession negotiation framework, as these are essential EU enlargement elements that will further advance Montenegro to the completion of the accession process (European Commission 2012c, 16–17, 2013b, 10–12, 2014b, 21–22, 2015b, 21–22, 2016b, 21–22)

The results of the applied analytical concept and the empirical findings will be beneficial not only for the case study of Montenegro but for the whole of the Western Balkans region as well. Primarily, and of great importance, this book is intended to provide scientific insights into whether Montenegro has truly earned its status as regional frontrunner due to its indisputable commitment to the EU accession processes, or whether it has noticeably moved forward due to the EU's permissiveness when the rest of the region, which lags substantially behind in the EU integration process, is taken into consideration. Also, following the new conditional accession approach that began in 2012, examining the case study of Montenegro will provide some explanations for the evolution of the EU enlargement conditional policy, reward-threat balance (positive-negative incentives), and advanced monitoring mechanisms as identically applied to the rest of the region due to regional political particularities. At the end, the study will also address the questions of whether and why the EU has prioritized its support of internal political stability, that is "stabilitocracy," instead of the adoption of the acquis and compliance with EU conditions, by taking into account that in most regional countries, Montenegro included, there are strong bonds between the domestic ruling elites (semi-autocracies) and the postcommunist legacy in opposing effective implementation of the political membership requirements.

STRUCTURE OF THE VOLUME

This research is split into *seven* sections and therefore organized in the following way:

In the *first section* of the book, the *introduction* is aimed at presenting the main argument of the book, the aim of the research, the main research question, and the significance of the research. In addition, the first section plays out the dilemmas of the research, the definition of the research subject, and past research contributions within the field. Based on the main research question, the book claims the EU essentially failed to induce pressure over Montenegro to comply with the political conditions in the accession process. This research argues that the enlargement process has become more like a movement without a goal and an accession without a credible membership perspective.

"Theoretical Background and Methodological Framework" is the *second section* of the book. It aims to present theoretical argumentations of Rational Institutionalism based on the logic of consequences and of Constructivist/Sociological Institutionalism based on the logic of appropriateness in the field of Europeanization provided by the Schimmelfennig and Sedelmeier theory of Europeanization. In addition, the methodological section further operationalizes the research by focusing on the single case study, direct content analysis, and normative and empirical analyses as methods of data collection.

Empirical findings are in the *third, fourth, and fifth sections* of the book ("Judicial Reform in Montenegro," "Fight against Corruption in Montenegro," and "Regional Cooperation and Developing Good Bilateral Relations with the Enlargement Countries and Member States"). In dividing each chapter into normative analysis, empirical observations and explanations, and conclusion, they offer a critical evaluation of the three membership criteria, namely, judicial reform, the fight against corruption, and strengthening regional cooperation and the development of good neighborly relations. Without any doubt, these three analytical sections represent the greatest value of the monograph, as they fill in existing gaps in the research and contribute to the existing scholarly literature.

In particular, the first parts of each section are both descriptive and analytical, providing an overview of various incentives, documents, and data originating from the EU incentive level and domestic normative response. This part is predominately covered by an analytical framework focusing on aspects of actions and reactions after Montenegrin alignment with the EU requirements. More precisely, the normative and analytical parts of the chapter(s) provide valuable insights and discussions about how certain EU initiatives came into being and what the reactions in Montenegro were, and perhaps far more importantly, what we learn from domestic responses and debates (i.e., intellectuals, policymakers, media outlets, NGOs, etc.) over the Montenegro's compliance with the EU acquis. The second parts of the chapters are fully analytical, providing empirical examinations of and explanations for why the state has (or has not) aligned with the EU conditions during the pre-negotiation and negotiation stages. Finally, the conclusion sections give an overview of the current state of Montenegro's advancement in the accession process after the accession conditions have been examined.

The *sixth section* of the book, "Discussion on Mechanisms of Europeanization Presented in the Case Study of Montenegro," is reserved for concluding remarks on the empirical results, a discussion about the applicability of the theoretical framework to the complexity of the Western Balkans, the interference of international factors in the region, primarily Russia and China, the insufficient interplay of the EU-domestic factors and the influence of Russia and China as undermining actors, as well as a final conclusion.

The *bibliography* is *the final section* of the book, comprising various primary and secondary sources.

POSITIONING THE RESEARCH AGENDA—THE RESEARCH DILEMMA

In 2005, when the French and Dutch referendum halted the adoption of the Treaty establishing a Constitution for Europe, it revealed and deepened a European crisis (Fuše 2009, 27). This crisis in EU integration has captured the attention and interest of both Europe and beyond, and it has resulted in devastating socioeconomic effects on the development of the member states. For the past fifty years, since the establishment of European projects, the process of EU integration has struggled with political and identity issues. Politically, particularly following the 2004 enlargement, there has been debate about the Union's inconsistency in deepening enlargement (sectoral) policies. This debate highlights the need to balance the policies with prospects for enlargement, sometimes at the expense of the enlargement prospects. In terms of orientation and identity, the EU has reached a point at which its values and founding treaties, its projects of peace and economic prosperity, are seen to have run their course. Therefore, the "Dutch and French no" to a new European Constitution opened a painful new chapter, spawning a wide range of various crises that have already shown their severity. From this crucial moment, the EU began to see serious structural problems (Fuše 2009, 27–33).

With the Union's failure to adopt the Constitution of Europe, numerous internal problems began to emerge and contours of new crises began to appear, such as the financial and economic crisis with particular problems in Eurozone functioning, unemployment, and public debt rising within the majority of the member states, the crisis of EU institutional functioning (problems related to institutional structure and its governance), and finally, crises of EU democratic qualities, of liberal democracy and of compromise-based decision-making and cooperation at the EU level (Rodrigues and Xiarchogiannopoulou 2014; Schweiger and Magone 2015; Ofe 2016; Zielonka 2014). Due to these comprehensive internal crises, which were highly visible and delicate as early as 2008, further development of the Union's integration agenda was postponed. The crisis primarily appeared as a financial crisis, but its important integration project—the monetary union—has shown all the vulnerabilities of the system, including in its main functions and sectoral policies. Based on their effects and their forms, these crises were not visible after the adoption of the Single European Act.[3] In fact, the process of widening (enlargement) combined with deepening sectoral policies were observed as purposeful and inevitable. The Maastricht Agreement (1993) successfully completed unification of the common market, consequently opening the prospect for further integration at the political level. The Economic and Monetary Union (EMU)—a European space with a common European currency and aligned economic policies—opened the opportunity for even greater integration. The states' cooperation in the field of security and judicial affairs, the establishment of Common Foreign and Security Policy (CFCP) and, logically, the European system of defense, only confirmed the Union's positive step forward toward further political integration. And finally, all these policies are to be implemented by the new member states based on proclamation of the successful EU enlargement policy (Samardžić 2016, 6–7).

Implementation of all integration projects has resulted in either partial or full failure. The EMU demonstrated a complete failure when the collapse of public finances and bank sectors in the majority of the member states occurred. This situation led to the severe debt crisis, the economic and financial consequences of which are still being felt by member states. The CFCP, primarily subordinate to the North Atlantic Treaty Organization (NATO), was not able to develop its own military capability strategy or its own security and defense mechanisms independent of US influence. The member states' cooperation in security and judicial affairs, which also includes integrated management of external borders, identified major deficiencies in addressing challenges of the migrant crisis. The introduction of a common visa policy, repressive states' actions against asylum seekers, transferring responsibility between member states and EU institutions, and building a physical fence between neighboring countries for the states' security reasons have shown a lack of commitment to common European values. Finally, following the outcomes of the last enlargement waves (2004, 2007, 2013), there is a substantial discrepancy between formally quantitative process of accession and the Union's capacity to absorb new member states, taking into account the complex functioning of its institutional structure, governance and decision-making procedures (Samardžić 2016, 15–24; Börzel 2016, 8–26).

All these indicators confirm that the Union is currently a system in crises. This crisis is systemic, deep, profound, and long-lasting. This being said, the reasons for the structural crisis could be elaborated in the combination of various factors. First, the EU has made a turnabout from an economic to a political concept of integration. Second, due to the effect of the turnabout, the Union still has not created another model as a replacement for economic integration. And finally, the reform of this hybrid model of integration has been in the works for more than twenty years—since the establishment of EMU and the Union's decision to continue with the massive enlargement influx of postcommunist countries. The Union has passed into an aggregate state of permanent crisis whose systemic problems require a comprehensive political and institutional reorganization by returning the integration project to its initial state of operation. Consequently, this structural crisis of the EU threatens to destroy the only healthy part of the economic integration project—the single market concept—therefore questioning the very existence of the Union (Samardžić 2016).

While the deep economic and financial collapse of the Union was seen as the main cause of the serious EU crises, it has also had a clear and profound impact on the EU enlargement process aimed at the Western Balkans. The EU financial and economic crisis of 2008 was a typical systemic problem within the Union, and as such, it was neither result of any particular EU policy nor in any way a decision of EU governing structures (BiEPAG 2016, 3; Ofe 2016, 9, 52–53). Simply, the combined crises had a profound effect on the generally negative mood of the Union in terms of further enlargement. This negative mood was significantly heightened among the EU member states due to the negative effects of the fifth wave of enlargement in both 2004 and 2007, which saw various problems in the complex functioning of institutions as well as the great burden of structural and cohesion funds on the EU itself. The EU also faced the even greater consequences of the employment policy and of labor migration from East to West (Samardžić 2016, 297–99, 333–34). The widespread enlargement fatigue among "older EU-15 Member States"[4] resulted from the belief that the reform processes in most postcommunist countries was not being effectively completed, leaving the issues of institutionally entrenched corruption and organized crime untouched. Although the Union introduced the Cooperation and Verification Mechanism against Bulgaria and Romania as a form of post-accession conditionality, the external incentive model did not bring tangible results in the area of judicial reform or in the fight against corruption and organized crime. In fact, the Commission's intention to apply targeted and differentiated conditionality by demanding six benchmarks for Bulgaria and four benchmarks for Romania to be addressed in the post-accession phase did not result in effective implementation or enforcement of EU rules and norms (Gateva 2015, 80–124; Grabbe 2006, 97–115).

Essentially, as a consequence of the negative outcomes of the previous enlargement waves, the EU has introduced a complex conditional strategy as a central part of its enlargement policy. The EU conditional policy entails a legal imposition and adoption of the EU rules and norms in domestic governing structures by following the principle of a reward-threat balance, as well as constant application of overall monitoring mechanisms aimed at assessing countries' advancement in the accession process. Under this instrument, the Union provides a reward if the target accession country aligns with the conditions, or it withholds the reward if it fails to align. Thus, the policy of conditionality demands full compliance with EU standards by aspiring countries, accompanied by a strict and precise procedure of monitoring and evaluation of each accession criterion during the whole accession phase. Through the accession conditionality, the EU has created highly asymmetrical and partially hierarchical relationships with the candidate countries by being actively engaged in the process of state building and democracy changes for which (potential) membership is to provide a key initiative (Börzel 2011, 12–15; Noutcheva 2009, 1081; Elbasani 2013, 8; Keil 2013, 348).

In comparison to previous enlargement rounds, it is evident that the EU conditional enlargement policy toward the Western Balkans has become stricter, more complex, and demanding. In that regard, the transformation of the EU enlargement conditionality toward the South-Eastern Europe is characterized by clarification and specification of a range and scope of conditions, all of which may be classified in the following way: (1) characterization of the political criteria, (2) introduction of opening and interim benchmarks, (3) transformation of the accession negotiations into an "open-ended process," and (4) introduction of the disequilibrium clauses. First, the EU has highlighted the growing relevance of the political criteria for the advancement of the enlargement process by emphasizing a full alignment with rule of law requirements (i.e., judicial reform, fight against corruption and organized crime), together with strict fulfillment of the stabilization and association process (SAP)-specific conditionality (i.e., cooperation with ICTY, regional cooperation, solving bilateral disputes, etc.). Second, the Union has introduced additional country-specific conditions as well as intensified benchmarks by highlighting the importance of meeting opening,[5] provisional closing and interim benchmarks, which emerge as an essential element of the EU enlargement strategy during all of the stages of the accession process, thus consequently transforming the dynamics of the membership talks. Third, over time, the accession negotiation framework has been transformed into an "open-ended process," which means that the EU has been opposed to setting target dates for the advancement of relations between the Union and candidate (and potential candidate) states. In other words, the Union has failed to ensure a credible membership perspective for the region due to its reluctance to provide any commitment toward a precise timetable for the accession of these countries to the Union. And finally, the Union has introduced both explicit and implicit threats, such as a wide range of preventive and remedial sanctions, that is, various EU measures in the form of suspending the implementation of SAA or postponing of membership talks, as well as the establishment of "disequilibrium cases" combined with the eroded credibility of the membership perspective that has strengthened the negative incentive structure. For instance, in the case of Serbia, the EU has established a disequilibrium clause that can potentially postpone the country's advancement in the accession process if the normalization of relations between Belgrade and Priština are compromised. The very same clause is being imposed toward Montenegro throughout the whole accession negotiation process in the event that domestic political leaders do not express political willingness to effectively address rule of law requirements (Gateva 2015, 124–73).

In line with the experience of the ongoing enlargement process, it is the EU strategy of conditional external initiatives based on "the principle of carrot and stick," which significantly undermines the Union's credibility as a normative power, and, at the same time, negatively reflects on the region's willingness and motivation to implement EU norms and rules as stipulated by the accession framework (Schimmelfennig and Sedelmeier 2005, 11; Börzel and Risse 2012, 203; Bieber 2011, 1791). The "EU enlargement fatigue" has demonstrated a discrepancy between the enlargement process and the need to deepen the Union policies (i.e., issue of widening vs. deepening), which raised questions of the so-called absorption capacity of enlargement for a certain period of time. Following the case of South-Eastern enlargement, this particularly means that the EU membership perspective of candidate (and potential candidate) countries has not changed in terms of the normative process of accession, but rather that it has changed in terms of the final goals of this process, that is, accession into the EU itself. This process has become more like a movement without a goal and a kind of accession without a credible membership perspective (Samardžić 2016, 299, 333–34).

However, we must not ignore the fact that the negative results of the previous enlargement waves have also had a substantial effect on EU public support concerning future integration. The data taken from the standard Eurobarometer surveys indicate a major trend in public opinion in the EU, and therefore, reveal important observations on further Union integration. From the point of view of European citizens, the ongoing EU enlargement process seems to be controversial. The data predominately shows that the majority of the EU population is opposed to furthering the EU enlargement process to the Western Balkan region, where the percentage of opposition among respondents varies from 45% to 49% according to surveys conducted between 2017 and 2019 (Eurobarometer 87, 2017; Eurobarometer 88, 2017;

Eurobarometer 89, 2018; Eurobarometer 90, 2019). This sort of fear (recognized in the lack of trust in contributing to national economic development and the EU budget, and threats to the loss of national identity) has remained a most important identity-related factor in EU citizens' opposition of the ongoing enlargement process. The lack of enthusiasm for furthering the enlargement process is predominately a consequence of inadequate knowledge among the EU citizens about the candidate countries, existing prejudices, and irrational fears of the Balkans as a troubled region (Taydas and Kentmen-Cin 2017, 613).

Also, the support for the EU integration process among the public substantially differs from one member state to another depending on which country respondents are from. Spain (71%) and Malta (61%), countries belonging to Mediterranean part of the Europe, as well as Poland (66%), Romania (65%), Lithuania (66%), and Hungary (62%), states with a common postcommunist heritage, largely support the continuation of the enlargement process. On the other hand, the strong opposition to EU expansion raises a serious concern of further continuation of the integration dynamics among the EU-15 states. In Austria (69%), Germany (68%), France (67%), the Netherlands (66%), and Finland (64%), the strong resistance toward EU enlargement calls into question the further use of the Union conditional policy, but perhaps far more importantly, it significantly endangers credibility of the current integration process. And finally, support for EU enlargement substantially depends on the particular candidate country in question. The public was, on one hand, strongly against the accession of Albania, Kosovo, and North Macedonia into the Union, and on the other hand favored and supported Montenegro and Serbia becoming new member states (Eurobarometer 87, 2017; Eurobarometer 88, 2017; Eurobarometer 89, 2018; Eurobarometer 90, 2019; Gateva 2015). This being said, the lack of support among the EU citizens for further enlargement raises a serious concern over the credibility of the EU integration process, taking into account the increasing relevance and active participation of the citizens in the decision-making process of the EU. This sort of rise of Euroscepticism within the member states does not necessarily mean abandoning the European integration perspective and a search for new alternatives, but simply a disagreement on the current methods, timing, and influence of the integration process (Belloni 2016, 530–47).

Besides the enlargement fatigue issues, the EU has demonstrated certain discrepancies in terms of fulfilling the promise of a European future for the Western Balkans from the beginning of the twenty-first century. The EU has proven not to be an effective state-building actor due to its lack of experience in state-building processes, absence of clear criteria within the acquis communautaire, as well as notable disagreements which exist between different Union institutions and the EU member states in terms of state-building process (Bieber 2011, 1785, 93; Keil 2013, 349; Börzel 2011, 11; Keil and Arkan 2015, 16).

As of the 2000s, the Union has been actively engaged in the state-building process in the Western Balkans mainly through the strategy of European integration. The state-building process has been largely interconnected with the process of democratization of the country (i.e., development of strong democratic institutions and establishment of democratic governance) by addressing an issue of effective implementation and enforcement of EU rule of law standards in the post-conflict region. In the case of the Western Balkans, the state-building process also includes institution building, which implies direct EU impact on domestic governance prerogatives, and therefore, direct interference in the sovereignty of the candidate state (Keil 2013, 344; Bieber 2011, 1791). However, the results of the EU's conditionality in the state-building process are limited due to the lack of political will on the part of the ruling elites to effectively address EU demands, and perhaps far more importantly, due to the Union's persistence in resolving status issues through the creation of tailor-made policies. The Union has focused on certain policies and their outcomes where no defined EU standards exist (Keil 2013, 349). Hence, the controversy of imposing state-building conditionality in the Western Balkans is twofold: first, there is an absence of clear criteria of imposition of conditionality rules, and second, there is a lack of understanding and cooperation between EU institutions and member states in the state-building process (Bieber 2011, 1793; Grim and Mathis 2018, 165). This sort of conflict between various EU actors has weakened the Union's leverage, and it has reduced its credibility in the region, thus resulting in the inability of the Union to promote democracy and strengthen governance prerogatives. At the same time, domestic alignment with EU accession criteria strives to be loose and shallow (Börzel and Grimm 2018, 122; De Bardeleben 2008, 205–16).

Although since the beginning of the twenty-first century, the Union has adopted a number of strategic documents which confirm the Western Balkans accession plan, the general impression is that this incentive has not resonated well enough among the regional countries (Anastasakis 2008; Noutcheva 2008). Taking into account the individual integration dynamics of each country, the Western Balkans have not adequately fulfilled the accession conditions stipulated by the SAA as an integral part of the SAP, nor have they adequately implemented the acquis communautaire (please see Table 1.1).[6] The current regional situation can best be described as "consolidation of unconsolidated democracy," demonstrating stagnation and backsliding in all key governance indicators, and therefore it is reasonable to claim that in all likelihood the Western Balkans membership in the EU is not viable, at least not in mid-term period (Kmezić 2017, 48–49). As a result, the progress of these countries toward EU membership is limited. The transformative effect of the current EU approach for the Western Balkans appears to be insufficient, mostly because conditionality does not work if the membership criteria are not clear, if the same criteria are not applied equally to all applicants, if they are not fairly monitored, if their findings are not transparently communicated, and if there is doubt that reward will come once conditions are met. Clearly, this is the case of the Western Balkans accession as such (BiEPAG 2017; Schimmelfennig and Sedelmeier 2005; Anastasakis 2008; Belloni 2008).

At the internal level, democracy in the Western Balkans has been in constant decline for decades. Democratic backsliding coupled with rising authoritarianism remains a key feature of the region, and therefore most of the Western Balkan states can best be described as defective democracies. The democratic backsliding can be explained "as the movement of a regime with democratic features away from democracy towards greater authoritarianism" (Bieber 2020, 3). This sort of democratic breakdown has appeared as a fairly new political phenomenon in the field of democratization of postcommunist societies, especially in the Western Balkans, where the emergence of various types of hybrid regimes have found their place between the consolidated democracy and fully authoritarian systems. The latest reports of Freedom House and Nations in Transit have classified the Montenegrin system of rule as a hybrid regime, while the Democracy Index has defined it as a flawed democracy, with distinctive characteristics of a defective democratic system or competitive authoritarian regime (Democracy Index 2019; Nations in Transit 2020). This hybrid regime is qualified by one distinctive characteristic, and that is the existence of formal democratic institutions and the election of regimes in more or less regular election conditions with the ultimate goal of undermining the functioning of democratic institutions by keeping them under autocratic control (Dolonec 2013; Levisky and Way 2010; Ahram and Goode 2016; Kmezić 2020).

None of these countries were considered to be consolidated democracies. Instead, they are mostly viewed as hybrid regimes and/or semi-authoritarian systems. As Ottaway (2003, 3) has claimed, semi-authoritarian regimes are "ambiguous systems that combine rhetorical acceptance of liberal democracy, the existence of some formal democratic institutions, and respect for a limited sphere of civil and political liberties with essentially illiberal or even authoritarian traits." According to her, they are not "imperfect democracies struggling towards improvement and consolidation, but regimes determined to maintain the appearance of democracy without exposing themselves to the political risks that free competition entails." For the sake of argument, there are two types of authoritarian regimes emerging in the Balkans: first, the autocrats who link autocratic tools of rule with declarative commitment to the EU accession process, and second, the nationalist autocrats who do not

Table 1.1 State of Play: Advancement of the Western Balkans in the Accession Process

First Steps to EU Membership	*Albania*	*Bosnia and Herzegovina*	*FYROM*	*Kosovo*	*Montenegro*	*Serbia*
SAA signed	12.06.2006	16.06.2008	09.04.2001	27.20.2015	15.10.2007	29.04.2008
SAA enforced	01.04.2009	01.06.2015	01.04.2004	01.04.2016	01.05.2010	01.09.2013
Membership application	24.04.2009	15.02.2016	22.03.2004		15.12.2008	22.12.2009
Commission opinion	09.11.2010		09.11.2005		15.12.2008	14.10.2011
Candidate status	27.06.2014		16.12.2005		17.12.2010	01.03.2012
Council decision to open accession negotiations					26.06.2012	28.06.2013
Starts of accession negotiations					29.06.2012	21.01.2014
Progress (June 2017)	Addressing key priorities for opening accession negotiations	Awaiting Commission opinion	Start of the accession negotiations blocked	Visa liberalization dialog	Chapters open: 26 Chapters closed: 2	Chapter open: 8 Chapter closed: 2

Source: Gateva (2015, 133)

possess external legitimacy, but they use nationalist discourse to remain in or consolidate power (Bieber 2020, 20; Keil 2018, 62–72; Levisky and Way 2010, 5; Dolonec 2013, 7–21). This region has been fruitful soil for the emergence and strengthening of semi-authoritarian regimes from the 2000s until now, as the post-Yugoslav space shares a common postcommunist heritage reflected in the collapse of the socialist system, the bloody conflict in the territory of former Yugoslavia, the lack of democratic political culture and praxis, and the existence of clientelism and informal networks. In fact, most of the structural apparatus and mechanisms of autocratic governance from the previous Yugoslav communist regimes remained intact, as they were easily transferred and adjusted to new post-transitional democratic realities (Radeljić 2012; Elbasani 2013).

There is no unique template of a semi-authoritarian regime in the Western Balkans based on which democratic backsliding features can best be described. However, what remains the same among the Western Balkan autocrats is their ability to adjust to current external incentives and, if necessary, to change their ideological profiles and foreign policy perspectives. Their chameleonic nature has been reflected in the formal support of the EU integration process as they have ultimately severed all ties with the radical and nationalist political past, proclaiming that their integration into the EU is their main foreign policy goal (Keil and Stahl 2015, 241–43). The autocrats have remained in power and built their statesmanship careers based on reputations as pragmatic reformists. They have justifiably realized that political survival is conditioned on the external support for the purpose of maintaining internal political stability. The so-called stabilitocracy supported by the Western powers allows semi-autocratic leaders to combine autocratic governance tools with declarative support to the EU integration process, consequently legitimizing the democratic backsliding and the erosion of democratic safeguards in the region (Bieber 2020, 7; Keil 2018, 59–82; BiEPAG 2017, 3–10). In fact, the regime in Montenegro can be described as a prototype of stabilitocracy—the existence of strong authoritarian levers of power combined with pro-Western rhetorical discourse and support from external actors. This strong pro-Western discourse, including the imposition of sanctions on Russia over the illegal annexation of Crimea in accordance with EU foreign policy regulations, the recognition of Kosovo, and active participation in NATO peace-building and peace-keeping missions in Afghanistan, Iraq, Libya, Mali, and Somalia, has positioned Montenegro as a reliable and important Western partner in the Balkans. This loyalty has been reflected in how the West ignores the democratic decline in all key governance indicators in the small Adriatic states. The gap between leaders' formal commitment to EU integration and rising authoritarianism has mitigated the prospect of the development of democratic procedure and practice. Hence, Montenegro (and other Western Balkan countries) has been faced with a certain paradox. While on one hand, Montenegro (and the Western Balkans) has demonstrated certain progress in EU accession, advancement in the accession process does not coincide with the process of internal democratization (Keil and Stahl 2015, 177–80; Džankić 2018, 83–100; Komar and Živković 2016, 785–04).

While the level of autocratic rule has varied from country to country, the mechanisms of control and influence remain largely the same. All Western Balkan semi-autocrats share a common characteristic that is profoundly visible in their intention to: (1) weaken democratic institutions by keeping them fragile and dependent, (2) politically interfere into the judiciary, (3) reckon with political opponents, and (4) create strong political polarization between the government and opposition. The autocrats such as Milo Đukanović, the president of Montenegro (as well as Aleksandar Vučić, president of Serbia and Milorad Dodik, Serb member of the State Presidency of Bosnia and Herzegovina) have predominately relied on mechanisms that spread fear and create artificial political crises to consolidate their power and strengthen their dominant position in the society. The peculiarity of this regime has been seen in its ability to change politics, policy orientations, and foreign policy priorities, thereby reducing the chances of losing dominance in the state (Keil 2018; Džankić 2018; Lavrič and Bieber 2020; Kmezić 2020).

The longevity of DPS rule and its more than thirty-year dominance has remained a pattern for the regional decline into authoritarianism. Since the introduction of a multiparty system in late 1989, and even before, since 1945, Montenegro has not witnessed a shift in power, as the ruling League of Communists was transformed into the DPS (Morrison 2009, 2018; Džankić 2014b; Bieber 2020). Džankić and Keil (2017, 409–13) have claimed that the DPS rule has established state-sponsored populism as a new form of populism, guided neither by far-left nor far-right beliefs and sentiments, but controlled by one ruling party whose main aim is to preserve their dominance in Montenegrin society. According to the authors, the DPS is not a populist party per se, however, this party relies heavily on populist mechanisms to maintain control of internal political processes and changes in the country. There are several elements that classify DPS as a state-sponsored populist party, namely "othering" political opponents both internal and external, commitment to and sympathies for the heartland, lack of party ideology, spreading fear and crises, the cult of personality, and the chameleonic nature of the party profile. Labeling with the so-called internal or external enemies, and the government's hostile political behavior toward these actors is one of the main characteristics of party-populist discourse. As a clientelistic party network, DPS uses a state-sponsored populist discourse to ensure a dominant position in society by capitalizing on identity conflict in the country and pushing a foreign policy that strongly distinguishes Montenegro from Serbia.

The connection between the citizens and the state of Montenegro as the "heartland," while the question of survival of statehood and national identity is at stake, has been misused by the party as a major rhetoric lever in the fight against internal dilettantes and external enemies. This kind of rhetoric was mainly used against opposition parties or critically oriented civil society organizations, which were portrayed as traitors and terrorists directly supported by the Serbian political establishment. The DPS does not have clear ideological principles or forms of action where the preservation of national identity and defense of achievements of statehood do not fit into the scope of the left-wing party. However, the DPS is characterized by its strong chameleonic nature, as the party easily adjusts to new circumstances and situations. While the party supported Milošević's expansionist war projects in the first half of the 1990s, the DPS made a gradual shift by establishing cooperation with the West during the second half.

In his latest volume, Morrison describes Milo Đukanović as "undoubtedly the most charismatic, pragmatic, single-minded (politically) intelligent and ruthless politician to emerge in Montenegro in the past few decades, [who] had survived the cut and thrust of Montenegrin politics through the most difficult times. His ability to adapt quickly and decisively in fluid political situations, his instinct for political survival and his ability to outwit his political opponents has been impressive" (Morrison 2018, 145). As a dominant force in internal political life for more than thirty years, the DPS and its leader Milo Đukanović has developed a number of effective mechanisms to maintain a continuity of rule in Montenegro. Control of the economy and black market along with the substantial financial support from the Western powers, especially during the period of confrontation with Milošević in 1997 and 1998, allowed Đukanović to consolidate his power mainly through patronage and clientelistic connections. The loyalty of the state security apparatus and financial support of postwar profiteers and transition tycoons have played a substantial role in positioning the party at the center of political changes and development to this day. The party has quickly positioned itself as a main controller of postcommunist privatization processes and economic transition developments of the state-owned industries and companies, choosing buyers, and deciding the price of certain entities (Džankić and Keil 2017, 408; Komar and Živković 2016, 785–87). Hence, his ruthlessness and political pragmatism have created a certain doubt in both Brussels and Washington as to whether Đukanović will demonstrate his political willingness to effectively address the political requirements of EU membership. In a way, both the EU and the United States have had a certain paradoxical relationship with Đukanović. While on one hand they felt certain doubts over Đukanović's willingness to meet conditions concerning widespread corruption issues and the de-politicization of the judicial sector, on the other hand, he was the sort of politician they could trust, a politician who is reliable and someone who can get things done (Morrison 2018, 145–46).

However, although Đukanović remains the most prominent political figure in contemporary Montenegrin politics, at the same time, his rule has been largely controversial. He has faced persistent accusations of links to the Italian mafia, and of an illicit cigarette smuggling business back to 2001 when the state was internationally and economically isolated due to the Yugoslav war of aggression on Bosnia and Herzegovina (BiH) and Croatia dating back to 1995 (Morrison 2018). Đukanović's rule has also been marked by numerous corruption scandals, that is, "Telecom" (2012), "Recording" (2013), "Can" (2016), "Envelop" (2019), "Apartment" (2019), and so on. The sense of omnipotence present in Đukanović's autocratic rule has been reflected in the absence of a final conviction for corruption allegations and abuses of power despite evidence which clearly pointed out the misuse of public funds for party purposes and the illicit enrichment of families close to Đukanović (IA and CGO and CRNVO and CeMI 2018; Kmezić 2017; Keil 2018).

The ruling party influences citizens through the process of extortion and pressure, especially those working in civil service. Many DPS party members have alleged connections with organized crime networks through financing party electoral campaigns and other activities, therefore cementing the DPS's grip on power (Freedom House 2018). The corruption is highly linked with patronage, where the DPS members and supporters have received preferential treatment when trying to find a job in state institutions (Džankić and Keil 2017, 409). The extensive informal patronage network is strongly connected with substantive corruption, where the loyalty to the ruling party plays a substantial role in the process of advancement in the party and its vertical hierarchy. Mocht'ak (2015, 111) has analyzed parliamentary and presidential elections in Montenegro from 1990 to 2013 and argues that there is a continuous escalation of electoral violence, identifying the DPS as a "potential incendiary factor igniting political conflict." Similarly, Džankić (2014b, 44) holds the view that the citizenship policy in Montenegro, as an "image of the nation" and an "image of politics," was an important mechanism that enabled the survival of the DPS rule: "By embedding the 'image of the nation' in the citizenship legislation, the ruling Montenegrin elite reinforced their political agenda. By entrenching the 'image of politics' in the citizenship law, they managed to produce conditions favouring their electoral victories and thus enabling the party's institutional dominance."

With all these claims, it should be kept in mind that Montenegrin society is a deeply divided society. The issues of statehood, nationhood, and national identity have continued to play a significant role in the political life of Montenegro, whereas different interpretations of these categories between Montenegrins and Serbs consequently affect the internal political dynamics and processes within the society as well as the development of the political situation (Morrison 2018). The national identity disputes between Serbs and Montenegrins have a long history of ethnic divisions. Interestingly, the history of nation building in Montenegro does not align with the institutionalist theory of nationalism based on which the establishment of national institutions will predominately strengthen and increase collective national identity. Clearly, this was not the case in Montenegro, where national identity sentiments gradually decreased from 91% in 1948 to 45% in 2011, based on the data from the latest census, despite the fact that the state had its own flag, coat of arms, parliament, national institutions, government, academy of science and art, and so on. Yet, the process of national identification was significantly slowed mostly because national institutions and elites were not persistent in enforcing national identity. The decline of the self-identified Montenegrin was predominantly the result of the lack of institutions and elites to further homogenize national identity, especially because of the needs of the domestic elites to promote the Yugoslav communist principle of "brotherhood and unity" (Jenne and Bieber 2014, 431, 452–53).

The self-identification issue still burdens complex Montenegrin-Serbian relationships even today. While the results of Montenegro's referendum from 2006 permanently changed its state-legal status, the issue of statehood and national identity continues to play a substantial role in public discourse even in the post-referendum period. The clear division on referendum winners and losers made even stronger antagonisms not just between the political parties but among citizens themselves. The country entered into a new political era characterized by a divided political body where a certain (substantial) national minority, namely Serbs, largely did not recognize the legitimacy of the referendum results. Constitutional issues, the position of the Serbian Orthodox Church, the use of state symbols, and the Montenegrin language all remained fertile ground for new political divisions between Montenegrins and Serbs (Morrison 2018, 133). The claims of Serbian national minority parties that Serbs and Montenegrins are part of the wider Serbian national corpus, and hence that Montenegrin national identity does not exist, has triggered a political revolt by the ruling DPS coalition which desperately sought, even in some cases quite artificially, to strengthen Montenegrin national identity. Consequently, the government used its levers of power to create critical divisions and clashes between the two nations. The intra-Orthodox conflict between the Serbian Orthodox Church and the Montenegrin Orthodox Church (largely supported by the ruling DPS party) over "autocephaly" has consequently been raised to the political level, bringing to the fore issues of Montenegrin nationhood, statehood, and identity as unfinished and problematic business. This sort of Orthodoxy, that is, one that is structured by state borders, has developed in the national context. It is often perceived as a symbol of nationality and a sign of culture and tradition, and is therefore politicized (Morrison 2018, 83; Ramet 1999, 109; Rastoder 2005, 117–25).

Also, several policies adopted by the DPS government in the post-referendum period aimed at reinforcing Montenegrin national identity (recognition of the Montenegrin language, adoption of new state symbols, and detachment of the government elite from the Serbian Orthodox Church) have also contributed to a large extent to the Serbian minority's rejection of Montenegro as their homeland (Džankić 2014a, 356, 362–71; Morrison 2009, 223). Furthermore, other issues and factors that have been seen by the Serb minority as clear examples of anti-Serb policy (Morrison 2018, 134–41) include the government's decision to recognize Kosovo as an independent state in 2008 and to join NATO in 2017, the issue of dual citizenship, official participation of the Montenegrin state delegation in the anniversary celebration of "Operation Storm" in Croatia, as well as the issue of the Serbian Orthodox Church and its limited ability to retain church property following the adoption of the Law on Religious Freedom in 2019. Interestingly enough, the anti-NATO stance has broad public support, with 42% of the population against Montenegro's membership in the Alliance and 38% for it (CEDEM Survey 2019, 18). Unlike the Serb minority, the Montenegrin Bosniak-Muslim and Albanian communities see Montenegro as their homeland mainly due to the adopted provisions in the Constitution of Montenegro that define the state as a civic rather than a national state (Džankić 2014a, 357; Morrison 2009, 224).

In short, the statehood problem continues to be the main domestic impediment toward EU membership, and it largely affects both the capacity and willingness of Montenegro (and rest of the Western Balkan countries) to effectively comply with the Copenhagen membership criteria. While, on the one hand, the EU has offered these countries a membership perspective to stabilize the region and overcome problems caused by weak and contested statehood, on the other hand, it is precisely the limited statehood of Montenegro that has undermined regional compliance with EU norms and rules (Börzel 2011, 5).

Essentially, although Montenegro has demonstrated visible progress in terms of formal institutional changes (adoption of EU rules and norms) aiming to strengthen democratic institutions and enhance capacity building, the main issue of effective implementation and its enforcement of the acquis communautaire has unfortunately remained unresolved (Börzel 2011, 9). In addition, the issue of the functional adoption of the acquis and policy alignment has been significantly hindered due to strong interference by autocratic leaders in all three branches, powerful influence of veto players, and lack of appropriate domestic administrative infrastructure, consequently resulting in the increase of corruption and clientelism within the state institutions. Furthermore, the lack of a credible EU membership perspective significantly challenges the successful completion of reforming the integration processes, where cost-benefit calculations play a dominant role with the domestic ruling elites. Consequently, all these domestic political issues have had negative repercussions for the effective implementation of EU requirements and on further consolidation of democracy in Montenegro (and the rest of the Western Balkans), especially in the case of functional democratic institution-building and capacity-building processes (Elbasani 2013, 12–13; Keil 2013, 347; Bieber 2011, 1785; Kmezić 2017, 48, 148–51; BiEPAG 2017, 8; Radeljić and Đorđević 2020).

DEFINITION OF THE RESEARCH SUBJECT

Based on the established research dilemma, this claim is further tested on the case of Montenegro as a "success story" of Europeanization of the Western Balkans. More precisely, this study has chosen to examine Montenegro as a good new case study of EU enlargement policy, with research outcomes that can be applied and transferred to the case of the Western Balkans as a whole, particularly due to its advancement in the EU accession process, and its particularities in the political system.

Hence, the *case study of Montenegro* has been used for this research for the following reasons:

First, shortly after the dissolution of the State Union of Serbia and Montenegro in 2006, Montenegro positioned itself as a regional frontrunner among the Western Balkans in the process of European integration. After signing the SAA on October 15, 2007, Montenegro successfully completed the first integration phase in a short period of time, and was granted the status of candidate country for EU membership on December 17, 2010 (Đurović 2016, 82–83). On June 29, 2012, the state began the second integration phase, namely the accession negotiation process. It is more complex than any of the other integration phases, especially in terms of its nature, content, scope, and range of conditions. As of June 30, 2020, thirty-three negotiating chapters had been opened (including Chapter 23—Judiciary and fundamental rights and Chapter 24—Justice, freedom and security, i.e., the rule of law chapters) and three chapters (Chapter 25—Science and research, Chapter 26—Education and culture, and Chapter 30—External relations) were provisionally closed (Delegation of the European Union to Montenegro 2020a).

Second, since 2012, and in line with opening the accession negotiation with Montenegro, new pre-conditions for the Western Balkans have been specified, with a focus on the dynamics of opening negotiation chapters: accession negotiation starts with Chapters 23 and 24, and they have become the very heart of the accession process, as they focus on the rule of law requirements together with constant evaluation and monitoring during the entire accession process (Đurović 2016, 69). Following provisions within the new approach from 2012, the accession negotiation operates on the principle "that nothing is agreed until everything is agreed," which means that provisional closure of individual chapters and agreements are finalized at the end of the accession negotiation process (Đurović 2012, 326; European Commission 2014b, 12). In line with one proclaimed principle, the EU has also set "interim benchmarks" and "suspensive and disequilibrium clauses" for the first time since opening accession negotiations with Montenegro. In the event of a serious violation of the Union's values or the nonfulfillment of the rule of law chapters, the European Commission may recommend suspending accession negotiations with Montenegro, on its own initiative or upon request from the member states (Đurović 2016, 87).

Third, there is unanimous consensus of all political parties toward EU membership. Correspondingly, the positive party attitudes toward the European integration process, where all the parliamentary parties strongly support the policy of Montenegrin accession to the EU, remain a novelty within the parliamentary systems of the Western Balkans. As a result of the achieved consensus among the parties on the issue of EU accession, the EU's influence on Montenegrin parties increased between the two electoral cycles (2009 and 2012). The majority of the relevant Montenegrin parties reached a noticeable level of Europeanization in their respective manifestos. Correspondingly, the EU's impact on relevant parties (KECG, SNP, PZP, DF, and BS)[7] was observable in the increased prominence of EU policies in their manifestos, which testifies to the perceptibility of EU transformative power on domestic changes (Vučković 2016a, 50–51).

Fourth, after an eight-year break in the NATO enlargement policy, on June 5, 2017, Montenegro became the twenty-ninth member state of the Alliance. This means that the country has fulfilled the necessary requirements on the rule of law reforms—a process equally as demanding and complex as that of the EU enlargement policy. Montenegro's commitment to defense reform has been especially visible in the two areas—democratic and civilian control of the armed forces and military reform—thus unequivocally proving that Montenegro's bid for NATO membership is not the result of internal political agreements in Brussels based on its geostrategic advantage or current international circumstances, but largely as a consequence of the state undergoing substantial democratic and military transformation according to the Alliance's requirements. This being said, Montenegro has become more democratically mature through the NATO enlargement policy, indicating that the state has reached an advanced level of democratic stabilization, particularly in the field of strengthening democratic institutions, which is the main precondition of building an effective and functional consolidated democracy (Vučković and Vučinić and Đorđević 2016b, 623).

Fifth, although the country has become the twenty-ninth NATO member and a leader in the EU enlargement process, the country still suffers from the weak governance and widely perceived corruption that is seen throughout the entire Western Balkans region (Kmezić 2017, 57). Corruption is prevalent in many sociopolitical areas, including all levels of state administration and state-owned enterprises, and remains an issue of serious concern (European Commission 2019, 4). For the sake of argument, the Corruption Perception Index scores Montenegro at 67 out of 180 world countries, above states such as Senegal, Belarus, Jamaica, Morocco, South Africa, and so on (Transparency International Index 2019). On the other hand, corruption remains one of the most important tools that the governing party has to remain in power. These conditions strengthened ruling elites' influence in the economic sphere and state-related contracts, resulting in the establishment of numerous private–public partnerships that are not subject to legal regulation or judicial control (Džankić and Keil 2017, 409). The existence of nonconsolidated democracy in Montenegro has opened opportunities for the political elite to use the decision-making process for private purposes, and to misuse government prerogatives to ensure that the adopted political decisions are largely in favor of clientelistic interests. As a result, widespread corruption substantially undermines the state capacity, weakens its legitimacy, and consequently results in ultimately weak states (Elbasani 2013, 12–13; BiEPAG 2015, 6; Keil 2018, 62–76; Džankić 2018, 90–98).

Sixth, as is the case with the region, Montenegro is strongly subject to the influence of "stabilitocracy," that is, weak democracy with autocratically minded leaders who govern through informal patronage networks and claim to provide pro-Western stability in the region. In the case of Montenegro, for instance, DPS, as the ruling party, has used NATO membership to portray itself as an indispensable "factor of stability" (BiEPAG 2017, 7). The country is continuously faced with democratic backsliding and erosion of Rule of Law through the strong influence of the informal power structure, state capture by the ruling party, patronage, and control of the media and institutions by the semi-authoritarian regime. The existence of democratic controlling mechanisms, namely independent media and democratic institutions, is both flawed and weak, mostly because they have been exposed to the strong political influence of autocratic leadership. Having thus claimed, the occurrence of the flawed democracy in Montenegro is both institutional and personal. The institutions have not been able to truly develop a more independent approach untouched by authoritarian influence, while the establishment of formal institutions has been (mis)used by the elite to obscure real reform progress, especially in the field of rule of law (Bieber 2020; Donno 2018; Kmezić 2020).

And finally, Montenegro is the only postcommunist country with one political party—DPS—which has ruled in continuity since the introduction of the multiparty system (Morrison 2009, 230; Džankić 2014b, 44). Besides his political capabilities to maintain and consolidate power in Montenegro, the former prime minister and president of Montenegro and of the ruling DPS, Milo Đukanović, has created a "tight-knit clan" of closely related allies who possess strong political and economic power and deeply affect domestic internal political processes in the society (Morrison 2009, 229). Đukanović, the most prominent figure in Montenegrin modern political history, has positioned himself as the main driver of political change by developing a mechanism based on which his family members acquire great wealth through control of the private sector, specifically through construction projects, investments, building small hydropower plants, bank and advocacy services, and so on (Džankić and Keil 2017, 406). The existence of a democratic system obscures the real situation in the country, where the ruling DPS controls many aspects of society, particularly by putting pressure on voters employed in state and public institutions and the private sector, as well as the sporadic pressure of DPS party activists on neutral voters and those with a poor financial status (Morrison 2009, 229; Freedom House 2018). Marginalized populations, mainly Roma, have been instrumentalized to vote for the ruling party through a vote-buying scheme (Freedom House 2018). Hence, clientelism and patronism have played a significant role in the DPS strategy for remaining in power for many years (Morrison 2009, 229; Keil 2018, 63–67; Džankić 2018, 85–95).

The results of the previously applied analytical framework, as well as the empirical findings, are beneficial for both the case study of Montenegro as well as for the entire Western Balkans region. Primarily, the research provides an explanation of special importance on whether Montenegro has substantially deserved its status as regional frontrunner because of its undisputable commitment to the EU integration reform processes, or whether the accession advancement of this small Adriatic country in the enlargement process has been the result of the permissiveness of the EU toward Montenegro in the light of the rest of the region significantly lagging behind in the accession process. In addition, in line with the new conditional enlargement approach from 2012, the analysis of the case study of Montenegro provides scientific insights in regard to the advancement of the EU enlargement conditionality, reward-threat balance (positive-negative incentives), and improved monitoring mechanism, which are identically applied to rest of the Western Balkans due to regional particularities. Finally, following the case of Montenegro and the rest of the Western Balkan states, the paper also addresses the question of whether and why the EU prioritizes the support of internal political stability, that is, "stabilitocracy," instead of the credible and sustainable adoption of

EU rules and norms, by taking into account that in most regional countries there are strong bonds between the domestic ruling elites (autocracies) and the postcommunist legacy in opposing effective implementation of political membership requirements.

AIM OF THE RESEARCH

The aim of this research is to examine the effectiveness of EU influence on domestic infrastructural changes in Montenegro. This particularly means to what extent and how the EU external initiatives have impacted domestic institutional and policy changes, and under what conditions the adoption of EU rules and norms has resulted in domestic structural changes.

The main objectives of this research are chiefly *empirical*. These objectives are vested in *description*, *analysis*, and *explanation* of the EU impact on domestic changes (institutions and policies) in Montenegro. Therefore, the aim of the study is to provide answers in regard to the role and significance of the EU transformative power resulting in domestic changes in Montenegro, as well as to clarify the scope and range of domestic factors to effectively enforce the EU requirements following the association and accession criteria.

THE MAIN RESEARCH QUESTION AND SPECIFIC RESEARCH QUESTIONS

The EU external incentive aims to achieve overall structural changes in Montenegro while keeping the criteria of positive experiences of enlargement and adding new criteria, conditions, and principles as a result of the negative ones. However, it might be reasonable to assert that due to cost-benefit calculations by the domestic actors, the EU conditional policy may cause an unwillingness of Montenegrin political elites to effectively implement the specific political requirements, consequently providing conditions for an outcome of unfinished EU impact on domestic infrastructural changes. Although Montenegro has chosen a path of stabilization and association and accession negotiation with the EU as the central pillar of its development strategy, further progress will depend solely on the Union itself to continue to influence the strengthening of the Montenegrin transformation (institutions, policies, politics, processes, actors, etc.) by promising a credible EU membership perspective.

Based on the aforementioned, the main research question has been formulated as follows: *To what extent and how has the EU transformative power resulted in institutional and policy changes in Montenegro?*

The following subset of specific research questions (SRQ) reflects the essence of the research focus. More specifically, the defined subset of particular research questions is strictly tied to the main research question, which seeks to provide scientific insights with reference to the effectiveness of the EU impact on institutional and policy preferences in Montenegro. In addition, the significance of the established subset of SRQ lies in their close relation to the following methodological framework of research, thus consequently providing guidelines for concrete operationalization of the research.

In accordance with the previous explanations and following the main conceptual principles of the theoretical framework of rational institutionalism, a subset of SRQ shall address the research issues:

- *What EU demands have been introduced during the accession process?*
- *Which EU incentives have been given?*
- *Which domestic institutional and policy reforms have been implemented so far, and how have these reforms evolved across different stages of the accession process?*
- *Are there any veto players who have opposed fulfillment of the EU conditions? If so, how has this particular issue affected the adoption of EU rules, to what extent, and how and why have these actors actually stood opposed to the given reforms?*
- *What are the motivations for the domestic ruling elites in adopting EU rules, whether and why has the process of Europeanization become an EU-driven rather than domestically driven agenda following by a logic of consequence versus a logic of appropriateness?*

NOTES

1. In using the term "EU charade," the author does not have any intention of slandering the EU, but rather to explain the circular and superficial character of EU engagement.

2. As an example, on the election day, October 16, 2016, the Government of Montenegro announced they were in possession of credible information indicating the organization of a so-called "state-coup." The whole case contains many gaps and unclear assumptions concerning the links between the opposition party member and plotters and their organized conspiracy attempt to overthrow the current Government. For more details, see Bieber (2020, 98).

3. Single European Act expanded a wide range of the policy areas such as common customs tariffs, free movement of capital and services, internal market, and so on.

4. Austria, Belgium, Denmark, Finland, France, Great Britain, Germany, Greece, Ireland, Italy, Luxemburg, Netherlands, Portugal, Spain, and Sweden.

5. Benchmarks are measurable and linked to key elements of acquis chapter. In general, opening benchmarks concern key preparatory steps for future alignment (such as strategies and action plans) and the fulfillment of contractual obligations that mirror acquis requirements. Closing benchmarks primarily concern legislative measures, administrative and judicial bodies, and a track record of implementation of the acquis. Interim benchmarks aim to further guide the reform process and keep the reforms on track. For more details, see Gateva (2015, 124–73).

6. So far, with the exception of the case of Croatia, none of the countries from the region is even close to completing accession process. BiH and Kosovo, as potential candidate countries, are still at the beginning of the integration phase, where the candidate status for the EU membership is still pending. After successful resolution of the open bilateral dispute with Greece and fulfilling the criteria related to independence and accountability of the judicial system and fight against organized crime, North Macedonia (and Albania) officially did not open accession negotiations until 2021. And finally, in the case of Montenegro and Serbia, which are currently positioned as regional frontrunners, the existence and strong political interference of semi-authoritarian leaders in legislative and judicial branches open the real question of the political willingness of the ruling elite to deliver tangible and sustainable results in the area of rule of law reform. For more details, see Radeljić (2013), Elbasani (2008), Keil and Stahl (2015).

7. A list of analyzed parties in Montenegro: Koalicija Evropska Crna Gora—KECG (Coalition European Montenegro) comprises the Democratic Party of Socialists (DPS), Social Democratic Party (SDP) and Liberal Party (LP); Socijalistička narodna partija—SNP (Socialist People's Party); Demokratski front—DF (Democratic Front) consists of New Serb Democracy (NOVA), Movement for Changes (PZP), Democratic Party of Unity and a group of citizens; and Bošnjačka stranka—BS (Bosniak Party). For more details, see Vučković (2016a).

Chapter 2

Theoretical Background and Methodological Framework

New institutionalism (March and Olsen, George Tsebelis, Geoffrey Garrett, Mark Polak, etc.) recognizes the European Union (EU) as a system of counterbalance institutions in which rational actors behave strategically to achieve desired results. The EU, as an institutional project in a nonaligned area where borders of political power intersect, is a defined institutional form that has permanent and connected sets of rules (formal and informal) that define behavior, create standards, limit countries, and shape expectations. Hence, following the main theoretical argumentations, it might be grounded to claim that the institutional theory is applicable to the Europeanization of the candidate countries.

The theoretical debate among the scholars in the field of Europeanization of candidate states predominantly lies in the framework of *neo-institutional theory*, especially the theoretical discussion between *rational and constructivist (or sociological) institutionalism*. Whereas rational institutionalism explains alignment by the use of positive and negative incentives which constrain or empower states and domestic actors by allocating different costs, constructivists highlight external socialization in which domestic actors change rules, norms, policies, and behavior as a result of imitation or persuasion (Schimmelfennig and Sedelmeier 2005, 6). Obviously, these theoretical approaches significantly differ in terms of the use of different mechanisms for EU norms adoption, that is, *EU conditionality* (for rationalism) or *persuasion and socialization* strategies (for constructivism). It is in this respect equally important to note the diversity in the context of logic of actions for alignment with EU policies, that is, *logic of consequences* (for rationalism) and *logic of appropriateness* (for constructivism) (Sedelmeier 2011, 11; Schimmelfennig and Sedelmeier 2005, 9).

The theoretical starting points are related to the *theory of rational institutionalism.* This theory argues that political institutions such as the EU itself are systems of rules and incentives within which individuals attempt to maximize their utility (Weingast 1996). In other words, rational institutionalists claim that institutions such as the EU have been purposefully designed to solve collective action problems (March and Stoker 2010, 66). According to rational choice institutionalism, the political institutions influence behavior by affecting the context in which individuals select strategies for the pursuit of their preferences, and these institutions provide information about others' likely future behavior and about the incentives (and disincentives) attached to different courses of action (Ostrom 1998, 1–22). While, due to the interdependence and reciprocity of the theoretical concepts, rational choice institutionalism is the most suitable theoretical framework for the study of Europeanization of Montenegro, it is useful to present both theoretical perspectives: rational institutionalism, based on the logic of consequences, and constructivist (or sociological) institutionalism, based on the logic of appropriateness.

EXPLANATORY MODELS AND MECHANISMS OF RULE ADOPTION

Schimmelfennig and Sedelmeier (2005, 8–10) developed three main explanatory models that determine different mechanisms of Europeanization and the conditions under which the target state complies with EU demands. According to the scholars, these models differ on two key dimensions. First, the process of the Europeanization of a potential/candidate country is either an EU-driven process (where the EU exerts pressure over the adoption of rules and norms), or a domestically driven process (where the nonmember state conducts reform activities). Second, scholars have defined a different logic of action of EU rules adoption by making a clear distinction between "logic of consequences" and "logic of appropriateness." The former case presumes that strategic rational actors aim to maximize their own power and welfare, while the latter identifies it logic of action with the EU identity, values, and norms.

The combination of the abovementioned logics creates different mechanisms of Europeanization or different explanatory models. In this respect, scholars have distinguished three different models of Europeanization of non-EU member states: *the external incentives model*, *the social learning model*, and *the lesson-drawing model*. The external incentives model is based on the logic of consequences as a course of action for EU rules adoption and uses EU conditionality as the main mechanism for inducing domestic changes,

Table 2.1 Alternative Mechanisms of Europeanization

Principle Actor in Rule Adoption Process	*Logic of Rule Adoption*	
	Logic of Consequences	*Logic of Appropriateness*
EU driven	External incentives model	Social learning model
CEEC driven	Lesson-drawing model	Lesson-drawing model

Source: Schimmelfennig and Sedelmeier (2005, 8)

followed by the strategy of reward-threat balance. The social learning model is based on the logic of appropriateness and assumes the state's identification with the EU and its values as being persuaded by the legitimacy of the EU demands and of the EU process through which the EU formulates conditions and promotes rules as such. And finally, *the lesson drawing model* presumes the creation and adoption of the rules and norms by the nonmember state consequently being reluctant to follow the EU initiatives (please see Table 2.1).

RATIONALIST INSTITUTIONALISM—LOGIC OF CONSEQUENCES

According to Schimmelfennig and Sedelmeier' theory (2005, 10–18), *the external incentive model*, as a rationalist bargaining model, uses the logic of consequences within the course of action for adopting EU standards, emphasizing the role of strategic, instrumentally rational actors who endeavor to maximize their own power and prosperity. According to the external incentive model, the EU established a certain set of rules and norms which the candidate country needs to adopt to receive a financial, technical, or institutional reward (or punishment) as proof of its (non-)advancement in the accession process. In this regard, the Union offers nonmember states two types of rewards if it aligns with the EU conditions: assistance and institutional ties. The Instruments for Pre-accession Assistance remains the most advanced assistance mechanism for the Western Balkans.[1] In addition, the Union introduced a wide range of institutional ties ranging from trade and cooperation agreements, association agreements (Europe Agreement and Stabilization and Association Agreement) to full membership in the EU. In any case, the external incentives model can be applied to the case of Montenegro, as well as to the entire region, as the target accession country is expected to adopt the EU rules and norms if the benefits received from the EU exceed domestic adoption costs (Schimmelfennig and Sedelmeier 2011, 663–67; Börzel and Risse 2012, 195; Sedelmeier 2011, 12–14).

EU conditionality is a central principle for examining EU impact on domestic changes because it introduces the strategy of reward-threat balance.

This particularly means that the EU grants a certain reward in the form of advancement in the accession process, as well as financial and technical assistance if the accession country complies with the EU requirements, but also introduces a specific threat in the form of sanctioning noncompliance by delaying the accession advancement or financial reward. The model particularly emphasizes the fact that the Union does not utilize the mechanisms of reinforcement as punishment for the nonfulfillment of the EU requirements. Rather, the target country is left behind in the integration process and simply denied the benefits of assistance and closer institutional ties with the EU. Therefore, compliance with the EU conditions remains solely a target country obligation, while the Union primarily serves to promote the integration process and monitors the country's advancement in the accession phase.

According to the theory of rational institutionalism, at the beginning of the bargaining process the target accession country is in status quo. The EU conditional process upsets continuous "domestic equilibrium" by exerting EU pressure on the country to comply with EU conditions. As a result, the conditional policy works in two ways: (1) through an intergovernmental bargaining process that directly affects the target accession country; or (2) through the differential empowerment of domestic actors. The intergovernmental bargaining process remains a profoundly "top-down" approach to the adoption of the acquis and alignment with EU policy, while the differential empowerment process is more oriented toward "bottom-up" EU rules adoption. In any case, the effective implementation and enforcement of the EU standards solely depend on the decision of domestic actors.

Based on the provided discussion and applying Schimmelfennig and Sedelmeier's definition, the general provision of the external incentives model under the strategy of reinforcing by reward is: *A government adopts EU rules if the benefits of the EU rewards exceed domestic adoption costs.*

However, the effectiveness of conditionality greatly depends on a number of other internal and external factors. In particular, the cost-benefit calculations of domestic actors largely depend on a certain set of other merit-based facilitating international factors, namely *determinacy of EU conditions*, *size and speed of rewards*, *credibility of threat and promises*, and *role of veto players and extent of adoption costs*.

The external incentives model indicates that the target accession country will not align with the EU requirements if the Union does not *determinate them as conditions for rewards*. Furthermore, determinacy of the EU conditions enhances the likelihood of the EU rules adoption by the nonmember state. In this regard, determinacy refers both to the clarity and formality of a rule. According to the theory, the clarity of the EU criteria is important for two reasons. First, it holds informational value. By defining the conditions, the target accession country knows exactly what needs to be done to receive a reward. Second, it strengthens the credibility of EU conditionality. On one hand, it sends a clear message to the nonmember state that there will not be a policy of permissiveness in the accession process, while on the other hand, it obliges the EU to provide a reward if the enlargement state effectively complies with EU requirements. In sum, according to Schimmelfennig and Sedelmeier, the determinacy hypothesis is: *The likelihood of rule adoption increases when rules are set as conditions for rewards and the more determinate they are.*

A second set of factors under the strategy of reinforcement by reward is *the size and the speed of the rewards.* Arguably, the credible membership perspective is a more powerful mechanism for domestic alignment than the other forms of institutional rewards such as association or assistance. On the other hand, the longer it takes to receive the reward, the less likely it is to expect that the nonmember state will adopt the EU rules. Moreover, previous enlargement waves have shown that EU impact on domestic changes is most effective just before the entry of these countries into the EU. In sum, according to Schimmelfennig and Sedelmeier, the reward hypothesis is: *The likelihood of rule adoption increases with the size and speed of rewards.*

Another source of discussion within the external explanatory model is the *credibility of conditionality.* This means that the Union has the credibility to impose threats and to withhold rewards if the target government does not align with EU conditions, and to introduce advancement or financial reward if the country fulfills the EU requirements. The credibility of conditionality depends on two factors, for example, the inability to endanger the EU's capabilities, and costs. The EU must have the ability to withhold the reward at no or little cost to itself, and it must be less interested in providing a reward than a nonmember state is in receiving it (power asymmetry). Secondarily, credibility primarily depends on the consistency of EU conditional policy. If the EU is perceived as an actor that subordinates conditionality to other political, economic, or strategic causes, then the target country might hope to receive a reward without addressing the conditions. Thus, according to Schimmelfennig and Sedelmeier, the credibility hypothesis is: *The likelihood of rule adoption increases with the credibility of conditional threats and promises.*

And finally, the external incentives model presumes that the EU acquis alignment includes domestic *adoption costs.* In this sense, adoption of the new EU rules and norms may produce opportunity costs, welfare, and power losses for certain public and private actors. As a result, the change in the current legal system may be perceived as a negative. Given the fact that effective implementation and enforcement of adopted rules primarily depends on domestic actors, the effectiveness of the EU conditional policy then relies on government will to comply with the EU conditions and influence other veto players.

Following Tsebelis' theory of veto players, they are public and private actors whose support is needed to change the domestic status quo. According to the theory, the more veto players perform in society, the less likely it is to expect that the status quo is going to change. In sum, according to Schimmelfennig and Sedelmeier, the adoption cost hypothesis is: *The likelihood of rule adoption decreases with the number of veto players incurring net adoption costs (opportunity costs, welfare, and power losses) from compliance.*

In addition, in terms of opportunity costs, the literature on Europeanization identifies domestic factors that create favorable conditions for national governments to adopt rules. They include the strength of EU domestic allies, the presence of a liberal democratic government, pro-EU parliamentary parties, the constraints of historical legacies, a low number of veto players, civil society organizations, and adequate administrative capacities, and so on (Elbasani 2013, 9; Sedelmeier 2011, 14–15). Furthermore, at an internal level, there are a number of domestic factors which significantly lessen functional introduction of the EU transformative power on domestic changes, such as the impact of historical legacies, weak statehood, strong role of authoritarian leaders, widespread clientelism, veto players, and the like (Elbasani 2013, 11–12; Börzel 2011, 8–9; BiEPAG 2017, 6).

CONSTRUCTIVIST/SOCIOLOGICAL INSTITUTIONALISM—LOGIC OF APPROPRIATENESS

Following Schimmelfennig and Sedelmeier's theory (2005, 18–20), *the social learning model* is a social constructivist model based on the logic of appropriateness. In contrast to external incentive models, the logic of appropriateness presumes the identification of the candidate country with EU identity and its values and norms, and it is persuaded by the EU to recognize the legitimacy and usefulness of adopting the EU rules and norms. Whether a target country adopts EU rules primarily depends on the level to which the government aligns with EU requirements and considers it appropriate in the context of collective identity, values, and rules. This model is/was particularly applicable to the process of accession of the CEE countries, but also to a certain extent to the Western Balkans, and it means that the target candidate country adopts the Union rules and norms if it is persuaded by the appropriateness of the Union legislation (Schimmelfennig and Sedelmeier 2011, 667–68; Sedelmeier 2011, 15).

Following the theoretical discussion and applying Schimmelfennig and Sedelmeier's definition, the general provision of the social learning model is: *a government adopts EU rules if it is persuaded of the appropriateness of the EU rules.*

Based on the logic of appropriateness, the EU may persuade a candidate country to align with the EU requirements chiefly through persuasion and socialization of the target government and also domestic social actors, groups, and organizations (Schimmelfennig and Sedelmeier 2005, 9). Similar to the previous model, within the social learning model there are a number of external factors affecting the domestic process of persuasion and socialization, namely *legitimacy of EU conditions* and *legitimacy of the EU process* through which the EU formulates demands and promotes rules as such, as well as *domestic identification* with the EU and *domestic rule resonance*.

Whether the target candidate country identifies with the Union's demands by being persuaded of the usefulness of EU norms primarily depends on the *quality of established rules* and the *process* through which they were established and transferred to the nonmember state. The scholars formulated certain factors which need to be satisfied if the enlargement country wants to be persuaded of the legitimacy of the EU rules and process. First, as was the case with rational institutionalism, the EU must determine the conditions for the given policy area. Second, the rule must be able to prompt change. And finally, the decision-making process must be legitimate for EU standards to be adopted. The creation of a specific policy for the region and awareness of the existence of special EU rules substantially increases the legitimacy of the EU rules and procedures, and therefore the likelihood of their adoption by the candidate country. In sum, according to Schimmelfennig and Sedelmeier, the legitimate hypothesis is: *The likelihood of rule adoption increases as the legitimacy of rules increases.*

Additionally, in terms of domestic facilitating factors, these factors include active participation of the target country in the process of setting conditions and making rules, but since this requirement is not applicable to the candidate country in the accession process, facilitating mechanisms should be oriented toward soft tactics rather than strong pressure from the Union. At the domestic level, certain sets of domestic factors influence the process of alignment with EU requirements, and they range from domestic identification with the Union to positive normative resonance with domestic rules (Sedelmeier 2011, 15).

A state's identification with the EU's identity, values, and norms has remained one of the most important domestic facilitating factors in the process of adopting EU rules. According to the social learning model, the likelihood of rule adoption increases with the identification of the candidate country by the EU, which has established the rules of the "game." Thus, according to Schimmelfennig and Sedelmeier, the basis of the identity hypothesis is: *The likelihood of rule adoption increases with the identification of the target government and society with the community that has established the rule.*

Table 2.2 Theoretical Framework: Europeanization of Candidate and New Member States

	Rational Institutionalism	*Sociological/Constructivist Institutionalism*
EU Strategy	*Conditionality—Western Balkans*	*Socialization—CCE*
International Facilitating Factors	• clarity of EU conditions • credibility of threat and promises • size and speed of rewards • power asymmetry • size of adoption costs	• legitimacy of EU conditions • legitimacy of the process through which the EU formulates demands and promotes rules
Domestic Facilitating Factors	• strength of EU domestic allies • liberal democratic government • pro-EU parties • constraints of historical legacies • low number of veto players • administrative capacities • civil society organizations	• identification with the EU • positive normative resonance with domestic rules
Domestic Mitigating Factors	• historical legacies • weak statehood • authoritarian leaders • clientelism • corruption • veto players	

Sources: Sedelmeier (2011, 13); domestic mitigating factors—Author's own elaboration

And finally, the social learning model emphasizes a positive normative resonance with domestic rules as the last factor. Under the term "positive normative resonance," the scholars imply domestic factors that facilitate or inhibit persuasion. The state's ability to adopt and comply with EU rules increases if domestic rules are absent or if they become delegated as a result of a crisis. Also, adoption increases if the EU rules correspond with a domestic perception that the policies are good. Hence, according to Schimmelfennig and Sedelmeier, the resonance hypothesis is: *The likelihood of rule adoption increases with domestic resonance*.

RESEARCH FOCUS

This research scrutinizes the three most prominent political membership conditions of the EU: *judicial reform, the fight against corruption,* and *strengthening regional cooperation and development of good neighborly relations*, all of which are stipulated in the Stabilization and Association Agreement (SAA) and the accession negotiation process. In addition, the three defined membership criteria at the same time represent *three dependent variables* that have been used as the basis for defining the analytical framework of this research.

Following the adoption of the Copenhagen criteria on the level of the Lisbon Treaty, various EU enlargement documents have been accepted, that is, "Agenda 2000: for stronger and wider Europe," the Council's improved policy of conditionality, Stabilization and Association Process (SAP), Zagreb Declaration, "Thessaloniki Agenda for the Western Balkans: moving towards European Integration," renewed consensus on enlargement, "A credible membership perspective for and enhanced EU engagement with the Western Balkans," and so on. In addition, due to the EU's particular focus on political membership criteria, experiences from the last waves of enlargement have also influenced the process of association, opening accession negotiations to become more complex and demanding for Montenegro and the rest of the Western Balkans (Lisbon Treaty 2007; Agenda 2000, 1997; SAP 1999; Zagreb Declaration 2000; Thessaloniki Agenda 2003; Renewed consensus on enlargement 2006c; A credible membership perspective for and enhanced EU engagement with the Western Balkans 2018). In addition, since 2012 and in line with opening accession negotiations with Montenegro, the Union has emphasized the growing relevance of political criteria for the advancement in the accession process by introducing new chapters on rule of law and linking the progress of the membership talks to progress made under Chapter 23 and Chapter 24 (Gateva 2015, 145). The selected political criteria significantly reduce the possibility of research limitations, as the EU sees these political requirements as crucial for Montenegro's membership in the bloc (European Commission 2013b, 2014b, 2015b, 2016b).

Furthermore, to assess the effectiveness of the institutionalization of the EU's political and good governance requirements in Montenegro, this paper examines a certain number of specific-dependent variables and/or dimensions within three political accession criteria, which are coupled with the following specific research questions:

- Three variables within the functioning of the judicial system:
  (1) *judicial independence;* (2) *judicial accountability;* (3) *judicial efficiency and effectiveness*[2]—are addressed in SRQ 1, SRQ 2, and SRQ 3.
- Two variables within the fight against corruption:
  (1) *prevention of corruption;* (2) *establishing a credible track record of investigation, prosecution, and final conviction of high-level corruption cases* are tackled in SRQ 1, SRQ 2, and SRQ 3.
- Two variables within strengthening regional cooperation and improving good neighborly relations:
  (1) *contribution to peace and stability in the region through active participation in the regional initiatives*; (2) *reconciliation and climate*

> *conducive to addressing open bilateral issues and legacies of the past*—are discussed in SRQ 1, SRQ 2, and SRQ 3 (European Commission 2016b, 9–18, 21–22).

From the methodological point of view, the author argues that the above-defined dependent variables and/or dimensions may provide the most appropriate explanations with reference to the real effects of EU transformative power in Montenegro.

Therefore, the Europeanization of Montenegro, as a variable that needs to be examined from the EU enlargement policy point of view, represents the process by which the target accession country adopts the EU standards with the intent to change its own institutional and domestic preferences.

Correspondingly, *the adoption of the EU rules and norms with the intent to change domestic institutions and policies in Montenegro* is defined as a dependent variable.

By focusing on the adoption of EU rules and norms, this research is oriented toward the process of institutionalization of the EU requirements within the Montenegrin government structure, which particularly means domestic alignment with the acquis communautaire, empowerment of domestic institutions through the EU rules and norms adoption, change of domestic political preferences, and actor behavior based on compliance with membership criteria (Schimmelfenning and Sedelmeier 2005, 7–8).

Based on the main research question, the study aims to measure or classify rule adoption in Montenegro in the following dimensions: (1) *EU rule transfer,* (2) *likelihood of EU rules adoption,* that is, conditions under which the state employs full or partial adoption, and (3) *effective implementation and enforcement of rules* rather than just formal adoption of the EU rules in the domestic legal system (this remains the key challenge in evaluating the EU's transformative power on domestic infrastructure changes) (Schimmelfenning and Sedelmeier 2005, 7–8; Kmezić 2017, 5; Börzel and Risse 2012, 199). In addition, this research distinguishes three forms of rule adoption that correspond to different levels of institutionalization of the EU rules: (1) *verbal adoption,* which is characterized by domestic actors' rhetorical endorsement of the EU rules and norms; (2) *legal adoption,* which represents the process by which the government attempts to pass legislation or establish formal institutions and procedures in line with the EU rules; and (3) *substantive adoption,* which goes beyond these two levels and refers to implementation as the process by which external norms are transposed, adhered to, and finally enforced at the domestic level (Elbasani 2013, 14–15).

In the context of the spatial framework of research, the study focuses solely on Montenegro, a candidate country for EU membership. In terms of the time frame of the research, the paper examines the outcomes of the adopted EU rules and norms in Montenegro *from 2007 to 2017*, that is, from the period when the country officially signed the SAA (2007) until the time when the country had officially opened twenty-six negotiating chapters (2017). Furthermore, based on the following four distinct stages of the accession process—the *pre-negotiation stage, negotiation stage, accession stage*, and *post-accession stage*—the study focuses only on the *first and second integration stages*. The pre-negotiation stage starts with the formal agreement of the European Council on the membership perspective of Montenegro as a candidate country and ends with the start of the accession negotiations. The start of accession negotiations makes up the second stage of the enlargement process (Gateva 2015, 27–28).

METHODS OF DATA COLLECTION

Based on the research focus, the study employs a combination of various qualitative methods of data collection including qualitative content analysis, text/document analysis, and other related methods. More specifically, to assess the effectiveness of the implemented reforms in the area of rule of law, and the improvement of regional cooperation as such, this paper seeks to examine effective shifts in institutional and policy preferences in Montenegro as an EU candidate country by using the *case study method, qualitative content analysis*, and *normative and empirical analyses*.

CASE STUDY METHOD

In terms of the operational methods of data collection, the study focuses on Montenegro's adoption of the EU rules and norms as a *single case study* by using the qualitative method, aiming to gain scientific insights based on the main research question.

Applying the single case study method on the case study of Montenegro undoubtedly has significant advantages. The qualitative single case study method seeks to explain outcomes of the main research question by focusing on certain elements of causality, such as growing EU conditional mechanisms, as well as the capacity and capability of domestic actors to effectively produce structural changes (Marsh and Stoker 2010, 255–56). Correspondingly, based on the defined subset of specific research questions, the advantage of this method is seen in its fundamental concept of the research as a whole, in its inclusion of a variety of sources and data, in its preservation of individuality as well as the elasticity of the research. By focusing only on the case study of Montenegro strictly in terms of content, space, and time, this method may provide scientific insights about the deepest layers of content and essence related to the process of institutionalization of EU requirements and its government effectiveness and democratic quality. In addition, the single case study method possesses characteristics of longitudinal research, and it includes periodic repetition of research of the same case study at various stages of its development process, which results in obtaining new data in regards to the domestic conditions undermining EU transformative power (Milosavljević and Radoslavljević 2006, 551–52; Gerring 2006, 43–60). Furthermore, as is the case with other methods of research in political science, limitations of the single case study are seen in insufficient validity, unreliability, and inability to be generalized. To sum up, the case study method is the most suitable, as it provides for more qualitative insights into the domestic institutionalization of EU norms and rules, and facilitates an examination of adopted EU and domestic legislation, as well as administrative and policy regulations.

QUALITATIVE CONTENT ANALYSIS—DIRECT CONTENT ANALYSIS

In addition to the single case study method, this research uses a *qualitative content analysis* as the operational method of collecting data to obtain research findings based on the main research question.

More precisely, the study relies on *direct content analysis*, a study design whose aim is to describe a phenomenon arising from the existing theory and prior research that is incomplete or would benefit from further description: in this case, the effectiveness of the EU's impact on domestic structural changes. By using preconceived categories and thus not allowing categories and names for categories to flow from the data, the goal of direct content analysis is to validate or conceptually extend a theoretical framework or theory. Thus, the existing theory or research can help focus the research question so that new insights can emerge (Hsieh and Shannon 2005, 1281).

Hence, direct content analysis, using observations and its method of description, remains an irreplaceable, indispensable, penetrating, and reliable method for collecting and sorting data in the context of the evolution of the EU enlargement conditionality toward Montenegro, and through its identification of main structural areas in which the EU intents to impose its adoption pressure (Milosavljević and Radoslavljević 2006, 556–60; Burnham and Gillard Lutz and Grant 2008, 259–64). In particular, the book relies heavily on description as a profound analytical framework that will acquaint the reader with basic information on the EU's pressure in the areas of judicial reform, fight against corruption, the strengthening regional cooperation, as well as the domestic response through institutional and policy changes. The substantial lack of literature using both top-town and bottom-up approaches in the given policy areas makes it necessary to provide background on the development of relations between the European Commission/EU and Montenegro during the state's integration phase.

The findings from a direct content analysis offer either supporting or non-supporting evidence for a theory. This particularly means that newly obtained insights either offer a contradictory view of the phenomena or might refine, extend, or enrich a current theory or theoretical framework. Therefore, the main advantage of the direct content approach to content analysis is extending or supporting an existing theory, which means that knowledge generated from content analysis is based on the researcher's unique analytical perspective and is grounded in the actual data. The disadvantages of this methodological approach are seen in a potential strong bias of the researcher's approach. This can result in collecting evidence that is supportive rather than non-supportive of the existing theory (Hsieh and Shannon 2005, 1282–83).

For the purposes of this research, the direct content approach examines a wide range of sources of scientific knowledge, such as the following primary sources:

- *Key EU documents*—Conclusions of the European Council, SAA, European Partnership, Enlargement Strategies, Progress Reports, European Parliament Resolutions, Specific Report on Montenegro's progress in the implementation of reforms, Commission Opinion on Montenegro's application for membership of the EU, Explanatory Screening Reports Montenegro for Chapter 23—Judiciary and Fundamental Rights, and Chapter 24—Justice, Freedom and Security;

Based on the main research question, the qualitative content analysis particularly addresses the subset of specific research questions (please see Table 1.3):

SRQ1—What EU demands have been introduced during the accession process?
SRQ2—Which EU incentives have been given?

NORMATIVE AND EMPIRICAL QUALITATIVE ANALYSIS

Normative and empirical qualitative analysis remains essential in gaining new scientific insights based on the defined main research question. Assessing the degree of effectiveness of the EU's impact on domestic structural changes in Montenegro by analyzing the adoption of the acquis communautaire, policy alignment, and the sustainability of reforms through credible track records of implementation, as well as scrutinizing the role and significance of domestic formal and informal "gatekeeper" elites who possibly mitigate EU transformative power greatly depends on the quality of sources of scientific knowledge.

The advantage of this analysis is particularly visible in its ability to provide accurate and merit-based scientific insights in regard to the research focus. However, the disadvantage of the normative and empirical approach can be seen in researcher's "selection bias," consequently prioritizing some sources over others for reasons of accessibility (Marsh and Stoker 2010, 262).

Nevertheless, to gain new insights into the Europeanization of Montenegro, this paper is particularly oriented toward strict selection and analysis of *primary sources* followed by different methodological techniques, primarily *methods of analysis* and *explanation.* Correspondingly, normative and empirical methods take the form of analysis of primary sources produced by EU institutions (European Council, European Commission, and European Parliament, etc.) and Montenegrin executive, parliamentary, and judicial branches, and policymaking agencies.

More precisely, well-defined normative analysis remains a prerequisite for merit-based empirical analysis. This particularly means that normative analysis takes the form of normative opinion as a value-based judgment, and this assertion will be confirmed or disproved depending on the obtained empirical data. The empirical analysis will either prove or disprove the following normative claim through an examination of EU and domestic documents, consequently reducing the possibility of potential bias in data selection.

The structure of the empirical and normative analysis is formulated as follows:

1. *Normative opinion as a value-based judgment:* Despite the fact that Montenegro has demonstrated visible progress in terms of formal institutional and policy change (adoption of EU rules and norms) aiming to strengthen democratic institutions and enhance capacity building, the main issue of effective implementation and its enforcement of the acquis communautaire still remains controversial (Börzel 2011, 9).
2. *Empirical analysis in the role of examiner of defined normative claim:* To prove or disprove the normative assertion, *empirical analysis,* coupled with the *method of analysis and explanation*, is used to select and examine a wide range of key EU and domestic documents (primary sources) in the mixture of top-down and bottom-up approaches:

Table 2.3 List of Methods of Data Collection, Coupled with Specific Research Questions

	SRQ1	*SRQ2*	*SRQ3*	*SRQ4*	*SRQ5*
Direct Content Analysis	✓	✓			
Nor/Emp. Analysis			✓	✓	✓

Source: Author's own elaboration

- *Key EU documents*: Conclusions of the European Council, SAA, European Partnership, Enlargement Strategies, Progress Reports, European Parliament Resolutions, Specific Report on Montenegro`s progress in the implementation of reforms, Commission Opinion on Montenegro`s application for membership of the EU, Explanatory Screening Reports Montenegro for Chapter 23 and Chapter 24;
- *Key domestic (Montenegrin) documents:* Constitution, domestic laws, reports on the fulfillment of obligations under SAA, action plans, reports, policy, and strategy documents on the fulfillment of membership criteria, National Program for Integration 2008–2012, declarations, information;

3. *Outcomes of empirical analysis* provide insights in reference to:
   - Whether and in which subset of the specific dependent variables within the three political membership conditions the state has not effectively complied with the EU requirements,
   - Reasons for ruling elites refusing to functionally implement EU rules and norms,
   - Changes to be introduced at the domestic level (agenda settings, policy choices, decision-making process, independence of institutions, administrative capacities, and similar) for Montenegro to successfully complete the process of institutionalization of the Union rules and norms.

In reference to the main research question, normative and empirical analysis addresses these specific research questions (please see Table 2.3):

SRQ3—Which domestic institutional and policy reforms have been conducted so far, and how have these reforms evolved across different stages of the accession process?

SRQ4—Are there any veto players who have opposed fulfillment of the EU conditions? If so, how has this affected the adoption of the EU rules, to what extent, and how and why have these actors actually stood opposed to the given reforms?

SRQ5—What are the domestic ruling elites' motivations for adopting the EU rules; whether and why the process of Europeanization has become an EU driven rather than domestically driven agenda following by different logic of consequence versus logic of appropriateness?

Finally, for the purposes of assessing Montenegro's overall progress in addressing judicial reform and fight against corruption membership criteria in a comprehensive and more detailed manner, this volume has also provided two appendices at the end of the empirical chapters on judicial reform and the fight against corruption in Montenegro. This being said, and in accordance with the defined methodological framework and the normative analysis, the evaluation of the process of Europeanization of Montenegro is divided into three categories: realized, semi-realized, and unrealized measures and/or activities.

NOTES

1. For Central European countries this was PHARE.

2. Under the term judicial independence, the study implies the establishment of new judicial institutions such as the Judicial and Prosecutorial Council whose members are appointed by judicial office holders liberated from political influence, appointment and dismissal of judges and prosecutors by the Councils, and introduction of a transparent and merit-based recruitment system of judges and prosecutors. Under the term judicial accountability, this research determines the accountability of judges and prosecutors in the performance of judicial affairs and the imposition of sanctions over other judicial office holders if they violate basic ethical judicial standards. Under the term judicial effectiveness, this volume implies resolving the issues related to backlog in both civil and criminal cases, the high number of pending cases and excessively lengthy procedures, and so on, while the term judicial efficiency refers to the capacity building process, that is, training of judges and prosecutors.

Chapter 3

Judicial Reform in Montenegro

THE EU-DRIVEN JUDICIAL REFORM PRESSURE AND THE DOMESTIC RESPONSE

Pre-Negotiating Stage

Judicial Independence

The introduction and adoption of the *European Partnership with Montenegro* by the Council of the European Union (EU, Council), which came into force on January 17, 2007, was an essential element of the pre-accession strategy, and it yielded novelties in the terms of addressing judicial reform issues. The European partnership as a means of supporting the European perspective of the Western Balkans strictly defines the main short-term and medium-term priorities, referring both to the adoption of legislative acts, as well as their implementation and institution building, all of which were expected to be accomplished within the period of 2–4 years. As a result, the Montenegrin track record in meeting the European partnership priorities was to be examined through the mechanisms established under the stabilization and association process (SAP), notably the annual progress reports presented by the Commission (Council of the European Union 2007, 2).

The Council placed considerable emphasis on judicial independence, stating that Montenegro needed to adopt a new Constitution which could prevent political interference into judicial affairs (Council of the European Union 2007, 3). The EU underlined the necessity of strengthening judicial independence and impartiality through the adoption of a Judicial Reform Strategy, the previously introduced provision of sustainable financing for the judicial sector and the autonomy of the Prosecutor's Office, highlighting the importance to "remove control of recruitment and career management from the parliament and establish transparent procedures based on professional and objective criteria for selection and career advancement" (Council of the European Union 2007, 6, 21). Consequently, it took only four months after the introduction of the European Partnership for the Montenegrin government to adopt *the Action Plan for Implementation of the European Partnership*. In line with the Council's recommendations for accomplishing the short-term and medium-term priorities on strengthening the country's judicial independence, the parliament initially adopted the new *Constitution* on October 19, 2007, consequently bringing new changes within the judiciary. New constitutional provisions were to reduce politicization of the judiciary through the active role of the parliament in appointing and dismissing judges and abolishing judicial immunity by transferring those competences to the Judicial Council, and further elaborating the principle organizational units in the judiciary Chapter 5—Courts, by articulating the difference between the Supreme Court and the composition and jurisdiction of the Judicial Council (Constitution of Montenegro 2007, Articles 123, 126, 127, 128).

The Union clearly stressed the reform of the judicial system that was taking place at the time was the beginning of the reform process, and therefore it required further strengthening of the judiciary, particularly in areas of judicial independence, accountability, efficiency, and effectiveness. Although the country demonstrated certain progress in reforming its judicial system through the adoption of the Judicial Reform Strategy and the new Constitution, the EU primarily outlined that the main problem within the judiciary predominantly lay with the insufficient independence of judicial institutions. Pending the entry into force of implementing legislation to the new constitution, the Commission raised serious concerns over the political influence of the parliament on the judicial system, particularly in terms of appointments to the Judicial and Prosecutorial Councils, as well as appointment, dismissal, promotion and disciplinary proceedings of judges and prosecutors (European Commission 2007b, 11, 2010b, 6).

One major problem in the effective functioning of the judicial sector was seen in the potentially strong interference of legislative and executive powers in judicial competences, where "the division of responsibility for supervision of the courts between the Ministry of Justice and the Judicial Council provided for in the new legislation and the participation of the Minister of Justice as a voting member of the Judicial Council are further factors putting the independence of the judiciary at risk" (European Commission 2008a, 43, 2008b, 6, 11). This being said, the Commission clearly indicated that there were still serious concerns regarding the independence of judges and prosecutors. This was particularly seen in the political influence exerted in the appointment of the Prosecutorial Council by parliament and the parliament's powers to appoint and dismiss state prosecutors, as well as the unclear division of responsibility between the Ministry of Justice and the Judicial Council for supervising the courts, the participation of the Minister of Justice as a member of the Judicial Council, and the election and dismissal of the president of the Judicial Council by parliament (European Commission 2009b, 11). Finally, the EU continued to express concerns regarding the independence of magistrates and prosecutors, as it was feared that they were not immune to political interference. This was because the Supreme Court president, the Supreme State Prosecutor, and judges of the Constitutional Court were appointed by a simple majority of parliament, which is not fully compliant with European standards. Furthermore, the EU highlighted that the limited mandates of the Supreme State Prosecutor and the Heads of Prosecutors' Offices remained problematic, while the merit-based elements of the career system needed to be substantially strengthened and a country-wide single recruitment system remained to be established (European Commission 2011b, 56).

In response, in June 2007, shortly after Montenegro declared independence from Serbia in 2006, the government adopted the *Judicial Reform Strategy 2007–2012*, along with the *Action Plan for Implementation of the Justice Reform Strategy 2007–2012* on December 27, 2007, and the *Commission for the Implementation of the Action Plan* on March 27, 2008. The Parliament of Montenegro (Parliament) adopted the *Law on salaries and other income of holders of judicial office and the rules and procedure of the state prosecutor's office* on June 15, 2007, the *Law on Amendments of the Law on Courts* on April 2, 2008, *and the Law on Amendments of the Law on State Prosecutors* on June 27, 2008, therefore providing adequate and sustainable financing for the judicial system. However, although some progress was indeed made in strengthening the legal framework over judicial independence, it needs to be mentioned that, when it comes to the Council's suggestion to remove control of recruitment and career management from the parliament and establish transparent procedures based on professional and objective criteria for selection and career advancement, the state bodies of Montenegro did not engage in any action to tackle this short-term priority.

In line with the Commission's recommendations over the appointment of the Judicial and Prosecutorial Councils, the parliament adopted the *Law on Judicial Council* on February 28, 2008, thus further regulating procedures for appointment and dismissal of members of the Judicial Council from the ranks of judges. Also, *Amendments to the Law on State Prosecutors* on June 27, 2008, which defined the jurisdiction of the Prosecutorial Council, were also adopted (Vlada Crne Gore 2008a, 3–5). The judicial sector also made additional efforts toward strengthening the institutional framework by establishing the *Judicial Council* on April 19, 2008, and the *Prosecutorial Council* on August 30, 2008 (Vlada Crne Gore 2009, 3). Also, the state bodies undertook certain activities toward strengthening the appropriate legal framework in respect to the Commission's requirement over appointment, dismissal, promotion, and disciplinary proceedings of judges and prosecutors by the parliament. Apart from constitutional provisions and amendments to the laws on courts, on the Judicial Council, and on state prosecutors, the Judicial and Prosecutorial Councils adopted the *Rules of Procedures of the Judicial and Prosecutorial Councils* on March 29, 2008, and on September 1, 2009, which further elaborated criteria for appointment, dismissal and disciplinary procedures of judges and prosecutors, and also established procedures for evaluating and promoting prosecutors (Vlada Crne Gore 2008a, 3, 2009, 11). Furthermore, the presidents of the courts submitted six recommendations for disciplinary proceedings and four recommendations for dismissal of judges in 2008, while no disciplinary measures were conducted against state or deputy state prosecutors in the given year (Vlada Crne Gore 2009, 4, 11, 14).

Parallel to the new Enlargement Strategy and its main challenges for 2010–2011, the Commission introduced its *Opinion on Montenegro's application for membership of the European Union* on November 9, 2010 (European Commission 2010a, b). The Commission announced that for Montenegro to advance to the negotiation stage of the accession process, it must meet the following key priorities:

> Strengthen rule of law, in particular through de-politicised and merit-based appointments of members of the judicial and prosecutorial council and of state prosecutors as well as through reinforcement of the independence, autonomy, efficiency and accountability of judges and prosecutors (European Commission 2010b, 11).

Based on the progress made toward fulfilling the criteria defined by the Copenhagen European Council in 1993 and the conditions of the SAP, the Commission recommended that the EU Council grant *Montenegro the status of candidate country*. As a result, and also following this positive turn of events, the European Council indeed did so and in its conclusion on December 17, 2010, agreed to assign *Montenegro with the status of candidate country* (European Council 2010, 3).

Following the decision of the European Council from December 17, 2010, to grant Montenegro candidate country status, the government in response adopted the *Action Plan for Monitoring Recommendations from the European Commission* on February 17, 2011 (Vlada Crne Gore 2011b, 2). The Action Plan was the subject of both internal and external monitoring, which meant that the plan had been originally submitted to the Commission (as well as to the Venice Commission or SIGMA, depending on the topic) for comments and suggestions after which the government itself (as well as the Assembly Committee for International Relations and European Integration and the National Council for European Integration) considered and evaluated monthly reports on the realization of obligations within the Action Plan (Vlada Crne Gore 2011c, 2). This being said, the parliament adopted the *Amendments to the Law on Judicial Council* and the *Amendments to the Law on State Prosecution Office* on August 4, 2011, to increase the independence of judges and prosecutors. The Amendments, along with the adopted *Rules of Procedures of the Judicial and Prosecutorial Councils* on November 30, 2011 and November 4, 2011, further improved the system of appointing members of the Judicial Council from the rank of judges, procedures for proposing candidates for the appointment of the president of the Supreme Court, appointment of judges, criteria for judges being elected for the first time, and procedures for promoting judges and presidents of courts. It also further developed the procedure for appointing deputies of state prosecutors, the special prosecutor and deputy special prosecutor, revising the existing criteria for election and their objective evaluation based on sub-criteria, and additionally established criteria and sub-criteria for the first appointment of the deputy state prosecutor, who advances and evaluates candidates (Vlada Crne Gore 2011d, 48–49, 2011c, 9). Also, the judicial system saw the strengthening of its institutional framework. The new *Commission for appointment of judges* was established on July 15, 2011, and based on new institutional amendments, the president of the Judicial Council is no longer a member of the Commission (Vlada Crne Gore 2011c, 9).[1]

Overall, in its *Report from the Commission to the European Parliament and the Council on Montenegro`s Progress in the Implementation of Reforms* from May 22, 2012, the Commission assessed that Montenegro had made steady progress during 2011 in meeting 7 defined priorities, including reform of the judicial system, and so in late June 2012, the European Council decided to *open accession negotiations* with the country (European Commission 2012a, 12).

Based on the Council's decision to start the process of accession negotiations with Montenegro in June 2012 and followed by the Commission's positive assessment of reforms within the 2011 Progress Report, the government adopted the *Annex to Report to European Commission on Montenegro`s Progress for 2012—for the period of September 1, 2011 to April 25, 2012* on April 25, 2012, as well as the *Annex to Report to European Commission on Montenegro`s Progress for 2012—for the period of April 25, 2012–September 1, 2012* on September 6, 2012. This was done to efficiently and adequately carry out the monitoring process of judicial reform in Montenegro prior to the opening of accession negotiations (European Council 2011, 5; Vlada Crne Gore 2012a, b). Having said this, Montenegrin state bodies had to undertake several activities toward strengthening the institutional and legal framework, particularly through the adoption of respective amendments to the constitution and appropriate legislation when it comes to the Commission's concerns surrounding judicial independence, which included de-politicized and merit-based appointments of the Judicial and Prosecutorial Councils and state prosecutors, as well as reinforcement of the independence and autonomy of judges and prosecutors. Thus, the government adopted the *Draft amendments to the Constitution* within the judiciary on June 3, 2011, as well as the *Procedure for constitutional amendments* on June 7, 2011. The draft amendments to the Constitution contained changes in terms of the composition of the Judicial and Prosecutorial Councils, appointment of the president of the Supreme Court, competences of the parliament in appointing and dismissing the president of the Supreme Court, Supreme State Prosecutor, state prosecutors and members of the Prosecutorial Council, as well as jurisdiction over appointment and dismissal of the president and judges of the Constitutional Court (Vlada Crne Gore 2001c, 8).

Furthermore, additional efforts in strengthening judicial independence were being conducted in the context of adopting legislation and improving the institutional setup at the sub-constitutional level. Consequently, in line with the amendments to the Law on Judicial Council (2011) and the Law on State Prosecution Office (2011), the Judicial and Prosecutorial Councils adopted the *Rules of Procedure* on November 30, 2011, and on November 4, 2011. Correspondingly, the rules of procedure established a set of criteria for the election and promotion of judges and court presidents and state prosecutors and deputies, and additionally prescribed the public vacancies, mandated the evaluation of candidates selected for the first time, and required the maintenance of a professional list of judges and prosecutors. Finally, in reference to the Commission's concerns surrounding the issue of limited mandates of the Supreme State Prosecutor and the Heads of Prosecutor Offices, the constitutional amendments foresaw appointments of the Supreme State Prosecutor and the Heads of Prosecutor Offices for five-year terms (Vlada Crne Gore 2012a, 71–72, 2012b, 71). Last, the Parliamentary Committee on the Constitutional Affairs and Legislations adopted the *Draft Amendments to the Constitution of Montenegro* and *Draft of Constitutional Law for the Implementation of the Amendments to the Constitution of Montenegro* on May 28, 2012, aiming to reduce political influence in the judiciary by the parliament, particularly over the appointment of the Supreme Court president and the Supreme State of the Prosecutor by the parliament by simple majority, and the appointment of judges to the Constitutional Court (Vlada Crne Gore 2012b, 3).

However, in respect to what has been said of changes on the domestic level and especially in regard to the Commission having serious concerns about judicial independence in relation to the active involvement of the parliament, that is, the appointment of the Prosecutorial Council, appointment and dismissal of the state prosecutor and the president of the Judicial Council, and the unclear division of responsibilities for supervision of the courts between the Ministry of Justice and the Judicial Council, as well as the participation of the Ministry of Justice as a voting member in the Judicial Council, the Montenegrin state bodies during the pre-negotiation phase failed to introduce any specific measures or recourse to tackle these particular issues.[2]

Judicial Accountability

The Union outlined the importance of enhancing judicial accountability through the improvement of the Code of Ethics during the pre-negotiation stage. In this sense, the state bodies of Montenegro had to consequently conduct several activities and take specific measures to further develop the judicial sector, primarily through the adoption of the *Code of Ethics of Judges* at the Conference of judges held on July 26, 2008. Furthermore, establishment of the *Commission for monitoring the implementation of the Judicial Code of Ethics* within the Judicial Council, as well as the *mechanism for Monitoring the Code of Ethics of state prosecutors and deputy state prosecutors* were also approved (Vlada Crne Gore 2008a, 6, 2010, 5). Also, the Judicial and Prosecutorial Councils at that time engaged in further activities toward introducing *Records for noncompliance with the Code of Ethics*, and, based on report period of 2008–2009, there were no violations of the Code of Ethics by judges, prosecutors, and deputy prosecutors (Vlada Crne Gore 2008a, 7, 2009, 15–16, 2010, 5)

In addition, in respect to the Commission's suggestion on increasing the accountability of judges and prosecutors in its Opinion in Montenegro`s application for membership (2010) and following the Action Plan of Monitoring Recommendations from the Opinion (2011), further activities were being conducted by Montenegrin state authorities to enhance the legislative measures and institutional framework. The Amendments to the Law on Judicial Council and Rules of Procedure further elaborated disciplinary measures and procedures against judges, as well as enhanced the system of objective evaluation. Consequently, based on the new legal provisions, the Judicial Council established the *Disciplinary Commission* on April 28, 2011, and the *Commission for monitoring implantation of the code of ethics for judges* on October 10, 2011. In contrast to 2010, when there were no code violations, these commissions resulted in the compilation of records of noncompliance (Vlada Crne Gore 2011c, 3, 9). Furthermore, the *Amendments to the Law on Courts* adopted on August 4, 2011, introduced clearer consequences for disciplinary violations, unprofessional behavior, and failure to perform duties, as well as procedures for the dismissal of judges. In 2011, based on these amendments, only one judge was dismissed and one disciplinary procedure was initiated (Vlada Crne Gore 2012c, 3). Furthermore, the new provisions within the Amendment to the Law on State Prosecution Office established who was responsible for disciplining state prosecutors. In this regard, the Prosecutorial Council had to take further steps to strengthen the institutional framework and thus introduced the *Disciplinary Commission* and the *Commission for monitoring implementation of the code of ethics for prosecutors.* In 2011, according to the records of noncompliance, there were no disciplinary procedures and/or dismissals of state or deputy state prosecutors, nor were there any violations of the code of ethics by prosecutors (Vlada Crne Gore 2011c, 9, 2012c, 3).[3]

In its 2011 Progress Report, Brussels noted that the adoption of the Codes of Ethics for judges and prosecutors had resulted in improvements in the legislative framework, and that the creation of the Commission for monitoring implementation of these Codes had improved overall judicial accountability. The Commission clearly pointed out, however, that "corruption and conflict of interest rules are still insufficiently monitored in the judiciary," while "both judges and prosecutors continue to enjoy functional immunity from prosecution" (European Commission 2011b, 11). This kind of comprehensive protection of judges and prosecutors remained a matter of concern. As a result, the EU suggested that "procedures for removing functional immunity need to be strengthened to ensure full accountability of judges and prosecutors under criminal law." Furthermore, the Commission indicated that the state authorities should devote more attention to the publication of court rulings, since, although foreseen, it was by that time still not implemented in practice (European Commission 2011b, 11).

As a response, concerning the Commission`s concern over insufficient monitoring of corruption and conflict of interest in the judiciary, no additional activities were conducted by the judiciary except for the annual performance reviews of judges and prosecutors by the Disciplinary Commission. Having said this, between September 2011 and the end of December 2012, the Disciplinary Commission launched only one disciplinary procedure against one judge, and only one disciplinary measure/warning was imposed. When it comes to the disciplinary proceedings against prosecutors, no disciplinary procedures were launched in either 2011 or 2012 (Vlada Crne Gore 2012b, 77). Also, the judicial system demonstrated efforts in strengthening and reinforcing the institutional setup in response to the Union's suggestion on devoting more attention to the issue of publicizing court rulings. All the cases, including the old ones, were transferred into the Judicial Information System—PRIS—by December 31, 2011, while the court website (www.sudovi.me) contained information regarding the work and organization of the courts and information on trial terms, judgments, and similar particularities (Vlada Crne Gore 2012a, 74). However, in relation to the Commission's demand for the comprehensive protection of judges and prosecutors through functional immunity, no further normative or institutional measures were carried out by Montenegrin state bodies.

Judicial Effectiveness and Efficiency

The Union underlined the wide-spread problem of judicial ineffectiveness in Montenegro. Following the short-term and medium-term priorities stipulated within the Council's European Partnership (2007), the Union specified further requirements on strengthening judicial effectiveness by noting that Montenegro needed to "rationalise the court system and modernise proceedings and improve administration" (Council of the European Union 2007, 21). In this sense, apart from the laws on courts and state prosecutors (2008), the parliament engaged in a number of actions aiming to reinforce the current legal system by adopting the new *Criminal Procedure Code* (CPC) on August 18, 2009, and the *Law on protection of the right to a trial within a reasonable time* on December 13, 2007. Also, the parliament adopted *the Law on Enforcement and Security of Claims* on July 27, 2011, which brought novelty within the legal system by notably simplifying the execution procedure of court decisions, facilitating court proceedings, reducing the backlog, and finally introducing the position of bailiff into the national legal system. Finally, the parliament adopted *Amendments to the Criminal Procedure Code (CPC)* on June 22, 2011, according to which the new law primarily incorporated the GRECO recommendations in reference to criminal corruption felonies related to bribery and trading influence (Vlada Crne Gore 2011c, 9–10, 2012c, 9).

The Union also noted that the issue of the significant backlog in both civil and criminal cases remained a matter of serious concern, and indicated a lack of strategy in solving this problem (European Commission 2007b, 11). As a reaction, continuous country efforts were made to resolve the high number of pending cases caused by excessively lengthy and insufficiently implemented execution procedures through the adoption of the *Law on Obligations* on August 7, 2008, and the implementation of the Law on protection of the right to a trial within a reasonable time (2007) (Vlada Crne Gore 2008a, 9, 2010, 8). This being said, to effectively deal with the high number of pending cases, excessively lengthy procedures, and insufficient execution procedures, the parliament adopted the *Amendments to the Law on Notaries* on August 15, 2008, followed by the establishment of the *Commission for taking notary exams* which consequently organized the first notary exam in 2009, as well as the *Law on Public Bailiffs* on November 23, 2011, after more than two years of delay. Furthermore, taking into account the Council of Europe's recommendation, the new law on the bailiff system was introduced, aimed at decreasing shortcomings in the systems of executions of law in place at the time, and, more importantly, tackling the issue of judicial ineffectiveness in reducing the significant number of backlog cases, the duration of proceedings, disputes over the collection of claims, and improvement of executive services (Vlada Crne Gore 2010, 10–11, 2011e, 12, 2012b, 12, 2011c, 10).

Additional attempts to improve the institutional setup by establishing measures of appointing notaries were made. Correspondingly, the first group of *34 notaries* swore an oath and the *Notary Chamber* was founded on April 29, 2011, and the first *notary offices* were opened on July 25, 2011 (Vlada Crne Gore 2011c, 11, 2012c, 7). Also, the *Mediation Centre* was established in 2008, and 255 out of 433 cases were successfully resolved using mediation procedures in 2008 (Vlada Crne Gore 2008a, 10). To further enhance the efficiency of mediators, as an alternative means of dispute settlement, the association of mediators adopted the *Mediator's Code* in 2011. In 2010, there were 742 mediation cases in total, out of which 570 cases were resolved by reaching a mediated agreement; 172 cases were not resolved, which consequently resulted in the release of 18 million EUR. Last, 623 mediations were registered in 2011, out of which 383 cases were resolved; 240 cases were not resolved, thus ultimately result in the release of 3,772,974 EUR (Vlada Crne Gore 2011c, 10–12).

The EU remarked that Montenegro showed progress in regard to judicial effectiveness, in particular in the context of reducing the backlog of cases based on the 2011 Progress Report. The Judicial Council and Supreme Court established the *Annual framework programs of backlog cases*, and in the period between January 1, 2007 and September 30, 2011, the backlog was significantly reduced to 75,000 cases (Sudski savjet 2008, 35; Vlada Crne Gore 2010, 8, 11–12, 2011c, 12, 2012c, 7, 28). However, the Union expressed concerns regarding the reliability of the methodological framework. Following the report's conclusion, the Commission highlighted its distrust in the given methods by emphasizing that "the statistical indicators do not provide complete information about courts' performance, the duration of case-handling and the human and financial resources allocated, thus creating problems with the consistency of data and effective follow-up" (European Commission 2011b, 11). Furthermore, the EU noted that enforcement of civil court decisions remained weak, while concerns persisted over the length of court proceedings (European Commission 2011b, 11). By the same token, the Commission indicated that future activities needed to be oriented toward streamlining the courts system by highlighting that "Montenegro continues to be one of the countries with the highest number of basic courts, magistrates, prosecutors and administrative staff in Europe" (European Commission 2011b, 12).

As for the Commission's suggestion regarding the random allocation of cases in courts, which needed to be implemented and also computerized, the judicial institutions had partially engaged in the implementation of the prescribed measure. The result of these reforms was that presidents of courts and state prosecutors now had the opportunity to follow cases through the judiciary, as the Judicial Information System (PRIS), a complete and functional information system, was introduced in 2010 (Vlada Crne Gore 2011e, 11). Finally, in line with Brussels' suggestion over the need to improve the reliability of court data, as well as introduce a computerized case management system in all courts, the parliament adopted the *Law on Information Security* on March 17, 2010. In 2010, activities aimed at introducing PRIS in the state prosecutors' offices were completed, thus allowing for data to be entered into the database, for the data to be used on a regular basis, and finally for it to be frequently updated. Training future users was already underway (Vlada Crne Gore 2011e, 49, 52–53).

The Union also outlined the importance of improving judicial efficiency through the implementation of legislation on "continuous training for judges, prosecutors and court support staff," thus enhancing the Judicial Training Center (JTC) that was established in 2006 (Council of the European Union 2007, 5–6). As a response, the JTC took additional measures to effectively reinforce the adoption of the *Law on Judicial Education* on April 27, 2006, based on which JTC was to be established as a special organizational unit within the Supreme Court of Montenegro (Vlada Crne Gore 2007a, 12–13). Further steps were taken toward the implementation of the Judicial Reform Strategy containing a special IT strategy, engagement of foreign experts in the education of judges and prosecutors, and similar issues (Council of the European Union 2007, 21; Vlada Crne Gore 2007a, 20).[4]

Regarding judicial efficiency, the Union also highlighted the importance of conducting properly structured initial and continuous training programs (European Commission 2008b, 11). This being said, the JTC carried out improvement measures for initial and continuous education in accordance with the Law on Judicial Education. Originally, the programs, designed to train people who held judicial functions, primarily focused on ongoing trainings, especially organized as seminars and workshops. The selection criteria for the initial training of candidates were established based on transparency and an evaluation of the candidates' knowledge. The JTC adopted its Annual plan and training program for 2009, which paid particular attention to educating the judiciary on the CPC and the European Convention of Human Rights. Apart from the judiciary trainings, further activities in strengthening the capacity of the JTC focused on employing domestic, regional, and EU lecturers, university professors and retired judiciary members (Vlada Crne Gore 2010, 24–26).

Finally, with reference to the given recommendations on strengthening judicial capacities stipulated within the Commission's Opinion (2010), the *Judicial Information System* (PRIS) went into operation on January 1, 2010, and the PRIS has so far been implemented in the Ministry of Justice, the state prosecutors' office, and the Institute for Execution of Criminal Sanctions within a centralized and unique database system. In addition, the judiciary established a web portal for the courts, www.sudovi.me, and it contains all decisions in a simple text format with anonymized data, regulations, trial schedule, basic information about courts and judges, facts, ads, and translated decisions of the European Court of Human Rights in Strasbourg (Vlada Crne Gore 2011c, 12, 2012c, 8). Furthermore, the JTC continuously implemented the training program for holders of judicial functions, and the training activities were conducted in cooperation with the Supreme Court, Supreme State Prosecutor's Office, United Nations Development Program (UNDP) Montenegro, OSCE Mission Montenegro, US Embassy to Montenegro, EIPA Institute from Luxemburg, and other relevant bodies. As a result, the *Annual training program of continuous education of judges and prosecutors* on the EU law was permanently implemented in cooperation with the EIPA Institute in Luxemburg (Vlada Crne Gore 2012c, 7, 18). However, although certain progress was seen in enhancing judicial capacity, the Commission indicated discernible deficits in the training of judges and prosecutors. The main issue identified was the lack of permanent mandatory courses and set curricula, but no additional JTC implementation measures or activities were seen in the given report period.

Negotiation Stage

On June 29, 2012, shortly after the Commission's spring report in which Montenegro's progress in the adoption of the acquis and alignment with EU policies was evaluated as good, the European Council endorsed the decision to open accession negotiations with Montenegro, confirming its further advancement in the accession process (European Council 2012, 4). Following the New Approach from 2012 (opening the accession negotiations by focusing on Chapter 23—Judiciary and Fundamental Rights, and Chapter 24—Justice, Freedom and Security), the Commission evaluated the Montenegrin legal and institutional framework before opening the accession negotiations. As of the Council's decision from December 9, 2011, to open accession negotiations with Montenegro in June 2012, and based on the analytical examination of the acquis communautaire with Montenegro on Chapter 23, the Commission itself launched the *Screening Report Montenegro on Chapter 23—Judiciary and Fundamental Rights* on November 12, 2012 (European Council 2011, 5, 2012d, 5).

This screening report provided an analysis of the Montenegrin legal framework and its alignment with the acquis communautaire in the area of the judiciary and fundamental rights, ultimately positioning itself as the most comprehensive document providing a detailed examination and evaluation of the scope of the judicial sector. The report outlined that Montenegro had engaged in important reform efforts to align with the acquis and meet European standards, but at the same time, it noted that further reform activities were needed in the area of independence of the judiciary. Thus, the EU specifically highlighted at that time that "despite the legislative and organisational changes that have been made, judicial reform in terms of concrete results is at an early stage and severe shortcomings have to be tackled, in particular at the constitutional level" (European Commission 2012d, 21).

Following the analytical outcomes, the Commission therefore stated that Montenegro should adopt one or more Action Plan(s), addressing in particular the following issues:

Independence

- Montenegro should amend its Constitution in line with the Venice Commission recommendations and European standards, ensuring independence and accountability of the judiciary. Changes should include, inter alia, the following points:
  - The Judicial Council and the Prosecutorial Council should be composed of at least 50% of members stemming from the judiciary. These members should be selected by their peers, representing different levels of jurisdiction, without involvement of the parliament (unless solely declaratory).
  - Prosecutors should not be appointed by the parliament.
  - Reasons for dismissal of judges and prosecutors should be included in the Constitutions.
- The recruitment process needs to be transparent and merit based. A single, nationwide recruitment system should be introduced, which could be based on anonymous tests for all candidates and obligatory training before being appointed judge/deputy prosecutor. The JTC could be involved in the testing process.
- A fair and transparent system of promotion of judges and prosecutors needs to be established together with a periodical professional assessment of judges' and prosecutors' performance.
- Ensure internal independence of judges and review the system of orders within the prosecution system.
- Sufficient administrative capacities and financial means need to be ensured to the Judicial and the Prosecutorial Councils to effectively perform their tasks.

Impartiality

- Improve the system of random allocation of cases, possibly also through streamlining the court.
- Review application of disqualification procedures and amend where necessary.
- Amend "conflict of interest" rules, ensuring that there is an effective monitoring of asset.
- Ensure effective monitoring of compliance with the code of ethics.
- Review the system of functional immunity for judges and prosecutors. Procedures for removing functional immunity need to be strengthened to ensure full accountability of judges and prosecutors under criminal law.

Professionalism/Competence/Efficiency

- Ensure reliable and consistent judicial statistics and introduce a system to monitor the length of trials.
- Review and rationalize the court network and ensure sufficient funding for the efficient functioning of the entire court system. Further reduce the existing backlog, especially as regard civic cases.
- Strengthen the enforcement of judgments in civil cases.
- Ensure effective functioning of the JTC.

(European Commission 2012d, 21–22, 2012a, b,[5] c, 10, 45, 2013b, 35–38, 2014b, 36–39, 2015a, b, 12, 50–52,[6] 2016b, 54–57).

Judicial Independence

At the bottom-up level, based on the completed screening process of Montenegrin legislation within the area of the judiciary, the Commission summarized the achievements, improvements, and further reform recommendations into the Screening Report for Chapter 23, and submitted it on December 25, 2012, to the newly established Working Group for Preparation on Negotiations on the Accession of Montenegro to the European Union in the area of the acquis related to negotiation Chapter 23—Judiciary and Fundamental Rights (Working Group 23), which consisted of the legislative, judicial and executive branches and included five representatives from the nongovernmental organization (NGO) sector (Vlada Crne Gore 2013). As a response, taking into account the interim benchmark introduced in the screening report by the Commission, the government introduced the *Action Plan for Chapter 23—Judiciary and Fundamental Rights* on June 27, 2013, almost a year after the official start of the accession negotiations.[7] Through the introduction of the Action Plan in June 2013, Montenegro addressed the last requirement to officially open the process of accession negotiations with the EU, and consequently opened the possibility to start fulfilling the recommendations stipulated in the Screening Report Montenegro for Chapter 23.

Primarily in line with the Commission's first recommendation in the Screening Report on judicial independence in regard to amending the Montenegrin Constitution as to ensure the independence and accountability of the judiciary, state authorities took several actions toward improving the legal system. First of all, the parliament adopted *Amendments I to XVI to the Constitution of Montenegro* and *the Constitutional Law for the enforcement of the Amendments to the Constitution* on July 31, 2013. Additionally, the Constitution was amended in the area of judicial independence following the opinion of the Venice Commission, especially when it comes to the composition of Judicial and Prosecutorial Councils, appointment of the president of the Supreme Court, the Supreme State Prosecutor and state prosecutors, reasons for dismissing judges and state prosecutors, and composition and method of electing Constitutional Court judges (European Commission 2012d, 21; Vlada Crne Gore 2013a, 16, 2013b, 3).

Concerning the Union's second recommendation stipulated in the Screening Report and Progress Reports, particularly in context of the recruitment process needing to be transparent and merit based, with a single, nationwide recruitment system to be introduced, Montenegrin state bodies engaged in additional actions to further strengthen the legislative framework. Primarily, the parliament:

1) adopted *the Laws on the Judicial Council and Rights and Duties of Judges and on State Prosecutor's Office* on March 12, 2015; enacted *the Rules of Procedure of the Judicial Council and of the Prosecutorial Council* on October 20, 2015, and November 12, 2015; as well as *the Rulebook for the evaluation of judges and presidents of courts* on December 9, 2015,
    a) proposed legislation regulating the procedure for appointing the Judicial and Prosecutorial Councils and members who are not judges or prosecutors,
    b) urged for the establishment of a single system of appointment of judges and state and deputy state prosecutors at the national level based on a transparent and merit-based procedure,
    c) supported the introduction of periodical evaluation of the work of judges and presidents of courts and prosecutors and a merit-based promotion system,
    d) called for the introduction of criteria for permanent reassignment of judges and deputy state prosecutors from one court to another on a voluntary basis, and finally,
    e) called for complete mandatory trainings as organized in the JTC as a condition for the election of deputy state prosecutors (European Commission 2012d, 21, 2013b, 36, 2014b, 36, 2015b, 12, 2016b, 12; Vlada Crne Gore 2013, 16–17, 19–20, 2015, 4, 2016a, 6–7).[8]

Furthermore, the parliament adopted the *Law on State Prosecutor's Office* on March 12, 2015, and along with it adopted the *Rules of Procedure of Prosecutorial Council* in a session held on November 12, 2015. These documents aimed to:

a) introduce changes in procedures for the appointment of members of the Prosecutorial Council in accordance with adopted constitutional amendments,
b) establish a single system for appointing state and deputy state prosecutors at the national level,
c) complete mandatory trainings as organized in the JTC as a condition for the election of deputy state prosecutors,
d) introduce a system for periodical professional evaluation of the performance of state prosecutors and their deputies within the merit-based promotion system, and finally,
e) improve criteria for greater voluntary mobility of deputy state prosecutors (Vlada Crne Gore 2013, 19–20, 2015, 4, 2016a, 7).[9]

In addition, the parliament also adopted the *Law on Courts* on March 12, 2015, with the intention, on the one hand, to further regulate conditions for appointing judges in terms of stipulating the obligation to complete mandatory training organized by the JTC following the constitutional amendments, and, on the other hand, to introduce the periodical professional assessment of performance of judges and presidents of courts as a condition for their promotion (Vlada Crne Gore 2013, 18, 2015, 4). Finally, following the constitutional amendments in the field of the judiciary, the parliament adopted the *Law on Constitutional Court* on March 12, 2015, thus aiming to further regulate the composition and appointment of judges of the Constitutional Court and the president of the Constitutional Court, as well as adjust the functional composition of judges in making decisions on constitutional complaints (Vlada Crne Gore 2013, 21, 2015, 7).

In regard to the third recommendation by the Commission over establishing a fair and transparent system of promoting judges and prosecutors along with a periodical professional assessment of judges and prosecutors' performance, the legislative and judicial branches realized a number of activities in this regard. Originally, apart from the aforementioned-adopted legislations, the Judicial and Prosecutorial Councils adopted the *Rulebook for the evaluation of judges and presidents of courts* in the session held on December 9, 2015. The *Rulebook for the evaluation of state prosecutors and heads of state prosecutor's office* was adopted in the session held on December 23, 2015, referring to further development of a system for merit-based promotion of judges and state prosecutors and their deputies, as well as their periodical evaluation in accordance with the criteria stipulated within the judicial and prosecutorial council and courts (European Commission 2012d, 22, 2013b, 36, 2015b, 12, 2016b, 12; Vlada Crne Gore 2013, 22–23, 2016a, 9–10).

Also, in reference to the fourth recommendation on judicial independence stipulated within the Screening Report, specifically in ensuring the internal independence of judges and reviewing the system of orders within the prosecution system, the state bodies of Montenegro conducted a number of activities aiming to adopt new legislative measures and to further enforce the current legal framework. More importantly, the parliament adopted the *Amendments to the Criminal Procedure Code* on August 13, 2013, and the amendments within Article 396a on the new criminal offense of obstruction of justice, which is intended to prevent unauthorized influence on judges and state prosecutors (European Commission 2012d, 22; Vlada Crne Gore 2013, 28, 2014, 35–36).

Finally, following the last of the Commission's suggestions on judicial independence as stipulated within the Screening Report, Montenegrin authorities took additional measures to further enhance the judicial institutional framework. This was done in response to the need to strengthen the administrative capacities and financial means within the Judicial and the Prosecutorial Councils. Primarily, in accordance with the adopted constitutional amendments and laws, the president of Montenegro announced decreed the composition of the *Judicial Council* on July 1, 2014, and the *Prosecutorial Council* on January 21, 2014 (European Commission 2012b, 22; Vlada Crne Gore 2013, 24, 2014, 26–30, 2015, 8–9, 2016b, 6–7).[10]

Judicial Accountability

In line with the first recommendation of the Commission on strengthening judicial accountability, in particular, toward amending conflict of interest rules and consequently ensuring effective monitoring of asset declarations and cross-checking with other relevant information, Montenegrin state bodies took action primarily toward the effective implementation and enforcement of the institutional framework. Originally, the Action Plan foresaw that presidents of courts, judges, state and deputy state prosecutors need to declare their assets in accordance with the Law on Prevention of Conflict of Interest, based on which the Commission for Prevention of Conflict of Interest (CPCI) introduced its report (European Commission 2012d, 22; Vlada Crne Gore 2013, 34). The control of judges' and prosecutors' declared assets was to be exercised in accordance with Article 20a of the Law on the Prevention of Conflict of Interests, which was the 2015 Annual Plan for review of public functionaries' property status and the Methodology of risk assessment. Therefore, in the period between January 1 and December 31, 2013, out of the total number of 359 judges and prosecutors (the CPCI initiated control of 266 reports of judges and 93 prosecutors regarding their income and assets), the CPCI launched misdemeanor proceedings against six judges and two prosecutors: four judges were sentenced with warnings and two were fined, while one procedure against a prosecutor was suspended and another was at that time still pending (Vlada Crne Gore 2014, 43–44). In addition, 478 judicial officials (338 judges and 140 prosecutors) submitted their Reports on income and assets in the period between July 1 and December 31, 2015, for the reporting period of the previous year. Of these, seven misdemeanor proceedings were initiated (against six judges and one prosecutor) for not submitting reports by the legally set deadline. Three of the cases resulted in sanctions and liability for court costs, but by the end of December 2015, four of the misdemeanor proceedings against judges had not been completed (Vlada Crne Gore 2016a, 27–29). Finally, in the period between January 1 and December 31, 2015, out of the total number of 338 judges and 140 prosecutors, the CPCI initiated control of 366 reports of income and assets of judges (the higher number of controls is the result of the increased number of judges who ceased their activity), and 112 reports on the income and assets of prosecutors. According to the report, out of 366 judges in total, 343 judges provided accurate data, while the remaining 23 provided inaccurate information. In the case of prosecutors, out of 112 individuals, 106 provided accurate data, while the remaining six prosecutors failed to provide accurate income and asset information. As a result, the CPCI initiated administrative and misdemeanor proceedings against twenty-three judges and six prosecutors who did not report or provide accurate or complete data (Vlada Crne Gore 2016a, 27–30).

In reference to the second concerns of the Commission provided within the Screening Report and the Progress Reports, particularly in terms of ensuring effective monitoring of compliance with the Code of Ethics, the state authorities introduced a number of measures aiming at effective enforcement of the legal system and institutional setup. Primarily, according to measures prescribed within the Action Plan, the Conference of Judges adopted a new *Code of Ethics of Judges* on March 22, 2014, and the Prosecutorial Council adopted the *Amendments to the Code of Ethics of State Prosecutors* on May 20, 2014, together with appointing the *Commission for monitoring of Code of Ethics* (European Commission 2012d, 22; Vlada Crne Gore 2013, 35, 2014, 52–54). By the same token, to ensure effective monitoring and compliance with the Code of Ethics, further efforts were directed toward enhancing the institutional setup through the establishment of the *Commissions for monitoring compliance with the Codes of Ethics of Judges and State Prosecutors,* as well as the Commission submitting semi-annual or annual reports on compliance with the Codes of Ethics to the Judicial and the Prosecutorial Councils (Vlada Crne Gore 2013, 35). In this sense, in 2012, no one was charged for violating the code of judges, while in 2013, the Commission charged three judges, determining a violation of the code of ethics of judges in one case. Furthermore, the Commission for monitoring took action in seven cases in 2014 and in fourteen cases in 2015, but found no violations of the code in the given period. Finally, the Commission acted in twenty cases in 2016 and found violations of the code in the case of four judges (three cases), while in 2017, the Commission took action on fifteen cases, but found no violations in the given period (Sudski Savjet 2012, 27, 2013, 22, 2014, 20, 2015, 15, 2016, 17). Furthermore, when it comes to state prosecutors, in 2015 the Commission for monitoring acted in one case against a deputy state prosecutor, and although the Commission determined violation of Code of Ethics, it remains unclear what the final verdict in this case was. Also, in 2016 and 2017, the Commission for monitoring took action in three cases against the code of violation of prosecutors and deputy prosecutors and found one in breach of the Code of Ethics (Tužilački Savjet 2015, 18–19).

In respect to the Commission's third suggestion, reviewing the rules on disciplinary and dismissal procedures and their implementation, as well as amendments where necessary, the state authorities of Montenegro continued to enhance the legal framework and institutional setup. In line with the Union's recommendations, the parliament adopted constitutional amendments, particularly Article 121 paragraph 3, on July 31, 2013, thus allowing for judges to be dismissed from their posts if:

a) they are sentenced for an act making them unworthy to perform a judicial function,
b) they unprofessionally and negligently conduct a judicial function, or
c) if they permanently lose the capacity to perform a judicial function in accordance with the terms of the Venice Commission.

In addition, following the constitutional amendments, the parliament adopted the laws on the Judicial Council and state prosecutor's office on March 12, 2015, aiming to further regulate both the competence to conduct disciplinary and dismissal procedures, as well as the role of the disciplinary commission, and to introduce the principle of proportionality between the disciplinary offense and the disciplinary sanctions (European Commission 2012d, 22, 2013b, 36–37, 2014b, 37, 2015b, 51, 2016b, 12; Vlada Crne Gore 2013, 38, 2014, 60–61, 2015, 19). Furthermore, the Judicial and Prosecutorial Councils continued to enhance the institutional framework by establishing the *Disciplinary Councils* on May 26, 2015, and May 14, 2016, as well by introducing databases on procedures conducted regarding the accountability of judges and state prosecutors within the PRIS in 2014 (Vlada Crne Gore 2013, 40, 2014, 66–67, 2016a, 16, 34).

Speaking in practical terms in respect to building a track record of disciplinary proceedings in the judiciary, the following ensued:

a) the Disciplinary Commission initiated five disciplinary procedures in 2013; these were submitted against judges and all the proceedings were qualified as unfounded and untimely, and there were no dismissal decisions;
b) in 2014, the Commission launched two disciplinary procedures against judges; in one case the judge was sentenced to a 20% reduction in monthly salary; there were no ongoing procedures on the dismissal of judges;
c) in 2015, the Commission initiated four disciplinary procedures; in all four cases warnings were issued as sanctions; no dismissal proceedings were initiated against judges; and
d) in 2016, no disciplinary procedures or dismissals were initiated against judges; in 2017 there was a disciplinary violation in one case (Sudski Savjet 2013, 28, 2014, 19, 2015, 15, 2016, 16).

By the same token, in regard to disciplinary procedures against prosecutors: in 2013, the Disciplinary Council imposed four disciplinary measures against one state prosecutor and three deputy prosecutors by reducing their monthly salaries by 20%, and one deputy prosecutor was dismissed; in 2014, 2015, 2016, and 2017, there were no disciplinary or dismissal procedures against prosecutors (Tužilači Savjet 2013, 5–6, 2014, 18, 2015, 19).[11]

Last but not least, in reference to the Union's final suggestion on reviewing the system of functional immunity for judges and prosecutors, the parliament adopted the Laws on Judicial Council and state prosecutor's office (2015) to ensure full accountability of judges and state prosecutors in terms of criminal offenses, in particular, criminal offenses against their official duty. Hence, the government reports stated that there were no cases in which the functional immunity of judges or state prosecutors prevented the implementation of the criminal proceedings in 2015 and 2016 (European Commission 2012d, 22, 2014b, 37; Vlada Crne Gore 2013, 40, 2016b, 16–17, 2017, 19–20).

Judicial Effectiveness and Efficiency

Several measures were introduced by Montenegro related to ensuring reliable and consistent judicial statistics, as well as introducing a system to monitor the length of trials in respect to the first EU concerns over judicial effectiveness provided within the Screening Report and the Progress Report.

Additional actions may be observed toward monitoring the backlog of cases within PRIS and establishing Annual programs for resolving the backlog of cases at all court levels. In this sense, the Judicial Council is now responsible for referring judges to other courts to resolve the issue of backlog of cases, while the PRIS system provides the ability to follow both the total number of backlog of cases and uncompleted cases. Therefore,

a) on December 31, 2013, Montenegrin courts were handling the backlog of 34,859 cases: the courts resolved 24,014 of these, while the number of unresolved cases remained at 10,845;
b) on December 31, 2014, there were 132,944 cases still to be dealt with: the courts completed 97,247 cases, while 35,697 cases remained unresolved;
c) on December 31, 2015, there was a backlog of 121,651 cases: 88,330 were resolved and 33,321 remained unresolved; and finally,
d) on December 31, 2016, there was a backlog of 122,850 cases: 90,537 were resolved, with 32,113 remaining unresolved (Vlada Crne Gore 2013, 53; Sudski Savjet 2013, 40, 2014, 48, 2015, 32, 2016, 37).[12]

Also, the *Amendments to the Law on Mediation*, which further regulate alternative dispute resolution, primarily through mediation, court settlement, and arbitration, were adopted on June 6, 2012. Following the strengthening of the legal system in 2013, there were in total 1,769 court settlements in front of the courts, while in 2014 1,269 cases in total were resolved by court settlement and the remaining 353 cases by mediation (European Commission 2012d, 22, 2015b, 51; Vlada Crne Gore 2014, 89–90). Furthermore, in 2014 the number of cases addressed through mediation was 1,722 (without labor disputes), based on which agreements were made in 869 cases.[13] The number of labor disputes addressed through mediation to the Agency for peaceful settlement of labor disputes was 89, while 1,859 cases were finalized through court settlement (Vlada Crne Gore 2016a, 48–49).

Also, concerning the Commission's second and third recommendations, Montenegrin authorities decided on a number of measures aiming to further enhance the current legislative framework and reinforce its information system in respect to strengthening the enforcement of judgments in civil cases. After the introduction of the bailiff system (following the adoption of the Law on Bailiffs on December 31, 2012), the Basic Courts in Montenegro had in total 184,107 enforcement cases (8,548 cases based on execution documents and 175,523 cases based on credible documents), based on which 4,451 cases were completed by execution document and 27,044 cases were completed by credible document. Furthermore, the Commercial Court in Montenegro had in total 2,602 enforcement cases after the introduction of the bailiff system (747 cases based on execution documents and 1,855 cases based on credible documents), consequently resulting in the completion of all enforcement cases (Vlada Crne Gore 2016a, 53–54).

Last, the government together with the parliament initiated further measures toward amending the legislative framework to transform the JTC into an independent and self–sustainable institution. In this sense, the parliament adopted the *Law on the Training Centre in the Judiciary and the State Prosecutor's Office* on September 23, 2015, according to which the status of the JTC as an organizational unit of the Supreme Court was transformed into an independent institution, named the Training Centre, in the Judiciary and the State Prosecution Office. The newly formed center has its own steering committee, while the funding, according to the law, is provided from the budget in the amount of 2% as dedicated to judiciary (Vlada Crne Gore 2013, 56; Vlada Crne Gore 2016a, 57).

The JTC organized continuous training programs on the implementation of the CPC¸ the Law on Civil Procedure, the Law on Obligations, the Law on Property Relations, the Family Law, the Criminal Code, and the Law on Enforcement and Security of Claims, and so on. In this respect, in the period between January and December 2015, the JTC organized 50 trainings with 241 participants from the Prosecutor's Office, 466 representatives from the judiciary, and 62 participants from other state bodies. The trainings were conducted by Montenegrin experts, regional countries, EU member states, and the United States. For the purpose of continuous education of judges and prosecutors, a total of 248,679 EUR was spent in 2015, which was more than expected. Finally, in the period between January 1 and December 31, 2016, the JTC conducted 51 trainings with 283 representatives from the Prosecutor's Office and 469 representatives from the judiciary, and for this purpose 353,369 EUR was spent in 2016[14] (Vlada Crne Gore 2013, 56, 2015, 32–33, 2016a, 55–57, 2016b, 28–29, 2017, 31–33).

To fully understand why the EU has failed to Europeanize Montenegro in the area of the judicial reform during the whole integration stage, a thorough empirical analysis is provided in the following section of this book.

CONDITIONAL INCONSISTENCY IN THE EU'S APPROACH AND THE STATE'S SELECTIVE FULFILLMENT OF JUDICIAL REFORM DEMANDS

Pre-Negotiation Stage

In a nutshell, empirical evidence of judicial reform in Montenegro during the pre-negotiation phase reveals two main observations. First, this phase is characterized by the Union's intention to improve all components within the judiciary in Montenegro in respect to independence, and to a lesser extent, to accountability, effectiveness and efficiency. However, although the Commission underlined the significance of addressing all judiciary reform criteria, it is clear that the Union demonstrated its most profound impact on enhancing judicial independence, particularly in reducing the politicization of judiciary by appointing the Judicial and Prosecutorial Councils, the Supreme Court president and the Supreme State Prosecutor by the parliament by simple majority, as well as judges of the Constitutional Court. Additionally, participation of the Minister of Justice as a voting member in the Judicial Council, strengthening the merit-based elements of the career system, and finally establishing the country-wide single recruitment system were also emphasized as such (European Commission 2008b, 2009b). Second, Montenegro achieved overall moderate results in judicial reform during the pre-negotiation phase. On the one hand, the potential candidate country showed considerable improvements in strengthening its judicial effectiveness and efficiency by adopting new legislation and introducing new institutions, but on the other hand, it also showed declining trends in enhancing judicial independence and accountability (European Commission 2010b, 2011b).

Noticeably, the state authorities achieved overall progress in developing a strategic framework, strengthening the legal system, and establishing a new institutional setup for judicial effectiveness and efficiency, primarily by introducing the new Judicial Reform Strategy 2007–2012 (2007), followed by the Action Plan for implementation (2007) and the monitoring Commission (2008), adoption of the Constitution of Montenegro (2007), Law on Judicial Education (2006), Law on protection of the right to a trial within a reasonable time (2007), CPC (2009), Law on Enforcement and Security of Claims (2011), Law on Public Bailiffs (2011), Amendments to Law on Notaries (2008), and the establishment of new institutions, namely the Judicial Training Centre—JTC (2006), Mediation Centre (2008), Notary Chamber (2011) and Judicial Information System—PRIS and the web portal of courts (2010), and the like. Rapid legislative growth together with increasing institutional development, consequently resulting in sustainable reforms in implementation, primarily in reducing the backlogs of cases and introducing continuous education of judicial office holders within the JTC. Hence, it is possible to confirm the existence of legal consistency in judicial effectiveness and efficiency in the pre-negotiation phase (Vlada Crne Gore 2011a, b, c).

However, the main concerns are still primarily related to the issue of politicization of the judiciary. The country made limited progress in improving judicial independence, particularly in reducing political influence over the judiciary by the parliament, specifically in the parliamentary appointment of the Judicial Council, the Supreme Court president and the Supreme State Prosecutor by simple majority, Constitutional Court judges, and introducing criteria and conditions for these appointments, disciplinary proceedings, and dismissal of judges and prosecutors. In particular, the adoption of the new Constitution (2007),[15] as well as numerous sub-constitutional provisions, namely amendments to the Law on Judicial Council (2008, 2011), amendments to the Law on Courts and the Law on State Prosecutors (2008, 2011), Rules of procedures of the Judicial and Prosecutorial Councils (2008, 2009, 2011), along with the establishment of Judicial and Prosecutorial Councils (2008, 2009), Commissions for appointment of judges (2011), Disciplinary Commissions for judges and prosecutors (2011), Commission for noncompliance of Code of Ethics of judges and prosecutors (2011), failed to address the required issues (Vlada Crne Gore 2011a, b, c).

Apparently, the new legislative framework brought minor changes to reinforcing judicial independence, while the problem of political interference by the parliament (and government) into the judicial sector, that is, the issue of politicization, remained a major challenge for establishing effective principles of impartiality of the judiciary and overall functionality of the Montenegrin judicial system (Council of the European Union 2007; European Commission 2007b, 2008b, 2009b, 2010b, 2011b). For the sake of the arguments, concerning the adopted constitutional provisions on the composition of the Judicial Council, which were supposed to reduce political influence by the parliament, the enacted provisions unfortunately fostered political interference of legislative bodies into the judiciary through the active role of the parliament and the president in procedures for the election and dismissal of judges and lawyers, together with the active participation of the Minister of Justice in the Council (CEDEM 2012, 7–8; HRA 2012, 11–19). Also, in terms of the ongoing and rather serious concerns of the Union over the politicization of the judiciary, especially through the appointment of the Prosecutorial Council, appointment and dismissal of the president of the Judicial Council (i.e., president of the Supreme Court) and the State Prosecutor by the parliament, active involvement of the Minister of Justice as a voting member in the Judicial Council, and finally, unclear division of responsibility for supervision of courts between the Ministry of Justice and the Judicial Council, it is more than clear that Montenegro did not manage to address the main judicial reform conditions during the pre-negotiation phase, although there were no adverse effects on the country's integration dynamics (HRA 2009, 21–28, 30–39; HRA and CeMI 2015a, 11–21). This being said, the adopted constitutional and legislative provisions did not contain clear and precise legal safeguard measures on the procedures for appointments, dismissal, promotions, and disciplinary proceedings of judges and prosecutors, nor did they managed to remove the established judiciary control of recruitment and career management from the parliament, consequently providing a visible risk for the continuous politicization of the judicial sector (HRA 2013, 16–27). Thus, the EU was not fully consistent in imposing its external pressure to meet judicial reform criteria. Rather, the Union had a negatively reinforcing impact on judicial independence, especially in the adoption of legislation and compliance with EU policies.

A visible inconsistency is also observed within the realm of judicial accountability. Although the country demonstrated improvements in its legal system and institutional setup during the pre-negotiation phase, substantial shortfalls are seen particularly in legal provisions allowing both judges and prosecutors to enjoy functional immunity from prosecution, and therefore not being subject to the criminal law, and, moreover, in insufficient monitoring of the judiciary in corruption and conflict of interest cases (CEDEM 2012, 6–8; HRA 2009, 39, 129, 137). The concerns over the insufficient number of disciplinary proceedings and dismissals against judges and prosecutors in the period between 2010 and 2012 remained, based on which the Disciplinary Commission of judges and prosecutors launched only four disciplinary procedures against judges, consequently resulting in only one dismissal and one disciplinary warning (HRA 2012, 74–75). It is evident that the EU-driven judicial reforms had a negatively reinforcing impact on judicial accountability, thus reflecting a decline in legal and institutional changes. Hence, the empirical findings reveal that Montenegro in the given period achieved visible progress in strengthening its legal framework and improving its institutional setup primarily through the reinforcement of judicial effectiveness and efficiency, thus creating a solid basis of legislative consistency and coherence within the legal system, while on the other hand, showing poor and lax reform progress in addressing the profound issue of politicization of the judiciary. Unequivocally, this integration period was primarily characterized by the state's weak results in reducing political influence over the judiciary by the parliament, as one of the key conditions for establishing a functional judiciary and advancing in the EU accession process (Appicciafuco 2010, 741–68; Memeti 2014, 58–67).

Brussels had both a deficient and reinforcing influence on judiciary reform in Montenegro in general during the pre-negotiation phase. Primarily, the EU-driven judiciary reforms had positive effects on judicial effectiveness and efficiency, but also rather negative effects on independence and accountability. Hence, the EU external incentives resulted in mixed influence on judiciary reform in Montenegro. However, if one presumes that judicial independence and accountability remain more important criteria for the enlargement policy than effectiveness and efficiency, then this study is in a position to argue that Brussels did not have a mixed impact on Montenegrin judicial reform in the given period. Rather, the EU-driven judicial reforms had a negatively reinforcing impact on empowerment of the judicial system, demonstrating at the same time inconsistency and lack of concern for the integration process. Visible progress was indeed made in strengthening judicial capacity, however, politicization of the judiciary in appointing and controlling judges and prosecutors, and also insufficient results in the performance of the Disciplinary Commissions remained matters of serious concern. Based on what is being argued, it is grounded to claim that the Union failed to Europeanize Montenegro, since this candidate country did not achieve concrete, sustainable results and failed to establish a convincing and credible track record in judicial reform during the pre-negotiation stage.

Paradoxically, the EU granted the status of candidate country to Montenegro based on partial fulfillment of judicial reform criteria by focusing mostly on judicial effectiveness and efficiency during the pre-negotiation phase. Looking from the current perspective, the Union demonstrated an obvious lack of interest as well as permissiveness in reinforcing judiciary reform in Montenegro, consequently applying the strategy of selective imposition of conditions. The EU reaffirmed further progress of Montenegro in the integration phase even though the Commission at that time on a number of occasions outlined many visible flaws and shortfalls in strengthening the Montenegrin legal and institutional framework of judges and prosecutors (Petrović 2013; Dallara 2014). Although the potential candidate country did not quickly, continuously, or purposefully commit to adopting the acquis and failed to align with the EU's requirements in the given area, the overall limited progress in reforming the state's judicial sector during the pre-negotiation stage did not however profoundly affect Montenegrin advancement in the accession process. On the contrary, Montenegro was allowed to take a step forward in the process of European integration, even though further efforts in reinforcing judicial impartiality and independence were a key condition for the advancement in the EU integration process (Renner and Trauner 2009; Kmezić 2017).

To sum up, it might be reasonable to conclude that, since the country has failed to effectively fortify judicial independence and accountability in accordance with the integration dynamics, this particular behavior may result in Montenegro not managing to properly comply with the obligations of EU membership during the period of accession negotiations over the long term.

Negotiation Stage

There are two main observations to be made when examining the negotiation phase. First of all, the Screening Report for Chapter 23 as launched by the Commission in 2012 represents the most comprehensive analytical document examining current levels of judicial reforms in Montenegro. It provides not only suggestions on enhancing the legal system and institutional setup of the reform of the judicial sector, but, perhaps far more importantly, also highlights the requirements for the sustainability of reforms, particularly in building a credible track record of implementation (European Commission 2012d). For instance, the issue of politicization of the judiciary in the parliament's active involvement in appointing the Judicial and Prosecutorial Councils, as well as selecting judges and prosecutors, remains a huge problem for overall judiciary reform and is thus a major challenge for successful completion of the accession process itself. In short, politicization undermines concrete, convincing, and sustainable results in reforming Montenegrin judicial sector. Second, Montenegro has in terms of its domestic politics achieved insufficiently satisfactory progress in meeting judicial reform requirements during the negotiation phase. On the one hand, the candidate country has demonstrated visible progress in strengthening judicial effectiveness and efficiency, while on the other hand, the state has suffered a declining trend in improving judicial independence, impartiality, and accountability.

The period between 2012 and 2017 was generally characterized by the state's advanced efforts in strengthening its legal system by adopting new legislation, implementation of already adopted legislative measures, as well as further reinforcement of judicial capacities to ensure the sustainability of reforms. The Montenegrin judiciary achieved satisfactory results in terms of further enhancing its legal system of judicial efficiency by adopting the Law on the Training Centre in the Judiciary and the State Prosecutor's office (2015), and in additional judicial activities oriented toward developing judicial capacities by means of ensuring necessary budget funds for financing continuous trainings and organizing training programs on implementing legislation: this was, for instance, done in terms of the CPC, the Law on Civil Procedure, the Law on Obligations, the Law on Property Relations, the Family Law, the Criminal Code and the Law on Enforcement and Security of Claims (European Commission 2013b, 2014b, 2015b, 2016b).

However, although the state has made solid progress in strengthening judicial effectiveness and efficiency, there are certain declining trends in addressing these dimensions. The Montenegrin judiciary continues to deal with serious issues regarding the reliability and credibility of data as well as the inconsistency of statistics due to the lack of a clear methodological framework, while the data on the overall length of judicial procedures is still not available (MANS 2017, 21–27). More than this, despite the country having demonstrated valuable outcomes in reinforcing its judicial capacities, there are still serious concerns related to insufficient funding for trainings. Noticeably, the new law on the JTC contains a legal provision of 2% of the dedicated budget for the judiciary and State Prosecutor's office to be allocated for effective functioning of the Centre (HRA and CeMI 2015b, 251; MANS 2017, 29). It appears that the lack of sustainable funds for continuous and initial training programs of the JTC still remains a substantial problem for strengthening judicial capacity even further. Given the fact that more than two-thirds of the budgeted funds for the JTC are provided by international donors, continuous training programs are brought into question, thus indicating the possibility for backsliding in terms of reinforcing judicial capacities. The issue of organizing initial training programs by the JTC still represents a major problem: due to the lack of financial resources, these programs are mostly of an ad hoc nature and organized without a set curricula (HRA and CeMI 2015b, 22–23, 123–24; MANS 2017, 29–30).

Essentially, Montenegro did not achieve satisfactory results in strengthening judicial independence during the negotiation phase (MANS 2018). Although the candidate country has introduced partial efforts in strengthening its legal system and establishing its institutional framework, there are additional concerns over the sustainability of reforms, that is, building having a credible track record of implementation, especially when it comes to issues over politicization of the judiciary. This enlargement state has taken partial steps in terms of amending its Constitution and ensuring the independence and accountability of its judiciary, especially in regard to reducing the political influence of Montenegrin Parliament and the government in the judiciary. Even though the constitutional provisions provide grounded measures in appointing the president of the Supreme Court, the Supreme State Prosecutor and state prosecutors, and election and dismissal of the Constitutional Court, visible flaws are particularly seen over the issue of the composition of the Judicial and Prosecutorial Council. According to new constitutional provisions, the Judicial Council is formed by the president of the Supreme Court, four judges are appointed and dismissed by the Conference of judges, four prominent lawyers appointed and dismissed by the parliament, and the Minister of Justice. Evidently, the new composition of the Judicial Council opens the possibility for strong political interference into the judiciary. First, there are no limits to the political engagement of the four elected prominent lawyers, thus allowing for these lawyers to be members of political parties. Secondly, participation of the Minister of Justice as a member of the Judicial Council remains a reason for serious concern due to the very real possibility of continuous political influence on the judiciary (HRA and CeMI 2015b, 72–73; HRA 2013, 21–25). A similar situation is observable in the composition of the Prosecutorial Council. According to a provision within the Law on State Prosecutor's office (2015), the Prosecutorial Council is staffed by the president of Prosecutorial Council (i.e., the Supreme State Prosecutor), five state prosecutors appointed and dismissed by the Conference of prosecutors, four prominent lawyers appointed and dismissed by the parliament, and one representative of the Ministry of Justice. Similarly, the composition of the Prosecutorial Council still leaves space for political influence by the parliament and the government, chiefly because current legislation does not provide limits to the political participation of the four elected lawyers in internal political processes, while at the same time the active involvement of the Ministry of Justice's representative creates space for strong political interference (HRA and CeMI 2015b, 116–17).

The reasons for serious concern over judicial independence still exist in the insufficiently defined rationale for dismissal of judges and state prosecutors as well. The constitutional provision does not provide enough insight in regard to the dismissal of judges, except for the statement that the Judicial Council dismisses judges, president of courts, and lay judges (Constitution of Montenegro, Amendment IX Point 4 2013). Also, the amendments do not contain enough information about the dismissal of state prosecutors, except for the assertion that the Prosecutorial Council elects and dismisses holders of the state prosecutor's office and state prosecutors. Hence, the constitutional provisions permit that holders of the state prosecutor's office and state prosecutors may be dismissed only if sentenced to unconditional imprisonment (Constitution of Montenegro, Amendments X, XI 2013).

The state authorities have also achieved partial results in strengthening the country's legal system over the recruitment process, which needs to be transparent and merit based, and Montenegro needs to introduce a single, nationwide recruitment system. The Law on the Judicial Council and Rights and Duties of Judges, the Law on Courts, and the Law on state prosecutor's office (2015) do not provide further legislative measures to improve judicial independence. Rather, the provisions within the Law on the Judicial Council do not contain sufficiently developed procedures for the election of judges, especially from the rank of judges and lawyers, because current legislation does not define clear measures preventing political interference. The law contains a periodic evaluation of the work of judges but not the periodic evaluation of judges of the Supreme Court. Therefore, the lack of accountability of Supreme Court judges calls into question the accountability of the entire Montenegrin judicial system, precisely because the Supreme Court judges are not subject to supervision or performance evaluation (HRA and CeMI 2015b, 71–76; MANS 2017, 13–14). Finally, the laws on courts and on state prosecutor's office do not have provisions particularly related to periodical professional assessment of the performance of judges and presidents of courts, state prosecutors and their deputies, as a condition for their promotion, nor are there conditions for the election of judges in terms of stipulating the obligation of completing mandatory trainings organized by the JTC, while the provisions within state prosecutor's office related to promotion do not possess clear and transparent merit-based promotion system (HRA and CeMI 2015, 20–21; MANS 2017, 13–14).

By the same token, Montenegro has selectively adopted measures toward strengthening its judicial accountability during the process of accession negotiations. Noticeably, although the state demonstrated visible results in improving its legal system and developing a new institutional setup, there remain serious concerns over achieving concrete and sustainable results and building a credible track record in the enforcement of the accountability of judges and prosecutors. In line with strengthening the legal and institutional framework for judicial accountability, the judicial bodies primarily adopted the amendments to the Code of Ethics of Judges and Public Prosecutors (2014), along with appointing Commissions for monitoring the Code of Ethics within the Councils (MANS 2017, 18–19). Also, during the accession negotiations, presidents of courts, judges, public prosecutors, and deputy public prosecutors continued to declare their assets in accordance with the Law on Prevention of Conflict of Interest, based on which the Commission for the Prevention of Conflict of Interest published its annual reports. However, there are still concerns primarily related to providing clear, precise, and sustainable results, as well as showing a convincing and credible track record on issues of judges' and prosecutors' performance violations. Based on the Commission's reports for monitoring the Code of Ethics of judicial office holders in the period between 2012 and 2017, out of the total number of fifty-nine initiated procedures, only four judges violated the code, while out of the total number of four procedures, in the period between 2015 and 2017, in only one case did a deputy state prosecutor violate the code. Noticeably, an unacceptably small number of conducted cases, alongside the extremely few violations of the Codes of Ethics raises serious doubts over judicial accountability (MANS 2018, 18, 2019, 12).

Limited progress has been achieved in strengthening disciplinary and dismissal procedures, as well as their implementation—one of the central pillars for establishing functional judicial accountability. Primarily, the constitutional amendments do not prescribe reasons for dismissing judges in accordance with the opinion of the Venice Commission. Rather, the amendments more likely provide general provisions in terms of the dismissal of judges, presidents of courts and lay judges (Constitution of Montenegro, Amendment IX Point 4 2013). Current mechanisms of judicial accountability do not ensure a credible track record of implementation, given the fact that in the period between 2013 and 2017, there was one dismissal procedure against a judge and one against a prosecutor (MANS 2018, 18, 20–21, 28–29). However, although the state bodies have not taken any concrete steps in terms of reviewing dismissal procedures, results can be seen in the case of strengthening legislation, particularly so in improving disciplinary proceedings. The laws on the Judicial Council and the state prosecutor's office have further enhanced disciplinary procedures by distinguishing between lighter, heavier, and serious disciplinary violations and disciplinary sanctions of judges and prosecutors (MANS 2017, 20, 2018, 14, 18). According to these laws, the procedure for determining disciplinary responsibility for disciplinary violations conducted by the disciplinary councils is based on the proposal by the newly established disciplinary prosecutors.

Last but not least, Montenegrin authorities have taken partial steps in eliminating functional immunity and ensuring full accountability of judges and prosecutors under the criminal law. The constitutional amendments provide the provisions of functional immunity only for holders of state prosecution office and state prosecutors by stating that they cannot be held liable for an opinion given or a decision taken while performing their duties unless it is a criminal offense (MANS 2017, 21). This particularly means that prosecutors are not protected by complete functional immunity and can be charged with criminal offenses committed during their prosecutorial duties. In line with the introduced legal provision, official government data indicate that there have been no cases in which the functional immunity of judges and prosecutors prevented the start of criminal procedures.

The empirical findings suggest that the Union showed both reinforcing and declining trends over judicial reform in Montenegro during the negotiation phase. In particular, the EU-driven rule of law reforms had a positively reinforcing impact over strengthening judicial effectiveness and efficiency, but also a negatively reinforcing impact on improving judicial independence and accountability. It is evident that Montenegro has achieved overall partial results in the reform of its judicial sector during the most demanding and dynamic integration phase. The candidate country has achieved satisfactory results in strengthening the legal and institutional framework of judicial effectiveness and efficiency, particularly in reviewing and rationalizing its court networks, enhancing the enforcement of judgments in civil cases, and ensuring the effective functioning of the JTC. Additional concerns over improvements in these areas still exist, however, particularly in terms of compiling reliable statistical data and consistent and valid judicial statistics, as well as the continuation of the ongoing and initial training programs of the JTC, which must be resolved with additional funding resources. On the other hand, the state has demonstrated limited progress toward reinforcing independence and accountability of its judicial system. Although the enlargement country has shown certain efforts over strengthening its legal system, particularly so by adopting constitutional provisions and legislations, and also by introducing a new institutional setup, major concerns still exist primarily in terms of the insufficiently defined or precise legal framework of judicial independence and accountability, and its effective implementation and enforcement.

Therefore, problems of judicial independence and accountability still exist in the active involvement and appointment of members of the Judicial and Prosecutorial Council by the parliament, and participation of the Minister of Justice in the Judicial Council, performance violations of judges and prosecutors, judicial capacity, functional immunity of the judiciary, and finally, dismissal procedures against judges and prosecutors.

EXPLAINING TRENDS IN PARTIAL FULFILMENT OF JUDICIAL REFORM REQUIREMENTS DURING THE INTEGRATION PHASE

Based on the discussion, there is one main question yet to be answered: How can one explain the given selective fulfillment in judicial reform during the entire integration stage? More precisely, what explains the state's achievement of visible results in fulfilling the judicial effectiveness and efficiency criteria? But, perhaps far more importantly, why did the state demonstrate substantially limited progress in the process of Europeanization in the given period, in particular when addressing judicial independence and accountability requirements as such?

Regarding the country's positive results in judicial effectiveness and efficiency during the integration phase, this study recognizes two applicable explanations for overall judiciary success. The first explanation is grounded in domestic reasons, primarily in the increase of the judicial budget (HRA and CeMI 2015a, 28–30; MANS 2017, 11, 14–15). After declaring its independence from Serbia in 2006, Montenegro started increasing its judicial budget to start fulfilling rule of law criteria, the main condition for further advancement in the EU accession process. The acceleration of the EU integration process and consequently addressing the Copenhagen political criteria stipulated within the Commission's Opinion from 2010 had a significant effect on reinforcing respective judicial funds and consequently meeting the respective requirements. Also, tackling easier judicial dimensions, for instance reducing the backlogs of cases, introducing the PRIS and introducing the continuous training for judiciary holders by the JTC, was the least painful way for the country to start the process of judicial reform to achieve visible results in this area (HRA and CeMI 2015a, 71–72; HRA and CeMI 2015b, 122–23; MANS 2017, 15). Arguably, by addressing certain judicial dimensions, such as capacity requirements, the state presented itself as a serious agent in the reform processes, consequently leading the state to further advance in the EU integration progress. Official data indicate that funds of judicial office holders were increased several times during the integration phase. The budget for the judiciary and the Prosecutor's Office for 2012 was 24.9 million EUR (which represents 0.75% of Montenegrin GDP); in 2013 the figure was 26.1 million EUR (0.80% of the GDP); in 2014 it was 26.6 million EUR (0.86% of the GDP); in 2015 it was 27.1 million EUR (0.78% of the GDP); and finally in 2016 it was 34.6 million EUR

(0.89% of the GDP), that is, 26% more than the 2015 budget (European Commission 2012c, 45–46; European Commission 2013b, 37, 2014b, 38, 2015b, 51, 2016b, 56). Apparently, the same logic is applicable to the functioning of the JTC. After the introduction of the law on the JTC in 2015, legally allotting 2% of the given budget toward the effective functioning of the Centre, judicial capacity recorded substantial improvements. Thus, in 2015, the JTC budget was allocated with 170,000 EUR, while in 2016 this budget was allocated 399,724 EUR: this is equal to 135.2% when compared to the year before (European Commission 2015b, 51, 2016b, 56).

The second and apparently more convincing explanation lays in the corelation with external factors, namely international donors. Evidently, the newly established state and insufficiently developed judicial sector requested financial support from various international donors, notably from the Union and its member states, non-EU member states (particularly Norway and the United States) and finally international organizations (UNDP and OSCE) (HRA and CeMI 2015a, 60, 2015b, 176). In fact, improving effectiveness in a country substantially suffering from weak judicial capacities was set as a judicial priority agenda by the EU and international donors. These actors aimed to build an efficient judicial sector in Montenegro by providing financial support in the areas of strengthening the legal framework of judicial capacity primarily through international assistance and expertise. In addition to this, it is not rare for the Union to push a country toward strengthening its institutional and structural system through the establishment of a Judicial Council during the integration phase. The same situation was applicable to the case study of Montenegro: the Union was substantially and actively involved in strengthening judicial capacity through supporting the establishment of the Judicial and Prosecutorial Councils and its Secretariats. Furthermore, legal and institutional improvements to please the international donors were also accompanied by technical capacity-building and overall support for IT equipment (strengthening the PRIS), technical and electronic adaptation of courts through audio-visual programs, technical and technological provisions for prosecutors' offices and judges' chambers, as well as the continuous and initial training programs for judicial office holders (HRA and CeMI 2015b, 250–51). Finally, the need to strengthen judicial efficiency, as expressed by the international donors, was also done through the implementation of information-communication technology within the courts system by means of financial support for informational equipment, various educational activities (trainings, study trips etc.), and strengthening human capacities (HRA and CeMI 2015a, 30). Thus, it may be reasonable to assume that all these capacity-building activities granted by the Union and the international donors aimed to support and stimulate Montenegro in continuing its overall judicial reform processes by facing and tackling the most difficult and demanding judicial dimensions such as judicial independence, impartiality, and accountability.

However, although the financial means have increased substantially, the impression is that judicial capacity still faces the problem of insufficient financial resources. Evidently, the lack of finances needed for consistent development of judicial capacities is a wide-spread systemic issue, especially in terms of introducing a system that measures and monitors the length of trials, establishes reliable and consistent judicial statistics, and secures funds for continuous and initial training programs of the JTC (HRA and CeMI 2015a, 70). Thus, Montenegrin authorities need to invest in further efforts so as to ensure reliable and additional financial resources to tackle the previously stated capacity requirements.

On the other hand, one question that has aroused much interest is why the state demonstrated limited progress or declining trends in the process of Europeanization, specifically in regard to strengthening judicial independence and accountability during the integration phase? Also, how can we explain the existence of continuous control and politicization of the judiciary by the state bodies despite the constant concerns of Brussels and repeated warnings to resolve this problem?

Three main explanations exist in this regard. First, the Montenegrin judicial system was characterized by rapid legislative growth and adoption and institutional transplantation during the whole integration phase. The adoption of a large number of constitutional amendments, laws, and by-laws has largely mitigated the process of effective implementation and enforcement of enacted legislation related to judicial independence and accountability. The available data indicate that more than fifty laws have been adopted, and more than twenty institutions established in this integration phase (HRA 2013; CEDEM 2012; MANS 2017; HRA and CeMI 2015a). Legislative growth, especially when it comes to the introduced legislative changes over the appointment of the Judicial and Prosecutorial Councils and state prosecutors, and dismissal and disciplinary procedures of judges and prosecutors, requires a longer implementation period and therefore its results can only be measured later (MANS 2017, 11–14). In a weak judicial system such as Montenegro's, accelerated and often late legislative growth substantially impacts not just undeveloped state institutions, but rather the whole judicial sector. This results in the overload and collapse of the entire legal and institutional system. Pressure from the EU to strengthen judicial independence overloaded the state administrative structure, while, at the same time, there was fast and formal adoption of legislation, although the legal changes were insufficiently effective. Most of these laws were adopted amendments to existing legislation that were supposed to introduce legal changes following the Commission's recommendations (HRA and CeMI 2015b; MANS

2018, 2019). However, the situation in judiciary at the time did not reflect the state's efforts to reinforce judicial independence. Instead, formal adoption of legislation and its incongruous effects merely created the illusion of legal changes and effective implementation. Therefore, one can assume that politicization of judiciary remained a major issue in the reform of judicial independence at that particular time. Following this domino effect, on the other hand, the artificially adopted legislation resulted in the creation of more rigid judicial institutions, often with only a fictitious role and use (Mendelski 2015; Elbasani 2013). The recently established Judicial and Prosecutorial Councils, financially supported by the Union and international donors, are good examples. Both of the Councils are artificially transplanted judicial bodies that are marred by the political influence of domestic elites. They are negatively reinforcing institutional pillars, a practice that is common to most Western Balkan countries suffering from profound issues of limited statehood (Dallara 2014; Džankić and Keil and Kmezić 2019).

Second, the lack of political will to substantially reduce politicization of judiciary is another explanation for declining trends in strengthening judicial independence and accountability. Evidently, the judiciary was still under strong and profound political influence of the parliament even during the integration phase, resulting in full control over the functioning of this body (Strekov 2016, 505–20). The political interference of the parliament into the judicial system affected the impartiality of prosecutors and judges, prosecution and final convictions, especially in respect to high-ranking politicians. Also, the dependency of judicial office holders on politicians had a strong influence on making impartial and fair decisions, especially in terms of the close family members of ruling elites using their influence to gain wealth illegally, or when using state budget funds for party purposes, that is, funding election campaigns (Vučković and Đorđević 2019, 158–69; Džankić 2018, 86–100; Keil 2018, 65–78; Elbasani and Šelo Šabić 2018, 1317–35). The politicization of the judiciary influences control over internal processes and trends in the judicial sector, a system in which the need for the establishment of impartial and accountable judiciary consequently results in sanctioning of judicial office holder(s). Thus, it is not rare that the need for judge(s) to perform more independently ends in the judges' dismissal. Profound political influence over the judiciary allows the domestic elite to assume the very comfortable position of being protected from prosecution and conviction. For the sake of the argument, Montenegro is the only EU candidate country in which the government has not changed since the introduction of the multiparty system (the end of 1980s), and corruption scandals within high-ranking government circles are quite common (Morrison 2018; Komar and Živković 2016; IA and CGO and CRNVO and CeMI 2018). It is evident, however, that the political elites do not effectively address those judicial independence and accountability requirements simply because this might jeopardize their positions of power.

Survey results from February 2017 indicate downward trends in overall public trust in the judiciary system; 41.7% of respondents do not believe that judges or prosecutors fight political corruption in the judiciary (CeMI and HRA 2017, 12). Compared to the results of a 2016 survey, the level of public confidence decreased from 52.6% (in 2016) to 44.6% (in 2017).[16] The lack of public trust in the Montenegrin judicial system remains a matter for serious concern for the government, as the official survey indicates that the majority of respondents (57.4%) believe that judges do not decide independently, while 30.4% of respondents believe that they perform without any political influence. On the issues of judicial independence and judicial professional advancement, 58.4% of respondents believe that the decisions of judges are influenced by the government, while 46.6% believe that judges are not elected and promoted based on their professional expertise, but rather on their strong political ties and kinship–friendship connections (CeMI and HRA 2016, 27–31). When asked about prosecution, 40% of respondents believe that that state prosecutor's office is not independent in deciding who to prosecute, and of those who believe that the Prosecutor's Office is not independent, more than 75.3% believe that prosecutorial decisions are influenced by the executive power (CeMI and HRA 2016, 34–37).

Political influence on judicial accountability also had a strong impact on maintaining a good track record of disciplinary proceedings and dismissals against judges and prosecutors. The low number of conducted disciplinary and dismissal procedures against judicial office holders in the period between 2010 and 2012 called into question any real progress in judicial accountability, taking into account the fact the judiciary reform in postcommunist countries was characterized by high levels of judicial corruption (MANS 2018, 18, 2019, 12). One cannot but mention the continuous downward trends in strengthening the impartiality and accountability of judges and prosecutors during the integration stage, particularly in terms of the composition of the Judicial and Prosecutorial Councils, insufficiently defined dismissal procedures for judicial office holders, the introduction of a nationwide recruitment system, and the periodical assessment of the performance of judges and presidents of courts, state prosecutors and their deputies as a condition for their promotion and election (HRA and CeMI 2015b; MANS 2017). Ultimately, the current trend in the judiciary indicates a win-win situation for both the judicial sector and domestic/political elites, becoming highly beneficial for both parties. On the one hand, a substantially small number of highly ranked politicians have been prosecuted and convicted, while on the other hand, a negligible number of judges and prosecutors have been dismissed so far (Vučković and Đorđević 2019; Elbasani and Šelo Šabić 2018). This assertion has been confirmed in the normative analysis presented here, and it highlights that thus far in the negotiation phase there has been only one disciplinary violation (2017) pursued by the Judicial and Prosecutorial Councils against judges and prosecutors (CGO and CRNVO and CeMI 2018; MANS 2018, 2019).

Finally, the insufficiently active role of the Union within the enlargement process during the integration phase was reflected in declining trends in reinforcing judicial independence and accountability in Montenegro. The conditional policy of the Union played a rather marginal role in reducing political influence by the parliament, particularly in the case of appointing the Judicial and Prosecutorial Councils, and also in appointing, promoting, and managing various disciplinary and dismissal proceedings of judges and prosecutors. Rather, the conditionality had more features of being a monitoring process, consequently undermining the power of this mechanism and reducing it to a mere technocratic repetition of recommendations without imposing clear and credible sanction policies of noncompliance with the Copenhagen political criteria (Gateva 2015). It is possible to assume that the Union's conditional inconsistency lay primarily in its internal and external political problems (enlargement fatigue, institutional reform issues, existence of political disagreements between member states about future internal and external perspectives, etc.), as well as the economic and financial issues that EU was facing at the time, consequently resulting in a lack of interest in the enlargement policy and credible fulfillment of the given political requirements (Samardžić 2016, 297–99, 333–34; Džankić and Keil and Kmezić 2019, 15–37). On the other hand, the challenges in the region at that time, as well as the insufficiently clear membership perspective for the Western Balkans, created a suitable climate for potential candidate countries to apply a selective approach in fulfilling judicial reform criteria and to successfully hide behind this tactic to avoid addressing the most difficult issues (IA and CGO and CRNVO and CeMI 2018, 3–4). Considering the fact that preserving internal political stability in the region was Brussel's highest priority (rather than any fulfillment of judicial reform requirements), Montenegro relied on the existing permissiveness of EU policy in maintaining steady progress in the accession process.

To conclude, the overall progress in fulfilling judicial effectiveness and efficiency requirements by Montenegro during the entire integration phase was the result of both external and internal factors. However, it might also be appropriate to conclude that external incentives and mechanisms, that is, EU conditional policy and international donors, were more coherent and congruent in having affected legal and institutional change through implementation and enforcement. On the other hand, the regress witnessed in strengthening judicial independence and accountability during the pre-negotiation phase was primarily the result of the incompatibility of both external and internal factors, that is, the EU itself and the domestic political leaders. In particular, the insufficiently reinforced EU conditional policy, along with the lack of political will on the part of domestic elites to effectively implement judiciary requirements, resulted in the rapid adoption of formal legislation and the transplantation of artificially created structures that did not result in effective legal and institutional changes. This is a selective approach toward promoting judicial reform that reinforces judicial effectiveness and efficiency, on the one hand, and on the other, negatively reinforces judicial independence and accountability. Moreover, the same approach has been limited by the domestic political elites who favor fulfilling less complicated judicial requirements, such as effectiveness and efficiency, to more difficult ones, that is, independence and accountability. The inconsistency in this regard has found its fertile ground among the domestic political elites who apply a very selective approach to fulfilling the judicial criteria, while at the same time are not sanctioned by the Union. Therefore, based on the empirical findings in this subchapter it is possible to confirm that the EU-driven judicial reforms had a negatively reinforcing impact on the empowerment of the judicial system in Montenegro.

CONCLUSION

Following the discussion presented in this chapter, this study has sought to provide a clearer picture on why Montenegro has failed to Europeanize its judicial system despite the long-lasting reform activities and substantial allocation of financial resources. More precisely, the discussion on what kind of conditions/factors influenced the visible decline in Montenegrin judicial reform and how these downward trends can be explained has been presented here. In this respect, there are four concluding points to be made.

First of all, since the time when Montenegro started reforming its judicial system, the Union has been faced with unfavorable domestic conditions, most notably in terms of the limited statehood issue. As was the case with many postcommunist transition societies, it was after gaining their independence that countries had to face their statehood issues, characterized by dysfunctional judicial institutions, institutionally entrenched corruption, and clientelism, as well as weak judicial capacities (Börzel 2011; Elbasani 2013; Keil and Arkan 2015). Correspondingly, the issue of limited statehood has influenced Montenegrin judicial sectors, a system in which independence and accountability of judges and prosecutors in the decision-making process remains extremely low, while monitoring judicial institutions exists only in formal and artificially transplanted bodies. We must not neglect the fact that

Montenegro has also been struggling with profound problems of politicization within its judiciary as well as being controlled by the semi-authoritarian political leaders. Institutions are not able to develop true independence or be free of autocratic leaders' rule in informal power structures, state capture by ruling parties, patronage, and control over the media. As a result, a limited statehood issue has been used as an advantage by autocrats to increase their political influence in fragile institutions as well as in the legislative sphere, while at the same time being supported by the West in their supposed roles as reformists who preserve internal political stability, that is, "stabilitocracy" (BiEPAG 2017; Bieber 2020; Kmezić 2020).

Second, the Montenegrin postcommunist legacy still plays a substantial role in the functioning of its judiciary, as has been witnessed in the accession process. The entire Western Balkan area is still a fertile ground for the establishment of strong authoritarian systems since they all share a common postcommunist heritage in the wake of the fall of their communist regimes, the wars in the former Yugoslavia, state capture by the party, decline of democratic institutions, weak state capacities, wide-spread corruption, and clientelism (Börzel 2011; Keil 2013; Noutcheva and Aydin-Düzgit 2012; Freyburg and Richter 2010; Dzihic and Wieser 2008). As a matter of fact, almost the entire authoritarian governing apparatus remained intact, as it was easily converted to present political circumstances (Radeljić 2012; Elbasani 2013). This being said, the strong influence of domestic veto players in this respect might explain the declining trends in impartiality and accountability of judges and prosecutors. These veto players (post-transition profiteers, business corruption elites, financial tycoons, etc.), originating from communist times, deeply infiltrated all spheres of public policy by having established various ties with the political elites and, therefore, the judiciary, and sought to consequently protect their interests. The very same veto players have long integrated with the ruling elites and have primarily tried, through active party participation, to secure and protect their roles and positions from any potential prosecution, often by providing party donations and financing election campaigns (Elbasani 2019; Radeljić and Đorđević 2020). This relatively limited circle of transitional winners and business elites, closely related to ruling parties' business ties or family relationships, has benefited from public procurement affairs and tenders, privatization and urbanization, and so on. Inter-dependence and mutual benefits for both sides have ensured their survival and cooperation by consequently protecting both parties from potential judicial investigation and conviction (Džankić and Keil and Kmezić 2019). It is clear that to maintain the illusion of progress in the accession process, these actors have allowed partial, limited achievements in the reinforcement of judicial independence and accountability, but only to the extent that their influence and power is not jeopardized. Hypothetically speaking, if one assumes a situation in which the state is pressured to further empower the independence and accountability of judges and prosecutors, it is reasonable to expect that the veto players would use all their influence to mitigate adoption of legislation and alignment with the given EU policies. In this sense, the state institutions have been engaged in formally adopting legislation in the form of laws and amendments, but without ensuring any effective legal changes in practice.

On the other hand, the existence of facilitating factors, namely civil society organizations (CSOs), that is, NGOs and representatives of academia, have not had any substantial impact thus far on internal judicial reform in terms of processes and changes, especially when it comes to providing recommendations or monitoring the process of strengthening independence and accountability. These domestic reformers, mainly supported by the Union, have strongly advocated in favor of the process of European integration, thus trying to play an active watchdog role in Montenegrin society (Wunch 2018; Salgado 2014). Clearly, strong ties exist between the Union and CSOs, especially in terms of monitoring the judicial reform process. A number of publications, analyses, policy reports, and such have been published by the NGO sector and have been used by the Commission as valuable input or feedback on the current level of judicial reforms in Montenegro (Freedom House 2020; Bojicic-Dzelilovic and Ker-Lindsay and Kostovicova 2013). However, the CSOs active role in the society does not have a particular impact on the decision-making process. In fact, conditions for critically oriented NGO's have been worsening at various levels, including their effective exclusion from the process of preparing a legislative act followed by the government decision to limit active participation of NGO representatives in Working Groups in preparing and conducting accession negotiation with the EU (IA and CGO and CRNVO and CeMI 2018, 3–4; CGO 2019, 4–5). Reasons for their isolation in this respect may particularly be seen in potential disclosure of judicial and corruption affairs within the state bodies, thus undermining the domestic political elites in their role of reformers ensuring their country's advance in the EU integration process. Ultimately, given the current level of politicization of the judiciary, as well as the inter-dependence between the veto players and the ruling elites, the CSOs, although financially supported by the EU and international donors, have been completely removed from judiciary processes and continue to play a rather formal and marginal role in relation to monitoring judicial reform performance.

Third, due to unfavorable domestic conditions, the political leaders have conducted formal judicial reform activities primarily through accelerated legislation and the establishment of a nonfunctional institutional setup, and at the same time have captured the Montenegrin judicial sector by means of politicization. These kinds of reform activities have been particularly designed and used to accelerate the Montenegrin accession process, as well as to present the international community with the notion that the political elites are indeed indispensable and purposeful reformers in this regard (Džankić and Keil and Kmezić 2019). Although the country has managed to reach a certain level of strengthening its judicial independence by amending its legal and institutional framework, the progress over reinforcing that judicial independence is slow and limited, with the country not achieving sustainable and merit-based results aiming to improve the independent status of its judges and prosecutors (Kmezić 2017; Mendelski 2015; HRA and CeMI 2015b; MANS 2017). Rather, the state has used the logic of partial fulfillment of requirements on impartiality by calculating and selecting which judicial reform measures are to be achieved in the given phase of the integration process.

The politicization of the judiciary is explainable through the substantial lack of political will of the ruling elites to functionally induce the EU rules and norms. There is an incontestable unwillingness of the political leaders to effectively comply with the acquis in suppressing political influence over the judicial sector by establishing a credible and impartial institutional system, consequently creating conditions for the potential elimination of the long-lasting corrupt political system that has existed in Montenegro for more than thirty years (CGO 2019; IA and CGO and CRNVO and CeMI 2018). Currently, when Montenegrin institutions have been primarily captured by political influence, judicial independence is not able to play an active role in overall democratization of the society and cannot foster democratic political processes in the country. Instead, the current political elites have toyed with political and legal changes, thus resulting in creating an illusion of overall internal sociopolitical development by fulfilling the EU political criteria. Apparently, this masking (fabricating) of formal legal and institutional changes, together with the Union's inconsistent conditional policy, has allowed the current political elites to stay in power and control political interference in the judiciary (Vučković and Đorđević 2019, 177–79). At a moment when the Montenegrin judicial system is being politicized, it is more than clear that the judiciary in Montenegro is not able to freely and independently investigate and prosecute high-ranking political figures who on reasonable grounds have been suspected of committing criminal offenses. Therefore, current political and legal processes are completely stagnating in the country, where the ruling elites have essentially captured the country's judicial institutions. This situation results in the survival of the current political establishment and allows for their support of those subjects (veto players) who would instead be facing legal prosecution.

The spiral of illusion of changes without concrete and sustainable results has in this regard had a profound effect on public confidence in Montenegrin judicial independence, ultimately leading to a decline in trust in the EU and the credibility of the integration process itself (CeMI and HRA 2016, 2017). In this case, there are two possible scenarios, that is, two challenges, that the current political elites are likely to face soon. The first scenario foresees a complete eradication of politicization of the judiciary and, therefore, independent and impartial enforcement of court proceedings. The second one assumes no change in the status quo, thus resulting in a complete failure in public trust in the EU enlargement process and a danger to current social peace. This would lead to an increase in public pressure on the decision-makers to achieve concrete and sustainable results in the judiciary so that the country is able to successfully complete the accession negotiation process. In either case, it is hard to expect that the domestic political elites will stay in power if political influence over judicial institutions continues to exist.

Fourth, another tendency can be observed at the EU level that may provide an explanation for why Montenegro has so far failed to further Europeanize its judiciary. Primarily, the Union-driven judicial reform model may be questioned in terms of its effectiveness. Noticeably, by using a monitoring approach the Union has aimed to reinforce the Montenegrin judicial system by providing recommendations for strengthening judicial independence, and to a lesser extent judicial accountability, as well as effectiveness and efficiency. Paradoxically, although the Union has imposed pressure for accountability and independence, the EU conditional policy has been insufficiently consistent or reinforcing, and has produced negatively empowering effects over the given judiciary reform, particularly in terms of reducing politicization of the judiciary by the parliament and substantially strengthening disciplinary and dismissal procedures against judges and prosecutors. During the process of judicial reform in Montenegro, the Union has primarily focused on the process itself rather than on results. Rather than being an effective driver in judicial reform processes, the EU conditional policy has largely served as a monitoring actor, constantly repeating the same recommendations not addressed by the candidate country (Gateva 2015; Džankić and Keil and Kmezić 2019; Noutcheva and Aydin-Düzgit 2012). Therefore, we can talk about the Union's lack of interest in further advancing its enlargement policy through the effective promotion of the judicial reform requirements. In addition, due to the Union's insufficient interest in the enlargement process on the one hand, and maintaining internal political stability on the other hand, the EU has supported domestic political leaders in the judicial reform process through the active cooperation of those agents. Noticeably, the Union has tried to play a constructive role in building an effective judicial system with postcommunist autocratic leaders who strongly interfere into judicial sector performance by using nondemocratic means, respectively, with those domestic agents suspected of having been involved in corruption and organized crime (Elbasani and Šelo Šabić 2018; Bieber 2020). Thus, the EU has not only supported domestic leaders in failing to meet judicial reform criteria, it has also helped strengthen their political position by providing them with funding through various instruments for pre-accession assistance. In return, the domestic political leaders have created the impression within international circles that they are irreplaceable by tackling some judicial dimensions, although not the dimensions that put their political survival at risk.

Hence, in line with the Union's inconsistent and insufficient conditional policy approach, it might be appropriate to discuss trends in the EU integration process of Montenegro. In particular, the research has indicated certain features inherent to the given judicial reform during the accession phase. Primarily, although Montenegro has advanced in the accession process, the country still faces issues of politicization and accountability of its judiciary. These problems are mainly related to: the parliament's active participation in appointing members of the Judicial and Prosecutorial Council and state prosecutors, the reasons for dismissing judges and prosecutors which should be included in the Constitution, introduction of a single, nationwide recruitment system and of a fair and transparent system for promoting judges and prosecutors (which needs to be introduced together with periodical professional assessment of judicial office holders' performance), and finally reviewing the system of functional immunity for judges and prosecutors (HRA and CeMI 2015b; MANS 2017). Second, the proposed model of the Union-driven rule of law reforms is being questioned particularly over strengthening judicial independence, consequently by positioning itself as the main monitoring agent. In a candidate country that lacks the political will to address the given independence dimensions, the problem of the active participation of the Minister of Justice in the Judicial Council has remained problematic since 2008 (Kmezić 2020; Appicciafuoco 2010; Ardit 2014).

Finally, and very much in regard to perhaps a far more important trend, although the Union has indicated visible inconsistencies regarding continuous external pressure, one may witness a situation in which Montenegro has continued to advance in the EU accession process while demonstrating reluctance to reduce political influence over its judiciary. As a result, the country's judiciary system is still dominated by political influence although more than ten years have passed since the beginning of the integration process. Evidently, the EU-driven rule of law reform promotion applies a strategy of permissiveness in judicial reform by allowing the candidate country to select and tackle certain judicial dimensions based on which it can advance in the given integration process (CGO 2019; IA and CGO and CRNVO and CeMI 2018). A candidate state may employ a selective approach to fulfilling judicial reform requirements by choosing to address easier requirements rather than harder ones. Therefore, one might observe the tendency of a state to tackle simpler judicial reform conditions, namely effectiveness and efficiency, instead of more demanding ones such as judicial independence and accountability. This in essence means confronting those judicial dimensions that do not question the issue of politicization of judiciary rather than those that do. In situations in which a country needs to reduce political interference in the judiciary, a candidate state may choose to hide behind relatively solid results achieved in improving its judicial capacity, therefore addressing the politicization dimension only superficially. As a result, the state's logic of calculations in avoiding the empowerment of judges' and prosecutors' independence and accountability can reach a level where opening accession negotiations with the Union seems highly probable.

Given the provided insights, this research claims that judicial system reform mostly depends on deep and inter-dependent relations between EU external incentives, domestic factors, and the efficiency of reform activities. More precisely, the effective EU external influence largely depends on the role of domestic leaders and their interest in complying with the EU requirements. In addition to the abovementioned factors, the way the reforms are carried out (formal or informal, quickly or continuously) is of utmost importance for the successful transplantation of external legal and institutional systems.

Consequently, Montenegro's overall results have been insufficiently satisfactory, as the positive reinforcing effects on judicial effectiveness and efficiency have been offset by the negatively reinforcing effects on judicial independence and accountability. If one assumes that judicial independence and accountability are more important dimensions than effectiveness and efficiency for the development of rule of law, then one may claim that the process of judicial reform in Montenegro imposed by the EU has failed to achieve a positive reinforcing effect in the given transformation process during the integration phase. Thus, the Union has empowered negative reinforcing effects, favoring domestic factors/conditions that systematically undermine the process of maintaining the impartiality and accountability of judges and prosecutors.

In line with the given empirical elaborations, the question that is being raised is whether the interdependency of both external and internal factors is sufficient for obtaining complete insights into why the Union has not succeeded in Europeanizing Montenegro in the field of judiciary reform.

This particular issue is addressed in the conclusion of this book: see Appendix 1.

NOTES

1. In 2011, the Commission appointed eight new judges. For more details, see Sudski Savjet Crne Gore (2012).

2. In 2010, the Judicial Council elected thirty-six judges, while the disciplinary commission had submitted three procedures against judges, based on which the commission also launched dismissal procedures against two judges. No information in regard to appointment, dismissal, and disciplinary procedures against prosecutors and deputy prosecutors could be found. For more details, see Sudski Savjet Crne Gore (2012).

3. No information regarding the appointment of prosecutors and deputy prosecutors, dismissal and disciplinary procedures against prosecutors and deputy prosecutors could be found.

4. For further information, please see Appendix 1—Judicial Reform in Montenegro—normative and empirical analysis of documents EU—Montenegro for the 2006–2017 period.

5. Following the introduction of the 2012 reports of the Commission and the Council`s conclusion, the European Parliament adopted the Resolution on the 2012 Montenegro Progress Report on April 18, 2013. For more details, see http://www.europarl.europa.eu/sides/getDoc.do?pubRef=-%2f%2fEP%2f%2fTEXT%2bTA%2bP7-TA-2013-0185%2b0%2bDOC%2bXML%2bV0%2f%2fEN&language=EN

6. Apart from the 2015 Montenegro Progress Report and the EU enlargement strategy 2015–2016, the European Parliament adopted the *Resolution on 2015 Montenegro Progress Report* on March 10, 2016. For more details, see http://www.europarl.europa.eu/sides/getDoc.do?pubRef=-%2f%2fEP%2f%2fTEXT%2bTA%2bP8-TA-2016-0092%2b0%2bDOC%2bXML%2bV0%2f%2fEN&language=EN

7. The Action Plan overall represents the most comprehensive document so far in the area of reform of the judicial system, which means that the provided measures for realization within the plan are being identically prescribed in other national documents, such as the Judicial Reform Strategy (2014–2018), Plan for Rationalization of the Judicial Network, Strategy for the Fight against Corruption and Organized Crime, and similar.

8. In 2012, the Judicial Council elected nineteen judges: one court president and eighteen judges. In 2013, the Judicial Council elected ten judges: one court president and nine judges. In 2014, the Judicial Council elected fourteen presidents, while in 2015 the Judicial Council elected ninety-seven judges: ten court presidents and eighty-seven judges (thirty-four judges and fifty-three misdemeanor judges). For more details, see Sudski Savjet Crne Gore (2012, 2013, 2014).

9. In 2013, the Prosecutor's Office appointed one state prosecutor and twenty-six deputy state prosecutors, while in 2014, the Prosecutorial Council appointed the Supreme State Prosecutor and fifteen state prosecutors. Furthermore, in 2015, the Prosecutorial Council appointed the Major Special State Prosecutor, eight Special State Prosecutors, and ninety-seven state prosecutors. No available information in regard to the appointment of prosecutors and deputy prosecutors for 2012 and 2016 is available. For more details, see Tužilački Savjet Crne Gore (2013, 2014, 2016).

10. Three officials were employed in the period between July 1, 2014, and June 30, 2016, in Secretary of the Judicial Council. In addition, six officials and one probationer were employed in the period between January and June 2016.

11. No available information in regard to the disciplinary procedures and dismissals against prosecutors, deputy prosecutors, and prosecutor holders in 2016 can be found.

12. During 2011, courts resolved 25,837 backlog cases, while the number of unresolved cases on December 31, 2011, was as high as 37,388. In addition, during 2012 courts resolved 25,652 backlog cases, while the number of unresolved cases was on December 31, 2012, standing at 35,811 cases. For more details, see Sudski Savjet (2011, 37, 42).

13. In 2011, 623 mediation procedures were registered and out of which 383 mediation cases were successful. The funds that were released amounted in total to 3,772,974 EUR. There is no available information to be found on the mediation process for 2012.

14. The JTC spent 47,459 EUR from its budget, while the rest of 305,910 EUR was provided by international organizations.

15. Particularly in terms of appointing members of the Judicial Council (i.e., four judges are elected and dismissed from duty by the Conference of Judges, two judges are elected and dismissed from duty by the Parliament, two renowned lawyers were appointed and dismissed by the President of Montenegro, and participation of the Minister of Justice), and appointment, dismissal, promotion and disciplinary proceedings of judges and prosecutors. For more details, see Constitution of Montenegro from 2007.

16. In 2013, the level of public trust in the judiciary was 38% and in 2014 was 47.8%. For more info, see HRA & CeMI Survey (2017, 13).

Chapter 4

Fight against Corruption in Montenegro

EU TRANSFORMATIVE POWER IN ANTI-CORRUPTION AND DOMESTIC CHANGE

Pre-Negotiation Stage

Prevention of Corruption

Introduction of the *European Partnership with Montenegro,* which came into force on January 17, 2007, represents a means of supporting the European perspective of the Western Balkan countries following the conclusion of the Thessaloniki European Council of June 19–20, 2003 (Council of the European Union 2007, 2). To be prepared to assume European Union (EU) membership obligations, potential candidate countries are requested to address both short-term priorities (expected to be accomplished within two years) and medium-term priorities (expected to be accomplished within three or four years) of the European Partnership (Council of the European Union 2007, 2). In this sense, concerning key short-term priorities, the Council urged Montenegro to strengthen its fight against organized crime and corruption at all levels. The European Partnership emphasized the need to amend and fully implement a law on conflict of interest to eliminate all possible cases of conflict of interest of its officials, especially when it comes to the management of public assets, and the significance of strengthening and implementing the law on political parties, thus aiming to ensure transparency and clarity in political party financing (Council of the European Union 2007, 6; European Commission 2007a, 41, 2007b, 12).

Only four months after the introduction of the European Partnership with Montenegro, the Montenegrin government adopted the *Action Plan for Implementation of the European Partnership* in its session held on May

17, 2007. By the same token, the Council and Commission emphasized two priorities, the first being political party financing and the second, judicial conflict of interest. In response, the Parliament adopted the Law on Financing of Political Parties on July 18, 2008, and the Law on Conflict of Interests of Public Servants on December 27, 2008, respectively. However, the state bodies did not engage in any actions in regard to the Union's demands to further strengthen the legislation on conflict of interest for public officials due to concerns over management of public assets. Finally, in response to the Council's demands, the state authorities introduced a number of measures and plans, including providing additional funds, to effectively prevent and suppress corruption at all levels, to fully align with the UN Convention on the fight against corruption and other relevant Council of Europe Conventions, as well as to show substantial results by establishing effective procedures for detection, treatment and follow-up of cases of suspected fraud, including the misappropriation of EU funds.[1]

Shortly after Montenegro submitted its application for EU membership, the Commission acknowledged some progress had been achieved in the fight against corruption, a key European Partnership priority, particularly in improving the strategic and administrative framework for combating corruption, addressing low-level corruption, and focusing on awareness-raising and training. However, the Union highlighted that corruption still remained widespread at that time and continued to be a serious problem in Montenegro, especially in the case of high-level corruption. Hence, the Commission raised additional concerns over the weak implementation and limited results in combating corruption (European Commission 2008a, 43, 2008b, 13). In this respect, the Union highlighted the importance of strengthening the legal framework against corruption, particularly through the adoption of the new Law on Conflicts of Interest, and the need for enhanced protection of whistleblowers in practice, even though the country had by that time already improved its legal framework in this regard (European Commission 2008a, 43, 2008b, 12). This being said, the Commission also underscored the need to strengthen the Montenegrin institutional framework. Although some progress had been made in enhancing preventive and investigative anti-corruption bodies such as the Directorate for Anti-Corruption Initiative (DACI), especially in cooperation with the police, the Union emphasized the importance of further improvements in the institutional setup. In this sense, the Union pointed out that "Montenegro lacks strong and independent supervisory and auditing authorities" needed to impartially and objectively assess asset declarations and funding of political parties (European Commission 2008b, 12).

Given the Commission's recommendation over strengthening the legal and institutional framework of anti-corruption policies in preventing corruption, the Government adopted the *Innovative Action Plan for implementation of the Program against the corruption and organized crime for 2008–2009* in 2008. In addition, the Parliament adopted the *Law on Prevention of Conflicts of Interest in Performing Public Functions* on December 27, 2008. Furthermore, the state authorities conducted additional efforts in improving the legal framework in tackling corruption issues by adopting the new *Criminal Procedure Code* on August 18, 2009, the *Law on Internal Financial Control* on December 2, 2008, and finally the *Law on Financing the Election Campaigns for the President, Mayors and Presidents of Municipalities of Montenegro* on January 21, 2009. However, concerning the Union's suggestions on improving legal protections for whistleblowers, the state bodies had by that time failed to conduct any recognizable activities aiming to enhance this measure, as they failed to adopt the Law on Protection of the Persons reporting Corruption and the Law on Integrity in Public Sector (MANS 2009a, 75). Nevertheless, in response to the Commission's call to improve independent supervisory and auditing authorities to impartially and objectively enforce and assess the asset statements of public officials, the State Auditing Institution (SAI) was tasked with reviewing the legality and effectiveness of the management of state property and obligations, budgets and financial affairs of entities whose sources of financing are public or stem from the use of state properties (MANS 2009a, 75). However, unlike the SAI, the state authorities failed to enact any legal measures to further strengthen the institutional supervisory anti-corruption framework so that it would be capable of independently monitoring political party funding and respective election campaigns.

As a result of state activities during 2008, the Union acknowledged in its 2009 Montenegro Progress Report, followed by the EU Enlargement Strategy 2009–2010, that Montenegro had made some progress in its fight against corruption, especially when strengthening the strategic, legal, and administrative framework was taken into consideration (European Commission 2009b, 11, 13). However, regardless of the results achieved, the Commission also underlined that corruption remained prevalent and thus continued to be a major issue (European Commission 2009b, 13). Therefore, the Union outlined the necessity of the state to achieve concrete results in the consolidation of rule of law, particularly in the areas of judicial reform and the fight against corruption (European Commission 2009a, 14). Primarily, the EU highlighted the need for Montenegro to improve its action plans for fighting organized crime and corruption by stating that risk assessments and the introduction of priorities for the respective action plans needed to be aligned (European Commission 2009b, 12). In addition, the Union noted that since the supervising authority monitoring compliance with the new Law on Financing of Political Parties and the Law on Financing of Election Campaigns for the president, mayors and presidents of Municipalities of Montenegro had still by that time not been implemented, political parties' alignment with the law was supported only by allocations from the state budget. Therefore, private donations for political parties were not being controlled due to the lack of monitoring bodies (European Commission 2009b, 12). The EU also remarked on the appointment of the supervising authority by the Parliament, and noted that the parliament's sanctioning power was limited due to potential political influence (European Commission 2009b, 12–13). By the same token, the Commission noted that although some improvements had been made through the adoption of the new Law on Prevention of Conflict of Interests in Performing Public Functions (2008), the same legislation contained serious shortfalls and loopholes. In this regard, the Union indicated the importance of further strengthening the Montenegrin legal system through major amendments of recently adopted laws, especially as the existing legal provisions foresaw "significant exemption for parliamentarians, who are allowed to hold executive powers in public companies or executive agencies" (European Commission 2009b, 12).

Following the bottom-up level, in regard to the Union's recommendations, the state bodies adopted a new *Strategy for the fight against Corruption and Organized Crime 2010–2014* and *Action Plan for Implementation 2010–2012* on July 29, 2010 (Ministarstvo unutrašnjih poslova i javne uprave Crne Gore 2010). The monitoring of achieved strategic activities during the 2010–2012 implementation period of the Action Plan was exercised by the *National Commission for implementation of Strategy for the fight against corruption and organized crime* (National Commission). However, concerning the Commission's suggestion on the need to improve the institutional framework by introducing independent supervisory authorities to evaluate the financing of political parties and asset declarations, Montenegrin legislative bodies failed to adopt any amendments to the Law on State Audit Institution, which was to follow the establishment of independent audit bodies outside the organizational structure of the SAI, nor did they adopt amendments to the Law on Prevention of Conflicts of Interest in Performing Public Functions that would strengthen the Commissions for the Prevention of the Conflict of Interest supervisory competences (Vlada Crne Gore 2011f, 14, 20–21).

Three years after the SAA with Montenegro was signed, the Commission introduced its *Opinion on Montenegro's application for membership of the European Union* on November 9, 2010, which was then followed by the EU Enlargement Strategy 2010–2011. The Union commended Montenegro's progress toward strengthening its legal system and institutional setup in combating corruption. However, regardless of visible results in the anti-corruption policy, implementation in the institutional fight against corruption remained insufficient, especially in terms of law enforcement. Primarily, the Union indicated that the anti-corruption legislation had not been fully implemented, particularly in the case of prevention of conflict of interest and on financing of political parties and electoral campaigns. Furthermore, the institutional framework contained visible flaws. Apparently, Montenegrin supervisory authorities did not have adequate legal mechanisms to ensure the enforcement of the laws on prevention of conflict of interest and control over funding of political parties and electoral campaigns (European Commission 2010b, 6).

The Commission also mentioned that further efforts were needed to:

> Improve the anti-corruption legal framework and implement the government's anti-corruption strategy and action plan; establish a solid track record of proactive investigations, prosecutions and convictions in corruption cases at all levels (European Commission 2010b, 11).

Based on the Council's decision from 2010 to grant Montenegro candidate country status for EU membership, the Government, in response, adopted the *Action Plan for Monitoring Recommendation from the European Commission* on February 17, 2011, along with the *Innovative Action Plan for implementation of the Strategy against Corruption and Organized Crime 2010–2012* on July 21, 2011 (Vlada Crne Gore 2011b, 2).[2] Originally, the Action Plan was subject to external and internal monitoring, which meant that the plan was originally submitted to the Commission (or to the Venice Commission, or SIGMA depending on the topic) for comments and suggestions after which the Government itself (but also the Assembly Committee for International Relations and European Integration, and the National Council for European Integration) evaluated monthly progress reports on meeting the obligations within the Action Plan (Vlada Crne Gore 2011c, 2). This being said, the Parliament adopted *Amendments to the Criminal Code* on June 22, 2011, thus incorporating the Group of States against Corruption (GRECO) recommendations on the criminal offenses of receiving and giving bribes and trading with influence, and the *Law on Civil Servants and State Employees* on July 22, 2011, foreseeing obligations to adopt integrity plans in the public sector and to institute protections for individuals who report corruption. The Parliament also enacted the *Amendments on the Law on Prevention of Conflicts of Interest in Performing Public Functions* on July 26, 2011, thus stipulating that individuals elected in elections cannot be members of management and supervisory boards. Also, the amendments strengthened the monitoring role of the Commission on Prevention of Conflicts of Interest (CPCI) in terms of data verification, with the given legislation also foreseeing stricter penal policy measures (Vlada Crne Gore 2011c, 15). Finally, the legislative body adopted the *Law on Financing of Political Parties* on July 29, 2012, and enacted financing rules for political party operations and election campaigns, in accordance with the GRECO recommendations. Also, the revision of financial reports was strengthened, thus enabling transparent financing and better control of the income, expense and assets of political parties (Vlada Crne Gore 2011c, 15).

Thus, based on the Commission's assessment of Montenegro's solid progress in the fight against corruption, the European Council on December 17, 2010, granted Montenegro the *status of the candidate country*.

In 2011, the Commission confirmed some progress had by that time been made in improving the anti-corruption policy, especially toward strengthening the institutional and administrative capacity of prosecutors and police to fight corruption by repressing it, with prevention also being heightened, and, perhaps far more importantly, satisfactory results being made in implementation of the Government's Anti-corruption Strategy and Action Plan, as the key priority set out in the Opinion (European Commission 2011a, 14, 2011b, 12–13). However, although the Union acknowledged that certain advances in strengthening the legal, institutional, and administrative framework had been made by the state authorities, this body also emphasized that corruption remained a serious problem in Montenegro and that it continued to be widespread in many fields. Therefore, according to the Commission's document, the implementation of the adopted institutional and legal framework remained deficient at the time. It underlined the significance of full entry into force of new provisions of the CPC and the Criminal Code that had not been sufficiently implemented by that time and also indicated the need for further training of judges. It also stated that problems with judicial independence continued to be a matter of concern, which significantly affected the fight against corruption (European Commission 2011b, 13–14).

By the same token, the lack of effective prevention of corruption was also seen in the limited implementation of new legislation on political party and election campaign financing. Thus, the Commission noted that "concern remains over the insufficiently dissuasive and undifferentiated sanctioning system, the regime and ceiling of membership fees, as well as the capacity of the State Electoral Commission (SEC) to ensure a fully effective independent oversight" (European Commission 2011b, 14). Additional flaws were also observable in terms of the functional adoption of conflict of interest politics. The report indicated that disciplinary provisions were being insufficiently implemented, as few sanctions for noncompliance had been initiated by the supervisory bodies (European Commission 2011b, 14).

At the domestic level, based on the Council's decision to start the process of accession negotiations with Montenegro in June 2012, a new incorporating negotiation approach was proposed by the Commission, focusing on Chapter 23—Judiciary and Fundamental Rights and Chapter 24—Justice, Freedom and Security. This influenced the Government to adopt the *Annex to Report to European Commission on Montenegro's Progress for 2012—for the period of September 1, 2011–April 25, 2012* on April 25, 2012, and the *Annex to*

Report to European Commission on Montenegro's Progress for 2012—for the period of April 25, 2012–September 1, 2012 on September 6, 2012, so as to quickly and adequately execute the monitoring process on the fight against corruption prior to the opening of the accession negotiations (European Council 2011, 5; Vlada Crne Gore 2012a, b). This being said, in the period from April 25 until December 15, 2012, the JTC engaged in twelve activities of continuous education and four activities of initial education for sixty-two representatives of the judiciary in the area of implementation of new criminal legislation of Montenegro, thus aligning with the Union's suggestions on the necessity for full entry into force of new provisions of the CPC and the Criminal Code that had not been sufficiently introduced by that time and the additional training of judges that was also required (Vlada Crne Gore 2012b, 84). However, regarding the Commission's recommendations on the limited implementation of new legislation on political party and election campaign financing and on the inability of the SEC to conduct effective independent oversight of and disciplinary measures against civil servants, the state bodies failed to take any particular action in this regard (Vlada Crne Gore 2012d, 26).

Therefore, based on the Commission's assessment of good progress made by Montenegro in 2011 in achieving overall satisfactory results in meeting seven defined priorities, including the fight against the corruption, as published in the document entitled *Report from the Commission to the European Parliament and the Council on Montenegro's Progress in the Implementation of Reforms* from May 22, 2012, the European Council decided to *open accession negotiations with Montenegro* in late June 2012 (European Commission 2012a, 12).

Investigation, Prosecution, and Final Conviction of High-Level Corruption Cases

Montenegro Progress Reports accompanied by EU enlargement strategies emphasized the importance of providing concrete and substantial results in the investigation, prosecution, and final conviction of high-level corruption cases by stating that "conviction rates in corruption cases are extremely low" while investigative capacities of the law enforcement bodies remained very limited, but also that there was a significant lack of expertise in financial investigation (European Commission 2007b, 12). Moreover, the problem of insufficiently developed capacities to fight corruption was also seen within the Special Prosecutor's Office and the special anti-corruption police task force, which lacked substantial capacity in terms of staffing, expertise, and equipment (European Commission 2008b, 13). As a response, the state authorities failed to introduce any activities to tackle this particular reform measure in 2007 and 2008, in spite of the Union's serious concerns over insufficient monitoring, prosecution and trial of high-level corruption cases, the need to enhance investigative capacities of the law enforcement bodies, the lack of expertise in financial investigations and insufficient capacities within the Special Prosecutor's Office and special anti-corruption police task force in terms of staffing, expertise and equipment, where no measures within the Action Plan anticipated the development of anti-corruption capacities of the abovementioned law enforcement bodies.

Following the 2009 Montenegro Progress Report and the Commission's Opinion on Montenegro's application for membership to the European Union from 2010, the Union indicated that the "track record of investigations, prosecutions and final convictions in corruption cases at all levels remains low," while "investigation capacities and law-enforcement co-ordination remain weak." Hence, the Commission underlined the need for strong political will to further strengthen the legal and institutional framework for combating corruption, especially in establishing a solid track record of proactive investigations, prosecutions, and convictions in corruption cases at all levels (European Commission 2009b, 13, 2010b, 6). The Union devoted special attention to improving investigative capacities of law enforcement bodies by noting that this authority "remains weak due to shortfalls in expertise, specialised equipment and working conditions" and because interagency cooperation needed to be further strengthened, and that the significant lack of expertise in modern financial investigation was to be remediated (European Commission 2009b, 13; Council of the European Union 2007, 4). Also, the Commission recognized that the administrative bodies for detecting and investigating corruption were faced with a substantial lack of staff and skills, particularly when it came to the performance of the Police Directorate's internal control unit, namely the Unit for combating organized crime and corruption, and the prosecution office (European Commission 2009b, 13).

At the domestic level, the state authorities intensified their activities in improving the strategic, legal and institutional and framework for combating corruption in 2010. Primarily, the state bodies intensified additional activities in strengthening investigation capacities and cooperation between the law enforcement bodies in repressing corruption through the establishment of the *Department for fight against organized crime, corruption, terrorism and war crimes*, managed by the State Special Prosecutor. In addition, the *Special Investigation Team (SIT)* was established as a specialized multidisciplinary and multi-institutional unit operating against the most complex issues of corruption, organized crime, and financial investigation (Vlada Crne Gore 2011c, 13, 15).[3] The SIT was spatially and technically equipped, and at that time it conducted investigations in four corruption cases and one financial case (Vlada Crne Gore 2011f, 47). Also, certain improvements were seen in the strengthening of investigative capacities of the law enforcement bodies in employing sixteen officials within the Police Directorate responsible for conducting financial investigations (Vlada Crne Gore 2011f, 39, 43). However, regarding the Commission's recommendation on strengthening interagency cooperation for combating corruption, the national coordination office had still not been established by that time. The same situation is observable in the Union's demand to further strengthen its administrative bodies for detecting and investigating corruption: no further activities were conducted by the state anti-corruption authorities.

Finally, certain results were seen in building a solid track record of proactive investigations, prosecutions, and convictions in corruption cases at all levels. In the case of "Komunalni redari," one investigation was conducted by the State Prosecutors Office against two communal officials over suspicions of having committed acts of corruption, specifically the criminal offense of giving and receiving bribes. Concerning another prosecution issues during 2010 and 2011 ("Auto moto društvo Budva,"[4] "dr Mikulić,"[5] "Signal,"[6] and "Zeta"[7]), the State Prosecutor's Office filed criminal charges against several individuals on suspicion of having engaged in giving and receiving bribes. Far more importantly, in the case of "Zavala," on March 21, 2011, the State Prosecutor's Office filed charges against twelve persons, three of whom were high officials of the ruling Democratic Party of Socialists (DPS) party: namely, the major of Budva Municipality, his deputy, and an MP were accused of abuse of official position and power in financial transactions and tax evasion. They were charged with the criminal offense of corruption for having illegally gained assets in the amount of 1,035,698.62 EUR. Last but not least, in response to the Union's request to carry out a number of high-level corruption cases in which the seizure or confiscation of assets was ordered by the law enforcement bodies (for instance in the case named "Šarić"), on May 14, 2011, the State Prosecutor's Office filed criminal charges against Duško Šarić and Jovica Lončar on suspicion of having engaged in money laundering. The defendants were charged because, in the period between 2006 and 2009, they used banking and financial operations to introduce "dirty money" in the amount of 21,353,879.22 EUR that originated from cocaine trade. As a result, the Higher Court in Bijelo Polje issued a decision on the temporary confiscation of property estimated at 12,483,577.54 EUR (Vlada Crne Gore 2011c, 39–40).

As a result of anti-corruption activities, the EU acknowledged that the candidate country had by that time achieved a solid track record of investigation, prosecution, and convictions in corruption cases at all levels, which remained one of the key priorities stipulated in the Commission's opinion. However, the number of final convictions remained low and limited, particularly for high-level corruption cases (European Commission 2011b, 14). The Union indicated that "the number of corruption cases in which seizure or confiscation of assets were ordered is still very low," while the adopted legal provisions within CPC and Criminal Code on extended confiscation of criminal assets were still not appropriately used (European Commission 2011b, 14). This being said, the Commission underlined the necessity of the state bodies to further enhance their institutional and administrative capacity. Primarily, the EU suggested that the capacity of prosecutors and police to conduct financial investigations, including into criminal assets, and presenting related evidence before the courts needed to be developed. Finally, the interagency cooperation and exchange of information between law bodies enforcement (police and prosecutors) needed to be further improved (European Commission 2011b, 14).

At the domestic level, the State Prosecutor's Office prosecuted the Major of Ulcinj Municipality on suspicion of having committed criminal offenses of abuse of official position following the EU's demand for achieving a convincing number of final convictions of high-level cases and a number of corruption cases in which seizure or confiscation of assets was ordered. A final conviction was made based on a plea agreement according to which the defendant was obliged to pay 10,000 EUR to charity. In addition, in the case of "Zavala," the Higher Court in Podgorica issued a final conviction, with the former mayor of Budva being sentenced to five years imprisonment, his deputy to four years, and the MP to three years (Vlada Crne Gore 2012b, 83). Furthermore, the Parliament adopted the *Amendments to the Law on Temporary Seized Assets* on June 15, 2012, thus foreseeing the possibility for the Directorate of Assets to temporarily seize assets placed under lease through public bidding (Vlada Crne Gore 2012b, 80). In this respect, the law enforcement bodies conducted procedures for temporarily seizing assets in three cases in 2012, namely in the cases of Šarić, Kalić, and Khvan, on the suspicion of money laundering. It is estimated that the value of temporarily seized assets was 47.3 million EUR (Vlada Crne Gore 2012b, 84, 2012e, 98, 2012d, 102).

Additionally, ten police officers were employed by the Police Directorate as a result of the Union's requirement to enhance the institutional and administrative capacity of law enforcement bodies to build a credible track record of corruption cases at all levels. Moreover, additional equipment, namely computers, encryption equipment, equipment for conducting investigations, specialized vehicles, and so on, was purchased for the police, thus aiming to provide better conditions for the detection and investigation of high-level corruption cases (Vlada Crne Gore 2012a, 78, 2012d, 87, 90). Also, certain improvements aimed toward strengthening administrative and institutional capacities of the law enforcement bodies were seen, particularly in providing 24 professional trainings in financial investigation by the JTC and Police

Academy for more than 132 participants (Vlada Crne Gore 2012e, 104, 2012d, 110, 2012f, 111). Finally, in response to the EU's request to improve interagency cooperation and the exchange of information between law enforcement bodies (police and prosecutors), the state authorities achieved limited progress through the introduction of the *Analysis of anti-corruptive institutional framework* and *Analysis of effects of establishment of the Agency for fight against the corruption* (Vlada Crne Gore 2012f, 206).

Negotiation Stage

Based on the Commission's positive assessment of Montenegro's fulfillment of seven key priorities, including rule of law requirements, the European Council endorsed the decision to open accession negotiations with Montenegro on June 29, 2012 (European Council 2012, 4). In line with the Council's conclusions from December 2011 inviting the Commission to start the process of building an analytical framework for an examination of the acquis with Montenegro on Chapters 23 and 24, this body launched the *Screening Report Montenegro on Chapter 23—Judiciary and Fundamental Rights* on November 12, 2012.

Overall, the Commission agreed that Montenegro had demonstrated good awareness of the EU's strategic and policy framework in combating corruption and conducted reforms toward the adoption of the acquis and alignment with the European policies (European Commission 2012d, 18). However, the Commission noted that "corruption in Montenegro is prevalent in many areas and continues to be a serious cause of concern" (European Commission 2012d, 22). Although the country demonstrated some progress in strengthening its legal and institutional framework, the implementation of reforms remained deficient. Thus, the Commission noted that further efforts were needed in ensuring a solid track record of investigations and convictions in corruption cases.

In line with the views above, the screening report originally recommended that Montenegro should adopt one or more Action Plan, addressing in particular the following problems:

<u>Preventive action against corruption:</u>

- Strengthen and possibly review the institutional framework for the fight against corruption. In particular, DACI's competences need to be upgraded and its capacities reinforced.
- Improve the system of asset declarations, strengthening in particular the supervisory competencies and the professional capacity of the Commission for prevention of conflict of interest to ensure effective and substantial checks on assets, and introduce measures preventing conflicts

of interest going beyond holding double public offices (such as public decision-makers holding stakes in private companies, etc.).

- Review the rules of procedure of the public administration, including appointment and internal control, to fully integrate prevention of corruption and conflicts of interest aspects.
- Improve the system of political party funding, ensuring reliable reporting as well as effective supervision and sanctioning powers by an independent authority. Strengthen the capacities of the monitoring bodies (the SAI and the SEC) and ensure a clear division of tasks and cooperation framework. Accounting obligations for political parties should be increased and all in-kind donations should be reported. The recommendations of GRECO should be followed-up.
- Ensure effective implementation of free access to information rules, inter alia, with regard to sensitive information with economic value. The provisions of the Law on prevailing public interest need to be clarified. Appropriate interaction between the Law on Free Access to Information and the Laws on Protection of Personal Data and on Data Secrecy should be ensured.
- The control system for public procurement is to be strengthened as well as the supervision of implementation of awarded contracts. Anti-corruption measures at local government level need to be stepped up.
- Develop specific measures to tackle corruption in particularly vulnerable areas, such as those identified in the findings of the risk assessment of July 2011. For these areas, separate action plans could be envisaged. Ensure that risk assessments are being used systematically.
- Strengthen the Parliament's role in fighting corruption by stepping up supervision of the executive. The Parliament should also pay specific attention to anti-corruption issues when revising and improving the legal framework. Ensure a thorough integrity system within the Parliament.
- Ensure that NGOs are involved in the anti-corruption agenda.

Repressive action against corruption:

- Ensure independent, effective specialized investigation/prosecution bodies, in particular through:
    - Constitutional and legal amendments strengthening the independence of the judiciary (see above) and to protect all investigative bodies from (potential) political pressure.
    - Provision of adequate resources (financial resources, staffing, etc.) to all investigation and judicial authorities involved in the fight against corruption, making corruption cases priority matters. A review of the definition of "high-level corruption" in view of the SSPO's area of competence would be recommendable.

    - Ensure that prosecutors have real-time access to relevant databases and sufficient capacity to effectively implement of the Criminal Procedure Code.
    - Review the competences of the Special Investigative Team and ensure its access to relevant databases.
    - Ensure sufficient training, well-qualified staff, and international exchange of expertise to allow for modern investigative techniques to be applied efficiently and on a regular basis. Similar training must be ensured for judicial authorities.
- Amend the Criminal Procedure Code where needed and ensure its effective implementation.
- Improve the use of financial investigations, possibly through establishing a team of highly qualified investigators for this purpose.
- Improve the cooperation and information exchange between authorities involved in the fight against corruption, including also tax and other only indirectly linked authorities.
- Improve the collection of unified statistics on corruption, distinguishing clearly between different types of criminal activities and allowing for a detailed assessment of length of the cases, outcome, and so on.
- The procedures for seizure, confiscation, and management of proceeds of crime need to be further regulated and the professional capacity of the relevant State Agency strengthened.
- Take the necessary steps to make the system of whistleblower protection more effective in practice.
- Review the system of immunities and ensure that effective procedures for lifting of immunities are in place.
- Review the procedure for closure of criminal cases and consider possibilities for appeals or complaints.

(European Commission 2012d, 25–27, 2012b, 12, 2012c, 11–12, 48, 2013a, 25, 2013b, 38–40, 2014a, 30, 2014b, 2–3, 11, 40–43, 2015a, 18, 2015b, 14–15, 2016a, 19, 2016b, 15–16)

Prevention of Corruption

From the bottom-up level, following the completed screening process of Montenegrin legislation within area of the fight against corruption, the Commission summarized achievements and improvements, and also provided further reform recommendations in the Screening Report for Chapter 23 and submitted it on December 25, 2012, to the newly established Working Group for Preparation of Negotiations on the Accession of Montenegro to the European Union in the area of the acquis related to negotiation Chapter 23—Judiciary and Fundamental Rights (Vlada Crne Gore 2013, 4). Based on the single interim benchmark introduced in the Screening Report by the Commission, almost one year after the official start of the accession negotiations the Government introduced the *Action Plan for Chapter 23—Judiciary and Fundamental Rights* on June 27, 2013.[8] Correspondingly, through the introduction of the Action Plan in June 2013, Montenegro addressed the last requirement to officially open the process of accession negotiations with the EU, thus consequently opening the possibility to start fulfilling the recommendations stipulated within the Screening Report Montenegro for Chapter 23.

Originally, in line with the first recommendation of the Commission stipulated in the Screening Report and 2015 Montenegro Progress Reports, particularly in strengthening and reviewing the institutional framework for the fight against corruption, the parliament adopted the *Law on Agency for Anti-Corruption* on December 9, 2014, in line with expert opinion from the European Commission foreseeing implementation of the enacted law on January 1, 2016, together with the established *Agency for preventing corruption*. In particular, the Law defined the following competences of the Agency, namely, coordination, supervision, and monitoring of the implementation of strategic documents for the fight against corruption with the supporting Action Plan, direct implementation and supervision over the Law on Prevention of Conflict of Interests and the Law on Financing of Political Subjects and Election Campaigns, protection of whistleblowers, and so on (European Commission 2012d, 25, 2015b, 14–15; Vlada Crne Gore 2013, 71, 2014, 125). In addition, the state also provided sufficient funds for technical resources and 55–60 personnel to carry out the work of the Agency and for the adoption of the new rules of procedures on organization and systematization of working places. As all open positions in the Agency had been filled and the IT systems were in a continuous process of development, the Government assessed the measure as being partly realized (European Commission 2012d, 25; Vlada Crne Gore 2013, 73, 2017, 46–47).

Concerning the second recommendation stipulated in the Screening Report and the 2012, 2013, 2014, 2015 Montenegro Progress Reports, and referring to improvement of the system of assets declaration, strengthening in particular supervisory competences and professional capacity of the CPCI to ensure effective and substantial checks on assets and introduce measures for preventing conflicts of interest going beyond holding double public offices, the Parliament adopted the *Amendments to the Law on the Prevention of Conflict of Interest* on December 16, 2014. According to the Action Plan provisions, the enacted law was to primarily expand the categories of persons obliged to report either property or work on managing boards of state-owned companies without remuneration, and it precisely prescribed which authorities would evaluate the asset statements of public officials (European Commission 2012d, 25, 2012c, 12, 2013b, 38–39, 2014b, 40–41, 2015b, 14–15; Vlada Crne Gore 2013, 73). In addition, in March 2015, the CPCI instituted a new form for checking asset data, thus improving the system of ensuring data accuracy in the reports of public officials. Additional activities were undertaken by the Commission to install software that would provide automatic networking and access to databases containing the asset and income information of public officials. Moreover, trainings for employees in the Commission and Agency for Anti-Corruption Initiative (CAACI) were improved, and they emphasized control competences and the use of databases as laid out in the Law (Vlada Crne Gore 2013, 79–81, 2017, 13–16, 57–61).

In response to the third suggestion mentioned in the Screening Report and the 2012, 2013, 2014, 2015 Montenegro Progress Reports (improving the system of funding political parties by ensuring reliable reporting, effective supervision, and sanctioning powers by an independent authority; strengthening capacities of the monitoring bodies such as the SAI and the SEC in accordance with the GRECO recommendations), the Parliament adopted the *Law on Financing Political Entities and Election Campaigns* on December 16, 2014. The enacted law clearly defined the competencies of the SAI and the SEC in legislative implementation, the involvement of independent audit houses in audit reports, the obligation of third parties to submit information upon request by competent authorities, the investigative powers of competent authorities, and the new system of sanctions (European Commission 2012d, 25, 2012c, 12, 2013b, 38–39, 2014b, 40–41, 2015b, 14–15; Vlada Crne Gore 2013, 92, 2014, 196–97).

Additional activities were oriented toward ensuring financial, technical, and personnel resources for the work of the Administrative and Technical Services of the SEC and the SAI through amendments of the Rulebooks on internal Organization and Job Descriptions of the SEC and SAI, thus specifying authorization and competence of staff, ensuring adequate budgetary funds and equipment for the Administrative and Technical Services of the SEC and the SAI, and drafting a specialization plan and continuous training plan in accordance with the given competences. In this respect, the SAI adopted on February 2015 the Rulebook on internal organization and systematization, resulting in the employment of one additional person in the SEC and eight persons in the SAI. Also, in accordance with the rulebook, the SAI employed ten out of thirteen individuals for monitoring Montenegrin political parties. Additional efforts were directed toward ensuring accommodation capacities, financial resources, and expert services the SAI. Furthermore, based on the draft budget for 2016, there was a total of 3.96 million EUR, which meant an increase of 2.51 million EUR when compared to the previous year. Likewise, based on the draft budget for 2016, the SEC received funds in the total of

0.24 million EUR for personnel and technical development (Vlada Crne Gore 2013, 93, 2014, 202–07).

Finally, the last of the Commission's recommendations in the Screening Report was intended to ensure that NGOs were involved in the anti-corruption agenda, and NGO representatives were thus included in the Anti-Corruption Committee, in line with set rules and procedures. In that regard, three NGO representatives attended the eleven Anti-Corruption Committee sessions held in 2015 (Institute Alternative, Centre for Civic Education, and MANS). In addition, in the period between January 1 and June 30, 2016, the Anti-Corruption Committee held three sessions that were attended by two NGO representatives (Institute Alternative and MANS). There was no information in regard to NGO attendance at the Anti-Corruption Committee in the period between July 1 and December 31, 2016 (European Commission 2012d, 26; Vlada Crne Gore 2013, 114, 2016a, 186, 2016b, 108).

Investigation, Prosecution, and Final Conviction of High-Level Corruption Cases

In line with the first of the Commission's recommendations on repressive action against corruption stipulated within the Screening Report and the 2014 and 2016 Montenegro Progress Reports (ensuring independent, effective specialized investigation/prosecution bodies), the Parliament adopted the *Law on Special Prosecutor's Office* on February 26, 2015, thus establishing a separate *Special Prosecutor's Office for fight against organized crime, corruption, terrorism and war crimes* to process cases of organized crime and corruption, especially high-level corruption cases.[9] Furthermore, strengthening staff capacities in the Division for the suppression of corruption, organized crime, terrorism, and war crimes was accomplished by employing twenty-eight individuals (European Commission 2012d, 26, 2014b, 42, 2016b, 15; Vlada Crne Gore 2013, 119–21; Vlada Crne Gore 2015, 115).

Concerning the second recommendation of the Commission as prescribed within the Screening Report, especially in regard to amending the Criminal Procedure Code where needed and ensuring its effective implementation, the Parliament adopted *Amendments to the Criminal Procedure Code* on July 7, 2015 (European Commission 2012d, 26; Vlada Crne Gore 2013, 208).

Also, in reference to the third of the Commission's demands over strengthening repressive action against corruption as prescribed within the Screening Report and the 2012, 2013, 2014, 2015, 2016 Montenegro Progress Reports (the use of financial investigation, possibly by establishing a team of highly qualified investigators for this purpose), the Parliament adopted the *Law on Confiscation of Asset Benefits Acquired by Criminal Activities* on November 9, 2015, to govern the procedure of conducting financial investigations and the confiscation of property (European Commission 2012d, 26, 2012c, 12, 2013b, 40, 2014b, 42, 2015b, 14–15, 2016b, 15; Vlada Crne Gore 2013, 133, 2016a, 210). Further activities were undertaken toward establishing specialized organizational units within the Criminal Investigation Police, specifically changes in organization and job descriptions. In this sense, in 2014, the group for conducting financial investigations, highly-technical crime, and human trafficking was established with five individuals employed, the group for the prevention of smuggling, human trafficking, and illegal migrations with three employees, the group for the prevention of high-tech crime with one employee, and the group for prevention of terrorism, weapons smuggling and explosive materials with three individuals. Finally, the JTC provided ongoing trainings for employees in the special unit of the Police Administration on the implementation of financial investigations, as well as for the multidisciplinary team and prosecutors and judges in combating corruption (Vlada Crne Gore 2013, 133–34, 2014, 367–68, 371–73, 2015, 129–30, 2016a, 212–13, 2016b, 125–27, 2017, 140–43).

Further actions were taken in terms of improving cooperation and information exchange between authorities, including tax and other indirectly linked authorities, involved in the fight against corruption. The state institutions signed the Protocol on Cooperation of the Supreme State Prosecutor's Office, Ministry of Interior and Police Directorate in pretrial and criminal procedures on April 9, 2014. This being said, additional activities were undertaken toward signing agreements between Montenegro and other state authorities including by the Tax Administration, Customs Administration, and the Harbor Master's Office, on exchange of information necessary for collecting data in pretrial and criminal procedures. In that respect, the Tax Administration and Police Directorate signed an agreement on standard operating procedures on June 1, 2015; additionally, an agreement was signed between the Ministry of Interior, Police Directorate, and Supreme State Prosecutor's Office on providing conditions for the smooth operation of the State Prosecutor's Office by the Police Administration, as well as an agreement between the Ministry of Interior, Police Directorate and Supreme State Prosecutor's Office on the smooth operation of courts and maintaining order. In 2016, there was no agreement of this type signed (European Commission 2012d, 26, 2012c, 12, 2016b, 15; Vlada Crne Gore 2013, 135–36, 2014, 377–80, 2016a, 215).

In respect to the next suggestion of the Commission stipulated within the Screening Report and the 2012 Montenegro Progress Report (procedures for seizure, confiscation, and management of proceeds of crime that needed to be further regulated and professional capacity of the relevant State Agency strengthened), the Parliament adopted the Law on Confiscation of Asset Benefits Acquired by Criminal Activities in 2015 (European Commission 2012d, 26, 2012c, 12; Vlada Crne Gore 2013, 139, 2017, 217). An electronic register of seized property was established in 2013 with information on the number of decisions, the name of the court or body responsible for conducting the proceedings, the type and the estimated value of the property, and the person from whom the property had been seized. Additional activities were conducted in strengthening the administrative capacities of the Public Property Administration by recruiting two additional civil servants for the management and custody of the temporarily seized or permanently confiscated property. Finally, further efforts were conducted toward strengthening the institutional framework by establishing the *Directorate of assets* on March 8, 2016, as an independent body in charge of the management and custody of seized property (Vlada Crne Gore 2013, 139–41, 2015, 133, 2016a, 217, 2014, 391–92, 2017, 149–50).

Finally, in reference to the last of the Commission's suggestions stipulated within the Screening Report (taking necessary steps to make the system of whistleblower protection more effective in practice), the Parliament adopted *Amendments to the Criminal Code* on July 30, 2013, thus ensuring the legal protection of whistleblowers. State reports indicated that there have been no charges, accusations or convictions since the introduction of the given legislation (European Commission 2012d, 26; Vlada Crne Gore 2013, 142–43, 2014, 151).

To fully understand why the EU has failed to Europeanize Montenegro in the area of the fight against corruption during the whole integration stage, a thorough empirical analysis is provided in the following section of this book.

CONDITIONALLY RELUCTANT PRESSURE BY THE EU AND THE COUNTRY'S POOR RESULTS IN THE FIGHT AGAINST CORRUPTION

The Pre-Negotiation Stage

Overall, the empirical findings in combating corruption in Montenegro during the pre-negotiation stage reveal two main observations. First, at the EU level, this phase is characterized by the Union's intention to improve both anti-corruption dimensions, that is, the prevention of corruption as well as building a credible track record of investigation, prosecution, and final conviction of all cases, especially those of high-level corruption. In particular, concerning pressure to improve anti-corruption preventive measures, the Union paid particular attention to strengthening the legal framework and the institutional framework of the DACI, the SEC, and the CPCI. This was due to serious concerns over the lack of transparency in political party financing and election campaigns and the lack of disclosure of various sources of income, as well as the legal shortcomings over the control of state assets with reference to the conflicts of interest of public officials. In addition, regarding the significance of improving the state's credible track record in investigation, prosecution, and final conviction at all levels, including high-level cases, during the pre-negotiation stage, the Union exerted constant pressure on Montenegro to develop the capacities of institutional and administrative bodies, namely the SIT (SIM), the Police Directorate's internal unit, the Department for the fight against organized crime, corruption, terrorism, and war crimes, to strengthen the investigative capacities of the law enforcement bodies, especially in providing staff, skills, expertise, and equipment (CeMI 2010, 11–26).

Second, on the domestic level, Montenegro achieved limited progress in the fight against corruption during the pre-negotiation phase. Evidently, some progress was made in strengthening the legal framework over preventive action against corruption through the adoption of the Amendments to the Criminal Procedure Code—CPC (2010) by introducing the concept of the prosecutors' investigation and the mechanism for combating corruption through the established measures of secret surveillance, as well as the legal provisions foreseeing confiscation of assets gained by criminal offenses (Vlada Crne Gore 2011c, 14). Further efforts were made in adopting the Amendments to the Criminal Code (2011) prescribing corruptive criminal offenses for bribery and trading in influence in line with the GRECO recommendations, and the Law on Civil Servants and State Employees (2011) introducing the institute for whistleblowers and their protection in cases of reporting corruption in public sector (Vlada Crne Gore 2011c, 15). Certain progress was also noted in the establishment of the institutional setup in preventing corruption, notably the DACI, the SEC, and the Commission, thus aiming to address the issue of political party and electoral campaign financing, as well as tackling the disclosure of sources of income of public officials. Finally, some results were achieved in building a track record in investigation, prosecution, and final conviction of all level of corruption cases, especially high-level corruption, as well as enhancing administrative capacities of law enforcement bodies for detecting and investigating corruption, particularly in terms of the development of skills, expertise, personnel, and so on (Vlada Crne Gore 2007b, 89).

However, corruption remained widespread and continued to be a matter of serious concern during the pre-negotiation stage. The state demonstrated insufficiently satisfactory results in the implementation and enforcement of its legal system and institutional framework in preventing corruption. The risk of political corruption could be seen in the legal provisions for the financing of political parties and election campaigns due to a lack of transparency of political subjects in terms of gaining financial assets. It is clear that the monitoring institution for controlling the finances of political subjects was insufficiently independent, which could be seen in the lack of legal provisions on controlling the allocations of private donations, as the emphasis was placed only on the state budget financial sources, and the lack of disciplinary procedures and sanctions for noncompliance with the law on providing accurate asset and political party funding information (CeMI 2011, 11–16). It was also evident that the monitoring institutions were under political influence, especially in terms of conflicts of interest. According to the legal provisions, the supervisory institution was appointed by the Parliament, and consequently, it lacked independent and impartial mechanisms to check the asset declarations of public officials. Additionally, there are other reasons to suspect that the political influence in the monitoring institution, specifically, the law that allowed members of Parliament to hold positions in state agencies and public companies while at the same time serving as parliamentary representatives (CeMI 2011, 17–20).

Although limited progress was made in strengthening the legal and institutional framework of preventing corruption before the country gained candidate status for EU membership, there were also visible shortcomings in improving the legal and institutional system of preventing anti-corruption after the state achieved the candidate status for EU membership. The state authorities also substantially delayed the adoption of legislation on strengthening anti-corruption measures on political party and election campaign financing and checking asset declarations of public officials. This was mainly reflected in the visible flaws in implementing the adopted laws in 2011 (Vlada Crne Gore 2011c). The state monitoring bodies, such as the SAI and SEC, did not possess effective independent check mechanisms to use in the event political parties provided false or inaccurate data in regard to the illegal allocation of financial resources mainly provided through private donations. This means that the supervising authorities did not possess effective sanctioning tools that could be used to impose penalties for noncompliance with the legal requirements over checking political party funding. Thus, it would be reasonable to claim that disciplinary procedures within the monitoring state authorities were not efficiently put into practice (CeMI 2010, 15, 21–23). The same situation was observable in the effectiveness of the Commission for prevention of conflicts of interest. Although new legal provisions further strengthened the control of the Commission's role in checking the submitted asset declarations of public officials, the empirical evidence outlined the substantial lack of legal provisions on illicit enrichment of state officials as the Commission did not have access to state officials' banking accounts, or their family members' accounts, nor could it access the exchange of information between other state authorities in regard to conflicts of interest. Hence, the state supervising institution(s) lacked the substantial independence and impartiality needed to assess asset declarations due to visible political influence in imposing disciplinary provisions against actors who did not comply with the given laws (CeMI 2010, 14–15, 23–25). As a result, political corruption remained prevalent in many anti-corruption institutional mechanisms mostly due to insufficient implementation and enforcement of the adopted legal measures and insufficient capacities of supervisory bodies to independently and impartially evaluate asset declarations of public officials while checking the origin of financial sources used by political parties in their election campaigns.

By the same token, Montenegro achieved overall poor reform results in building a credible track record of investigations, prosecutions, and final convictions of all corruption cases, especially high-level cases during the pre-negotiation phase. Evidently, the state demonstrated substantially low progress in enhancing its administrative capacities for detecting and investigating corruption (SIT, Police Directorate internal control units, Unit for fight against the organized crime, corruption, terrorism, and war crimes, etc.), particularly in terms of improving its investigative capacities through providing additional personnel, equipment, and expertise (Vlada Crne Gore 2011f, 47, 2011c, 15). In addition, law enforcement bodies, namely the Police Directorate, the State Prosecutor's Office, and the DACI displayed substantial shortcomings and loopholes in conducting investigations into financial corruption. There was a significant lack of expertise and equipment, and interagency cooperation, and the exchange of information between law enforcement bodies remained undeveloped (Council of the European Union 2007, 4; Vlada Crne Gore 2007b, 69–70, 2012f, 106). Consequently, the country also achieved insufficiently satisfactory results in building a concrete and sustainable track record in monitoring, prosecution and trial of corruption cases, including high priority cases. Although the state authorities took certain actions to strengthen the legal system in combating corruption through the adoption of the new CPC and the Criminal Code, it was evident that the law enforcement bodies chiefly had issues with implementation and empowerment. In other words, the legal framework for repressing corruption was built, and the administrative and institutional bodies were established, but the sustainability of corruption reform through building a credible track record of implementation was missing (IA and CGO and CRNVO and CeMI 2018, 4–6). In line with this assertion, only one judge from the High Court was convicted to seven years of imprisonment for passive bribery in December 2010, and three individuals (the mayor of Budva, his deputy, and a member of the Parliament) were sentenced to a total of twelve years imprisonment for high-level corruption for abuse of official position and bribery during the ten-year integration period (MANS 2009b).[10] Furthermore, the High Court made only three decisions in regard to temporary confiscation of assets for the criminal offense of money laundering and one decision against the Major of Ulcinj, sentencing him to pay 10,000 EUR to charity for the criminal offense of abuse of official position. Therefore, given the research findings one may claim that the fight against corruption in relation to high-level cases remained extremely low during the pre-negotiation phase, mainly because of the lack of commitment of both investigative and prosecution law enforcement bodies to tackle the prevalent corruption issues (Vlada Crne Gore 2012b, 83).

Based on the empirical observations, it seems credible to talk about certain tendencies existing within the area of combating corruption during the pre-negotiation stage. Primarily, Montenegro continued to experience the same problems in the implementation and reinforcement of the adopted legal system and established institutional framework designed to progressively combat corruption. On the one hand, the country did provide convincing and sustainable results in adoption of the acquis and alignment with the EU policies to ensure sustainability of reform through building a credible track record of implementation in the prevention of corruption, as well as in the investigation, prosecution, and conviction of high-level corruption cases. On the other hand, not having fulfilled certain Union requirements did not, although it should have, affect the integration dynamics of the country in question. In particular, this claim can be tested by observing the Commission's demands contained in the 2007, 2008, and 2009 Progress Reports in which the Union continuously underlined the importance of resolving the issue of prevention of corruption (amending the laws on conflict of interest and political party financing) and repression of corruption (credible track record of investigation, prosecution, and conviction of high-level cases), which consequently resulted in the state's unwillingness to comply with the EU requirements (European Commission 2007b, 2008b, 2009b). Thus, it might be reasonable to argue that the Union was inconsistent and ineffective in pressuring the state to tackle the corruption issues. Instead, the EU had negative reinforcing effects on preventing and repressing corruption, particularly in the adoption of legislation and alignment with EU policies (Vučković and Đorđević 2019; Elbasani and Šelo Šabić 2018; Mendelski 2015; Keil 2013; Noutcheva 2009).

It is more than clear from Montenegro's implementation track record in the area of fight against the corruption during the pre-negotiation stage that the sustainability of reforms was not credibly ensured. Although the state demonstrated some progress in strengthening its legal system and institutional setup in combating corruption, it is also evident that the enlargement country showed weak progress in tackling corruption. However, the country advanced in the accession process, gaining candidate status for EU membership, regardless of its insufficiently satisfactory results in the fight against corruption. Thus, the progress of the candidate country in the EU integration opens the question of the Union's real range of interests in and scope of conditions for the enlargement state. It is more than clear that the Union had a negative reinforcing impact on the strengthening of the anti-corruption policy when it applied a strategy of permissiveness toward the candidate country. As a result, the target accession state conducted patchy and loose reform activities in combating corruption during the pre-negotiation stage, predominantly maintaining the political corruption in the state anti-corruption institutions (DACI, CPCI, SEC, SAI), while at the same time refusing to deliver convincing results in the prosecution and conviction of high-ranking persons. However, the state's reluctance to effectively implement the anti-corruption measures requested by the EU did not affect its further progress in the EU integration process. On the contrary, the EU strongly supported Montenegro on its integration path, although the Commission continued to raise serious concerns over the effects of widespread corruption at all levels of governance and administration.

The Negotiation Stage

In a nutshell, two main empirical observations can be made on the fight against corruption in Montenegro during the negotiation stage. First, the Screening Report for Chapter 23 is, as far as the EU is concerned, the most comprehensive analytical document investigating the current level of the state's alignment with the EU rules and norms in combating corruption. It provides not only recommendations for enhancing the legal and institutional framework for tackling corruption, but, perhaps far more importantly, it requires the achievement of concrete and sustainable results in the field of the fight against corruption in Montenegro. Having thus claimed, the Screening Report outlines the importance of meeting the requirements on preventing corruption and establishing a convincing and credible track record in the investigation, prosecution, and final conviction on all corruption levels, especially high-level corruption cases. Moreover, in terms of the state's continuous declining trends in combating corruption, the Union has paid the most attention to both anti-corruption requirements, that is, strengthening preventive and repressive anti-corruption activities. This includes the problem of strengthening the legal and institutional framework in terms of conflict of interest and financing of political parties and election campaigns, building credible track record in prosecution and investigation of high-level corruption cases, as well as having a substantial number of cases of seizure or confiscation of assets, as these issues have remained matters of serious concern in Montenegro's fight against corruption so far (European Commission 2012d; MANS 2017).

Second, the empirical findings outline that on the domestic level Montenegro has achieved overall limited progress in the fight against corruption during the negotiation phase. Although the state has shown some results in strengthening the legal system and institutional framework and administrative and institutional capacities to tackle the given problem, the empirical evidence indicates that overall moderate progress in fulfilling anti-corruption demands during the second integration stage has taken place so far. Originally, the accession negotiation period between the EU and Montenegro, specifically the time frame between 2012 and 2017, is characterized by the state's effort to enact new legislation, reinforce already adopted legislative measures, and strengthen its anti-corruption institutional and administrative capacities. In this sense, concerning the Union's requirements over strengthening the anti-corruptive preventive actions, the state primarily adopted the Law on Agency for Anti-Corruption (2014), thus foreseeing the establishment of the Agency for preventing corruption from 2016. Correspondingly, the Agency holds the competences of coordination, supervision, and monitoring of implementation of strategic documents for the fight against corruption, that is, repression of corruption with the supporting Action Plan, as well as coordination of direct implementation and supervision over the laws on prevention of conflict of interests and financing of political parties. Additional improvements have been particularly observable in providing trainings for employees in the CAACI in terms of control competences and use of databases prescribed within the Law. In addition, in regard to enhancing repressive anti-corruption activities, particularly in ensuring independent and effective specialized investigation and/or prosecution bodies, further improvements have been seen in strengthening the Montenegrin legal system and development of administrative capacities through the adoption of the Law on Special Prosecutor's Office (2015), thus establishing a separate Special Prosecutor's Office for the fight against organized crime, corruption, terrorism and war crimes to process cases of corruption and organized crime, especially high-level corruption cases, and strengthen staff capacities of the Division for Suppression of Corruption, Organized Crime, Terrorism and War Crimes (CeMI 2014; MANS 2017).

By the same token, the Montenegrin anti-corruption system has demonstrated visible results in strengthening procedures for seizure, confiscation, and management of processing crimes that need to be further regulated, along with the establishment of a financial investigation team governing the procedure of conducting financial investigations and the institute of confiscation of property by adopting the Law on Confiscation of Asset Benefits Acquired by Criminal Activities (2015). Additional activities have been oriented toward strengthening the institutional framework through the establishment of the Directorate of assets (2016) as an independent body in charge of management and custody of seized property. Furthermore, the state has demonstrated visible achievements in improving administrative (professional) capacities of the relevant State Agency based on the Law on Confiscation of Asset Benefits Acquired by Criminal Activities as well as capacities of the Public Property Administration through increase in the number of jobs for civil servants for management and custody of temporarily seized or permanently confiscated property (MANS 2017, 72–73). Moreover, the JTC has provided continuous training for the employees in the special unit of the Police Administration for implementation of financial investigations, as well as to the multidisciplinary team and prosecutors and judges in combating corruption (MANS 2017, 29–30). However, although Montenegro has made some progress in strengthening its legal system and has established an institutional setup for preventing and repressing corruption, the problem of corruption remains prevalent in many areas and continues to be a problem of serious concern in the negotiation stage. In particular, the country does not demonstrate sufficient dedication to reform activities in the fight against corruption, particularly so in the prevention of corruption and proving a credible track record in investigation, prosecution, and final conviction of all corruption cases, especially high-level cases through effective implementation and enforcement of already adopted measures. In short, the implementation remains deficient (CeMI 2014; MANS 2018).

In this sense, concerning the Union's recommendation over strengthening preventive anti-corruption activities, particularly in improving the system of asset declarations by strengthening supervisory competences and professional capacity of the Commission for prevention of the conflict of interest to ensure a substantially effective check of assets, the new adopted law from 2014 has shown substantial shortfalls in terms of effective prevention of corruption. Visibly, based on five areas prescribed by the action plan in prevention of the conflict of interest, only three are covered by the respective law. Following already-defined measures in preventing corruption, the newly enacted law does not ensure that the work of public officials in state-owned companies is being performed without remuneration, and, perhaps far more importantly, respective legal provisions do not contain more concrete or strict sanctions related to violations of the rules on conflict of interest, especially in cases when there is no reporting of assets or when there are incorrect data in asset declarations (MANS 2017, 40–42). Furthermore, although the system of reporting properties has been improved since March 2015, the performance of the Commission in checking data accuracy from reports of public officials contains visible shortcomings and loopholes. During the first half of 2015, the Commission found more than 600 violations of the respective Law. However, information on the exact number of conducted misdemeanor procedures against public officials and the outcomes of these procedures remain unknown.[11] Also, the Commission has also indicated insufficient progress toward developing institutional capacity, with reference to checking correct data in the asset declarations of state officials by establishing automatic networking and access to databases only to the Ministry of Interior and not to, as it was initially described within the Action Plan, the Ministry of Maritime Affairs and Transport, the Ministry of Finance, the Commission for the Control of Public Procurement Procedure, that is, those bodies and institutions possessing data on the property and income of public officials (MANS 2017, 40–42; CeMI 2014, 17–20). Therefore, based on the empirical observations it seems reasonable to claim that there is a strong influence of political corruption in the anti-corruption monitoring authority in terms of prevention of conflict of interest due to problems of implementation and empowerment of legal provisions, as well as a lack of transparency on the part of supervisory bodies in accurately reporting data and already-conducted disciplinary procedures.

The same reasons for serious concern over political influence within the anti-corruption supervisory authority also apply to the insufficiently improved system of political party funding, which does not ensure reliable reporting, effective supervision, or sanctioning power by independent authorities following the GRECO recommendations. Evidently, the issue of further strengthening the Montenegrin legal system of preventing corruption raises doubts over the independence of the SAI and the SEC to impartially check and monitor mechanisms of political party financing and the ability to impose the sanctions if needed. In line with the adopted law on financing of political parties and election campaigns, the monitoring anti-corruption bodies, namely the SAI and the SEC (responsible for the implementation of the law), have not adopted substantially important by-laws as prescribed by the Action Plan, which are needed to further regulate the use of public resources for the activities of political parties during election campaigns and likewise determine the manner of accounting of political entities. In addition, the anti-corruption supervisory authorities face the profound problem of lack of professional capacities. The SAI has employed 70% of its capacities within the sector controlling illicit financing of political parties, whereas the SEC has not yet fully completed this process (MANS 2017, 44–45). Hence, the anti-corruption preventive bodies are characterized by prevailing political corruption in controlling the illegal financing of political parties due to the lack of professional capacities and legal provisions to prevent possible misuse of public resources for political party purposes during election campaigns.

The research findings also reveal that Montenegro achieved insufficiently satisfactory results in strengthening its anti-corruption measures during the negotiation phase. Primarily, the amendments to the CPC (2015) introduced novelties regarding obstruction of the legal system and perpetrators avoiding criminal sentences, especially in terms of high-level cases serving appropriate sentences. Based on the adoption of the amendments to the CPC, it is possible to claim that plea bargaining, even for the most serious criminal offenses, including those of corruption, has been applied even more in high-level corruption cases. The amendments to the CPC do not foresee that the final sentence of parties accused of a high-level corruption criminal offense cannot be lower than the legal minimum for other corruption offenses, and that the final sentence for a high-level criminal corruption offense can only exceptionally be decreased under the conditions prescribed within the CPC (MANS 2017, 68–69). This legal loophole in the current amendments to the CPC has been substantially used by defendants convicted of high-level corruption and organized crime, and allowed them to receive a minor penalty. For instance, in 2015, in the case of "Zavala," the High Court in Podgorica upheld a previous sentence of 3–5 years of imprisonment for the former mayor of Budva, his deputy, and a former DPS MP, while in the case of "Košljun" another individual who was also a former mayor of Budva received a six-year prison sentence from the High Court in Podgorica as a result of a plea-bargaining agreement (Freedom House 2017; Monitor 2015; Radio Slobodna Evropa 2015). Also, in 2016, the High Court in Podgorica concluded a bargaining agreement with former president of the State Union of Serbia and Montenegro and high-ranking DPS party official Svetozar Marović. He was sentenced to three years and nine months of imprisonment for high-level corruption offenses, with a 1.1 million EUR fine and 100,000 EUR to be provided by him to charity (European Commission 2016b, 15; Vijesti 2019; Radio Slobodna Evropa 2016). Last but not the least, with reference to misuse of public funds for political party purposes—in the "Audio Recording" affair, the Basic Court in Pljevlja in 2014 issued a final sentence of six months imprisonment against a director of the Social Welfare Centre in Pljevlja and one of its employees (European Commission 2014b, 42–43; MANS 2018, 8–10).

Hence, based on the provided data, the empirical observation suggests that the EU has shown substantially declining trends in strengthening the anti-corruption policy in Montenegro during the negotiation phase. The Union-driven rule of law pressure has had negatively reinforcing impact on the enhancement of prevention of corruption and realizing a credible track record in investigation, prosecution, and final conviction of all cases, including high-level ones, therefore, producing profoundly negative empowerment effects in combating corruption in Montenegro since 2012. As a consequence of such Union activities, the candidate country has shown profoundly limited progress in combating corruption during the whole negotiation phase. The state has made some progress in strengthening its legal and institutional framework, as well as built up its institutional and administrative capacities to tackle corruption issues; however, the implementation remains deficient.

EXPLAINING TRENDS OF THE STATE'S NONFULFILLMENT OF THE ANTI-CORRUPTION POLICY REQUIREMENTS DURING THE INTEGRATION PHASE

Following the provided empirical observations in combating corruption in Montenegro during the whole integration phase, the main question that arises here is how can we explain declining or downgrading trends in strengthening of the anti-corruption policy? More precisely, what are the main reasons for the state's achievement of poor reform results in preventing corruption and providing convincing results in investigation, prosecution, and conviction of high-level corruption cases?

Four main explanations may be provided in this regard. First, strengthening of the anti-corruption policy in Montenegro during the accession process was primarily characterized by accelerated growth in legislation followed by a high number of adopted anti-corruption strategic frameworks. Available information shows that more than five different versions of the action plans for the strategy against the corruption and organized crime, along with one defined anti-corruption strategy, were introduced during the integration process (Vlada Crne Gore 2007a, 2011a, 2011b, 2013). So many adopted strategic documents in such a short period of time may have influenced the quality of the enacted legislation due to the constant changing of reform priorities within the anti-corruption strategy. As a result, the accelerated adoption of the anti-corruption strategic documents had a profound impact on rapid legislative growth, resulting in legal changes that were ineffective in the fight against corruption. Obviously, the Union-driven pressure for rule of law that would induce effective anti-corruption changes resulted in the enactment of uneven, fast, and inadequate laws (more than seventy), which were substantially limited in their scope of influence (MANS 2017). This being said, the accelerated legislative growth led to an insufficiently developed administrative apparatus that was unable to cope with the vast amount of legal changes, especially when it comes to changes in anti-corruption policy and the overall effects on the independent functioning of the state anti-corruption institutions (CeMI 2013). Also, the system created both formal and ineffective legal regulations that were not in a position to credibly strengthen the legal system in the fight against corruption or to ensure sustainable results in investigation, prosecution, and final conviction of corruption cases. Due to inefficient legal changes, the anti-corruption monitoring institutions became profoundly limited in scope, and therefore not able to pro-actively approach the preventing corruption. The examples of the SAI and the Commission suggest that those supervisory institutions did not hold any real power to evaluate the asset declarations of political party funding or public officials. This was due to the limitations of mechanisms for checking the accuracy of provided data (MANS 2017, 44–45). By that time, the monitoring institutions for preventing corruption were merely artificial and formal institutions, not independent in their scope of influence, and were characterized by overwhelming political influence. This was justified by the formal fulfillment of the EU requirements as such.

The substantial lack of administrative and institutional capacities of anti-corruption bodies can be seen as the second reason for the state's declining trends in fighting corruption, as the state monitoring institutions for preventing corruption, such as the SAI and the Commission, were faced with profound issues of professional capacity. Although the country strengthened its legal and institutional framework in tackling corruption issues, the implementation remained deficient due to the lack of staff and additional expertise in effectively evaluating the asset declarations of public officials and the financing of political parties. It was a visible lack of administrative capacities in the state monitoring institutions that substantially impacted the impartiality and independence of the anti-corruption bodies to address corruption issues, chiefly the political corruption and organized crime existing at all levels of governance and administration, as well as the prosecution and investigation of high-level corruption cases (CeMI 2013, 13–15).

The substantial lack of financial resources for strengthening the administrative and institutional capacities of law enforcement bodies is also used as additional explanation for the declining trends in curbing corruption at that time. Those independent and effective (financial) investigation teams and prosecution bodies largely depended on the support of international donors, given the fact that the state's budget did not cover the need for building specialized law enforcement bodies (CEMI 2013). Therefore, although there was some improvement in the state's administrative and institutional capacities in tackling corruption, an increase in domestic budgetary funds, and Union financial support provided through the Instruments for Pre-Accession Assistance I and II (IPA I and II), it is evident that the overall strengthening of the capacity of law enforcement bodies was extremely low. If one considers that the financial support of the EU through the IPA I funds was in total 173.1 million EUR for the whole Transition Assistance and Institution Building component,[12] and IPA II through the component of "Democracy and Rule of Law" totaled 80.1 million EUR for the period of 2014–2017,[13] one can estimate that the financial support for the overall fight against corruption in Montenegro was substantially insufficient during the whole accession process (Đurović 2012, 343; European Commission 2020). As a result, the significant lack of financial resources deeply affected the development of capacity of investigative and prosecutorial bodies, especially when it comes to the lack of appropriate skills, adequate equipment, and human resources, to curb corruption and address high-level corruption cases (European Commission 2015b, 14, 2016b, 16).

Strong opposition of the ruling elites to strengthening anti-corruption preventive measures as well as to building a credible track record in investigation, prosecution, and final conviction of high-level cases is the third explanation for the declining trends in the fight against corruption. In the case of Montenegro, the entire integration period has been characterized by prevalent corruption in all levels of government and administration, as well as by rather strong infiltration in many public and private spheres (European Commission 2014b, 2, 2015b, 14, 2016b, 15). It has not been a rare occurrence to see political corruption in Montenegro in terms of the use of state or public resources for financing the ruling political party and its election campaigns. Serious allegations of the misuse of state financial resources for internal political party purposes during the parliamentary elections in 2012 and the presidential elections in 2013 did not result in prosecution or conviction of those responsible, even though evidence was presented to the appropriate authorities (Vučković and Đorđević 2019, 163–69; Radio Slobodna Evropa 2009, 2013; Vijesti 2013). Corruption in this small Adriatic state is strongly linked to and influenced by the politicization of its judiciary, specifically by having political influence in judicial independence and accountability that ensures that all potential corruption affairs involving government officials remain unaddressed (MANS 2017, 7–13). The "Audio Recording" affair from 2013 may be used as a suitable example to support the given claim. The "Audio Recording" affair is related to the release of audio recordings of a session of the ruling DPS in which talks on the use of state resources for party purposes and employment by party affiliation during the 2012 parliamentary and 2013 presidential elections were recorded. There is reasonable suspicion that the DPS had purchased ID cards from citizens, especially from those who were facing poor financial conditions, to ensure the survival of the ruling elite (DAN 2014). The serious concerns over violations of political party finance laws by the ruling political party center around the ruthless pressure placed on undecided voters and state employees to vote for said party, in order that they could remain in power. This visible political influence remains a cornerstone for survival in power, as both legislative and executive branches formally adopt legislation or by-laws related to ensuring transparency of financing of political parties and election campaigns, but in practice implementation and enforcement does not actually exist.

Also, the law on financing of political parties contains substantial flaws and loopholes regarding political party funding. The current law foresees individuals contributing to financing of political parties and election campaigns from private sources with a maximum of 2,000 EUR per year. The problem arises due insufficient control of the Agency for preventing corruption, as it does not possess the capacity to check financial donations or contributions to political parties, as strong political interference influences the activities of the anti-corruption bodies. Obviously, any politicization of the Agency that controls party donations from private sources unequivocally opens a large space for money laundering, which consequently jeopardizes public interest in suppressing corruption, especially when it comes to, for instance, elections. The allegations of money laundering against the ruling DPS party and its donors in the previous parliamentary elections have caused public controversy. Apparently, the DPS provided a list of two thousand donors who had paid 654,000 EUR in support of DPS election campaigns, although some of those named in the report publicly denied their donation and claimed that their names and data had been misused (Vijesti 2011; Kovačević 2014; IA and CGO and CRNVNO and CeMI 2018).

The cluster of domestic ruling elites and corruption is a major issue in Montenegro, a country where material benefits are being gained through corruption-based affairs (Börzel 2011; Morrison 2009; Bieber 2020). For as small as Montenegrin society is, the principle of acquaintance and gaining merit-based personal relationships represents a daily pattern of functioning that applies to all aspects of society, that is, from employment in state institutions, public procurement, to various tenders, and so on (Džankić 2018; Keil 2018). Hence, protection by the domestic political elites of domestic and public actors suspected of corruption is the most common characteristic of widespread corruption. The significantly small number of prosecutions and final convictions of high-level corruption cases during the whole integration phase presents a serious concern over the political elites' deep involvement in corruption and possible scandals that could be utterly compromising for these actors (Radeljić and Đorđević 2020). For the sake of argument, in the period between 2013 and 2018, the Montenegrin courts convicted only five state officials for high-level corruption crimes, while one individual had his assets seized and/or confiscated (MANS 2018, 11). The politicization of the judiciary raises serious concerns surrounding the effort to provide convincing results in high-level corruption cases, as there has been a constant decline in prosecutions and convictions of high-level corruption felony cases against high-ranking government officials. Investigations and prosecutions are more often conducted against state administrators and small and medium businessmen for cases of petty corruption (more than 56% compared to 20% of high-level corruption). Proceedings against government officials, on the other hand, are rare—generally the lowest among all those accused of corruption. Of course, exceptions have been made in the cases of the defendants Svetozar Marović (former speaker of the Montenegrin Assembly and vice president of ruling DPS and president of the former State Union of Serbia and Montenegro), and Đorđe Pinjatić (former member of the Parliament) who were sentenced to three years and nine months and one year in prison, respectively, due to their criminal involvement in the so-called Zavala Affair (MANS 2018, 8, 11). Interestingly enough, in the case of other potential corruption affairs widely familiar to Montenegrin public, such as "Can," "Telecom of Montenegro," and so on, the Special State Prosecutor's Office failed to find any evidence for an indictment against other DPS-party-related officials and their family members (IA and CGO and CRNVNO and CeMI 2018, 5).

One can claim that the court's penalizing policy against high-ranking state officials for high-level corruption was mild and low, as in all six cases the courts imposed minimum sentences or sentences below the statutory minimum (MANS 2018, 8, 11).[14] Visibly, concerning the Union-driven rule of law pressure on the state to show convincing and sustainable results in repressing corruption, the ruling elites in Montenegro, to satisfy the Union, have resorted to the logic or principle of the weakest link. The DPS, as the most dominant and highly corrupt political party, has had to "sacrifice" its "weakest" high-profile individual(s) to formally meet the EU requirements during the negotiation phase. In a gesture of gratitude, the governing power has also adopted legal provisions enabling those high-profile individuals to be only lightly sentenced. The case of Svetozar Marović confirms this claim. Apparently, before the start of the process of investigation, prosecution, and final conviction of Marović for his involvement in a criminal corruption affair that syphoned off several million euros from the local and state budget, the Parliament adopted the amendments to the CPC, thus essentially helping the defendant. This new legal provision introduced the instrument of plea-bargaining agreements for most corruption offenses, including, of course, high-level corruption cases as well. Consequently, the amendments to the CPC allow for a substantial decrease in the sentences of high-level corruption cases with a given sentence not being below the legal minimum that applies in all other cases (non-high-profile cases, that is) (MANS 2017, 68–71; MANS 2018, 12–13). Obviously, this legal loophole was used by Svetozar Marović to get a minor penalty, and he was sentenced to a total of three years and nine months for corruption. Even today, the use of the plea bargaining opens various questions related to the range and scope of law enforcement investigation and prosecution capacities, as well as probes the lack of transparency in conducted procedures due to the fact that Montenegrin public still does not have access to precise information on these and similar matters.

Consequently, Montenegro continues to face a decline in public trust in the judiciary despite the paradoxical fact that the candidate country is currently in the advanced stage of the integration process. There is substantial mistrust of the Special State Prosecutor's Office in prosecuting high-level corruption cases, as it has been perceived that prosecutors are deeply linked with the ruling DPS party. According to polls, the unwillingness of SDT to open investigations into the "Audio Recording," "Can," and "Telekom Montenegro" corruption scandals, among others, against high-raking ruling party officials and their relatives, despite clear and credible evidence, confirms strong political influence on the judiciary and state capture by one party (BIRN 2013; IA and CGO and CRNVNO and CeMI 2018, 7).

Finally, the Union's visible lack of interest in the EU enlargement process represents the fourth explanation in regard to corruption. Obviously, profound internal and external issues of the EU, that is, the strong influence of economic and financial crisis, institutional reform issues, visible disagreements among the member states regarding the future development of the Union, the rise of populism, right-wing political parties, and semi-authoritarian leaders, and finally enlargement fatigue, have had a profound impact on the lack of consensus within the EU institutions about the future of the enlargement policy (Samardžić 2016; Elbasani and Šelo Šabić 2018; Džankić and Keil and Kmezić 2019). Although the EU has provided the region with an opportunity for membership, Brussels has been, on the other hand, reluctant to confirm a date for the accession of the Western Balkan countries. In fact, this lack of interest on the part of the Union in its integration process for Montenegro has been characterized by clarification and specification of both range and scope of conditions observed in three points: characterization of the political criteria with a special focus on the rule of law, introduction of the opening and interim benchmarks, and transformation of the accession process into an "open-ended process" (Gateva 2015; Laursen 2013). Thus, one is able to claim that the EU conditional policy has had a substantial negative impact on the political transformation in Montenegro during the negotiation stage, due to the insufficiency and inefficiency of its policy for effectively fighting corruption. In particular, the negatively reinforcing impact of the EU has substantially affected conditions surrounding tackling corruption, especially when it comes to achieving concrete and convincing results in the prevention of corruption and establishing a credible track record in investigation, prosecution, and final conviction of high-level cases. Hence, it can be easily argued that the inadequate results in combating corruption have primarily stemmed from the Union's reluctance to hold domestic ruling elites accountable for strengthening the state's anti-corruption policy through the implementation of anti-corruption measures. On the one hand, it is the reluctance of the EU to put stronger pressure on Montenegro to reduce corruption that has consequently negatively impacted anti-corruption measures and caused problems in building a credible track record in the prosecution and investigation of high-level cases. Last of all, the given approach has thus resulted in very limited progress in the fight against corruption in Montenegro.

CONCLUSION

Based on the given explanations, this chapter has sought to provide answers on the question of Montenegro's failure to Europeanize despite the long-lasting reform process. In particular, the issues of external or internal conditions/factors influencing visible decline within the fight against corruption and respective downgrading trends have been assessed.

In that regard, since 2007 when the country started combating corruption, the Union has been confronted with profoundly unfavorable domestic conditions, particularly the limited statehood issue. As was the case in many post-communist transition societies, Montenegro has been faced with the problem of having a weak democracy and strongly dependent institutions, institutionally entrenched corruption and clientelism, and an insufficiently developed administrative structure unable to effectively tackle corruption issues (Börzel 2016; Kmezić 2020; Bieber 2020; Keil and Arkan 2015). The problems of limited statehood have had a profound impact on widespread political corruption within the anti-corruption supervisory institutions created to mitigate political influence in relation to the conflict of interest of public officials and the monitoring mechanisms used to ensure transparent political party funding and election campaigns. Due to the lack of expertise, funding, and staff, as well as an insufficiently developed administrative and institutional capacities of the law enforcement bodies, there has also been a failure to effectively address corruption issues, particularly in achieving concrete and sustainable results in investigation, prosecution, and final conviction of all corruption cases, especially high-level ones (MANS 2017, 2018, 2019).

Second, remnants of the postcommunist legacy have continued to play an active role in the fight against corruption during the entire EU integration phase (Elbasani 2013; Radeljić 2012). The strong influence of veto players in combating corruption might account for the downward trends in the prevention of corruption and achieving convincing and sustainable results in prosecution and final conviction of high-level corruption cases. The veto players (post-transition profiteers, corrupt business elites, financial tycoons, etc.) originating from the postcommunist period and continuing with the financial support of the governing party, have deeply infiltrated all levels of governance and administration (Elbasani 2019; Noutcheva and Aydin-Düzgit 2012; Freyburg and Richter 2010; Dzihic and Wieser 2008). Close (and criminal) cooperation between the corrupt political elite and the veto players primarily ensures the political protection of these players from possible investigation, prosecution, and final conviction through the strong political influence over the judiciary, especially over the independence and impartiality of judges and prosecutors (Vučković and Đorđević 2019, 177–79; Keil 2018, 59–82; Džankić 2018, 83–106). Having thus claimed, the corruption in the Montenegrin judiciary primarily reinforces the status of the corrupt political elites and veto players as legally untouchable for their corrupt actions and maneuvers. By providing financial support and other donations for the ruling party's election campaigns, these organized criminal clans realize their private interests through a corrupt executive power that remains a suitable tool for increasing their illegal wealth. It is this close circle of post-transitional winners that are criminally tied to the ruling party, which consequently benefits from corruption in privatization, urbanization, public tenders, and public procurements (Radeljić and Đorđević 2020; IA and CGO and CRNVO and CeMI 2018, 8). Due to the strong interdependence between the domestic ruling elites and the veto players, this corrupt and criminal clan alliance is able to stave off potential prosecution and conviction of high-level corruption offenses (Bieber 2020; MANS 2018). Therefore, it would be reasonable to claim that long-lasting criminal ties will continue to exist until the Union-driven rule of law pressure imposes positively reinforcing effects in achieving a credible and convincing track record in monitoring, prosecution, and trials of corruption. One might argue that the veto players still have had a strong impact in undermining the process of effectively fighting against corruption during the negotiation stage (Vučković and Đorđević 2019).

On the other hand, the existence of facilitating factors, namely civil society organizations (CSOs)—primarily NGOs and representatives from academia—still does not have any concrete influence in providing assistance in the fight against corruption, particularly over providing recommendations and/or monitoring activities toward strengthening preventive and repressive anti-corruption activities (Wunch 2018; Salgado 2014). These domestic reformers, largely linked with the Union and its accession perspective, have been trying to play an active role in the fight against corruption mostly through the National Commission for implementation of the Strategy for the fight against corruption and organized crime and the Working Group for Preparation on Negotiations on the Accession of Montenegro to the European Union in the area of the acquis related to negotiation of Chapter 23—Judiciary and Fundamental Rights, and so on, without, however, any convincing results. A number of critically oriented NGOs have been prevented by the state from actively performing their role as watchdogs during the accession process by effectively cutting them off from the process of preparing legal acts.[15] Campaigns to discredit critically oriented NGO's by the media have become a strong mechanism widely used by the Government. During 2017 and 2018, the pro-government daily newspaper "Pobjeda" continuously published information of alleged savings in NGO bank accounts in the total amount of 45.7 million EUR. This sort of propaganda was used as a means of manipulation and deception against those NGOs that have a critical attitude toward the Government and its corruption affairs, aiming to undermine the importance of their work as watchdogs and to decrease public trust, and perhaps far more importantly, to damage their sustainability, independence, and impact (IA and CGO and CRNVO and CeMI 2018, 8, 10–11). However, although they make substantial efforts in monitoring the process of combating corruption, CSOs do not have any particular influence in the decision-making process, and consequently play a rather marginal role in improving government performance (Freedom House 2020; Bojicic-Dzelilovic and Ker-Lindsay and Kostovicova 2013). One reason for eliminating the CSOs from the process of strengthening the given anti-corruption reform activities can be seen in their disclosure of corruption affairs among the ruling elites, which might mitigate further progress of the state in the process of accession negotiations.

Due to unfavorable domestic conditions, the political elites have undertaken profoundly limited activities in enhancing the prevention and suppression of corruption, at the same time undertaking state capture measures over the state's anti-corruption institutions. Following the current state integration dynamics in combating corruption, it is evident that corruption remains a prevalent problem and continues to be a matter of serious concern even after five years have passed since Montenegro opened the accession negotiations with the EU by opening the Chapter 23 and focusing on the rule of law requirements (Kmezić 2017; Mendelski 2015; Keil 2018; MANS 2017). These profound problems are particularly seen in the strong political influence on the anti-corruption institutional setup, as well as in issues with the law enforcement bodies being continuously stopped from effectively tackling widespread corruption issues. The monitoring and supervisory anti-corruption institutions, as well as prosecution and police, show visible elements of state capture, mostly because many of these accusations do not get a legal epilogue in any particular way (Vučković and Đorđević 2019). Therefore, one is in the position to talk about the political capture of anti-corruption authorities not using legally provided sanctioning measures to prevent party corruption. Also, the substantial lack of a credible track record in investigation, prosecution, and conviction of high-level cases during the whole integration phase provides a clear picture of the overall corruption status in Montenegro. So far, five individuals have been legally convicted in high-level corruption cases, although the Union-driven rule of law pressure for this demand has been in existence for more than ten years. If one takes into account that many convicted persons use the established mechanism of plea bargaining to significantly reduce first instance verdicts, then one may claim that the state has not achieved concrete and sustainable results toward meeting the Union's demands over establishing a convincing and credible track record in prosecution and conviction of high-level corruption cases (MANS 2018, 8, 11).

The results of the organized crime cases against Šarić and Kalić, accused of money laundering and illegally smuggling tons of cocaine, remained a humiliation to the state, as the defendants were released by the Appellate Court, and the country now faces requests for damages. Those cases, mostly used to boost the statistics, were often cited by the Government as a positive example of the fight against organized crime and the seizure and confiscation of criminal assets. Needless to say, no one in executive or judiciary power wants to take responsibility for this failure. Also, the state's failure to impose sentences is clear in the case of Svetozar Marović and his son Miloš Marović, who admitted that they were in charge of a criminal group. While their signed plea agreement with the state was lauded as the purest example of judicial success in the fight against corruption and organized crime, in reality it was a fiasco, as no one has yet served prison time nor paid any fines (IA and CGO and CRNVO and CeMI 2018, 4–5).

Thus, political corruption remains widespread at all levels of government and administration and continues to be a profound problem in terms of future EU membership. Obviously, the main reason for rooted corruption in many areas lies in the rather strong unwillingness of the political ruling elites to effectively tackle corruption by releasing the anti-corruption authorities from state capture and political influence (Džankić and Keil and Kmezić 2019; Bieber 2020). However, the current perception of the long-lasting political regime, one characterized by numerous accusations of corruption and scandal in the 30-year rule of Montenegro, does not sound so convincing when government officials claim that the fight against corruption will be successful regardless of the cost (CGO 2019, 4–5). In fact, current trends in providing convincing and credible results in the fight against corruption have proven the exact opposite. Apparently, the masking (fabricating) of formal and institutional changes together with the EU's reluctance to induce anti-corruption measures has allowed the political elites to remain in power and undermine addressing corruption issues (Vučković and Đorđević 2019). As a result, overall legal and political anti-corruption changes are unequivocally stagnating in the country, demonstrating the same insufficient commitment in providing clear and sustainable results in the fight against corruption.

Last but not the least, reluctance of the Union-driven rule of law pressure to set anti-corruption standards is the final explanation for why Montenegro has failed to Europeanize despite the long-lasting reform process. Evidently, during the process of strengthening the anti-corruption policy in Montenegro, the Union has mostly focused on processes themselves rather than on achieving real progress. Rather than being an effective driver of the anti-corruption system, the EU conditional policy has largely played the role of a monitoring actor constantly repeating the same recommendations not addressed by the candidate country, but on the other hand, without introducing additional measures on how to prevent the given problems (Gateva 2015; Keil and Arkan 2015; Noutcheva and Aydin-Düzgit 2012). Therefore, one can talk about the Union's lack of interest in advancing the EU enlargement policy further toward effective promotion of the anti-corruption requirements. In addition, due to the Union's reluctance to advance the enlargement process on the one hand, and maintain internal political stability on the other, the EU has consequently supported domestic political leaders in fighting corruption by means of active cooperation with those agents. Noticeably, the Union has tried to play a constructive role in strengthening the anti-corruption system by building ties with the postcommunist autocratic leaders, who strongly interfere into the anti-corruption institutions by using nondemocratic means, that is, with those domestic agents suspected of being involved in corruption and organized crime affairs (Elbasani and Šelo Šabić 2018; Kmezić 2020). Thus, the EU has not only supported domestic leaders in failing to meet the anti-corruption criteria, but it has also strengthened their political position by providing them with funds through various Instruments for Pre-Accession Assistance. In return, domestic political leaders have developed a sense of irreplaceability with international circles in terms of tackling those anti-corruption dimensions that do not jeopardize their survival in power.

In line with the Union's inconsistent and insufficiently conditional policy approach, it might be appropriate to also mention the country's current trends in the EU integration process. In particular, this research has highlighted certain features inherent to combating corruption in Montenegro during the accession phase. Primarily, although Montenegro has advanced in the accession process, the country has also continuously met the same problems mainly related to the issue of strengthening anti-corruption measures, ensuring independence of the country's supervisory authorities, and achieving a credible track record in investigation, prosecution, and conviction of high-level corruption cases. In addition, and being perhaps a far more important trend, although the Union has indicated visible inconsistencies regarding continuous external pressure, Montenegro has nevertheless managed to continuously advance in the EU accession process while at the same time demonstrating reluctance to effectively address prevention of corruption measures and establish convincing and credible results in prosecution and final conviction of high-level corruption cases (MANS 2017, 2018). As a result, political corruption has remained widespread and continues to be a matter of serious concern. Evidently, the EU-driven rule of law promotion has applied a strategy of permissiveness in strengthening the anti-corruption policy, while at the same time allowing the candidate country to advance in the EU integration process even though it has not provided sufficient results in combating corruption (CGO 2019; IA and CGO and CRNVO and CeMI 2018). Therefore, there has been a tendency in the state to demonstrate limited progress in preventing corruption and providing concrete and sustainable results in fighting high-level corruption, paradoxically resulting in advancement in the accession process.

Based on the provided discussion, this chapter has argued that the fight against corruption in Montenegro during the accession process has depended on three interdependent factors, namely the EU conditional policy, the domestic factors, and the efficiency of conducted reform activities. Given the outcomes in combating corruption in the fight against corruption during the pre-negotiation and negotiation phase, the candidate country has achieved profoundly limited progress in the fight against corruption by having negatively reinforcing effects on prevention of corruption and achieving a credible track record in investigation, prosecution, and final conviction of high-level corruption cases. In particular, the Union's reluctance to effectively impose anti-corruption measures to prevent and suppress corruption, and the strong lack of political will to tackle profound corruption issues have consequently resulted in weak reform progress due to political elites' selective approach in fulfilling those anti-corruption dimensions, while failing to examine the existence of political corruption within the anti-corruption supervisory authorities or the judiciary. As a result, the EU's lack of interest in improving the given anti-corruption framework has contributed not only to the survival of semi-authoritarian elites, but, far more seriously, it has assisted the state capture, as the corrupt ruling party has clear ties with organized crime structures (BiEPAG 2017; Appicciafuoco 2010; Ardit 2014).

In line with the given empirical findings, the question that is being raised is whether the interdependency between both external and internal factors is sufficient for obtaining complete insights into why the Union has not succeeded in Europeanizing Montenegro in the field of the fight against corruption.

This particular issue is addressed in the conclusion of this book: see Appendix 2.

NOTES

1. The medium-term priorities have not been specifically explained because the fulfillment of these measures is carried out during the whole pre-negotiating phase. For more details, see Appendix 2—Anti-corruption policy in Montenegro—Normative and empirical analysis of EU—Montenegro documents for 2006–2017.

2. The Action Plan also contains the Action Plan of the Parliament of Montenegro.

3. The unit is comprised of representatives of the Directorate of Police, Directorate for Prevention of Money Laundering and Terrorist Financing, Directorate of Revenues, and Customs Administration, and for their performances they are responsible to the State Special Prosecutor.

4. The State Prosecutor's Office filed criminal charges against eleven persons on March 11, 2011, for the criminal offense of attempted abuse of economic power, due

to suspicions that in the period from 2007 to 2010 they tried to transfer state property to private ownership, and therefore acquired unlawful material benefits in the amount of 3,344,870.00 EUR.

5. The State Prosecutor's Office filed criminal charges against five persons on March 9, 2011, for the criminal offense against one recipient of a bribe, a specialist doctor, in the total amount of 500 EUR, and against a judge, lawyer, doctor, and one citizen for the crime of giving a bribe.

6. The State Prosecutor's Office filed criminal charges against twenty-one individuals on August 23, 2010, for the criminal offense of abuse of official position—enabling physical and legal persons to transfer goods over the customs line without paying customs, receiving bribes, and receiving cash compensation for the purpose of performing official duties.

7. The State Prosecutor's Office filed criminal charges against two individuals—authorized police officers on October 27, 2011, for the criminal offense of receiving a bribe.

8. The Action Plan overall represents the most comprehensive document so far in the area of reform of combating corruption, and it provides for realization in plans that are identically prescribed in other national documents, such as: Strategy for the Fight against Corruption and Organized Crime, Action Plan for implementation of Strategy for the Fight against Corruption and Organized Crime for 2013–2014, and others.

9. Except for the Special's Prosecutor's Office, two specialized divisions merged in high courts into one for the purpose of centralizing competences for criminal offenses of organized crime, corruption, terrorism, and war crimes. Detailed activities, competent bodies, and deadlines are envisaged by the Plan of rationalization of the judicial network.

10. Mayor of Budva was sentenced to five years imprisonment, his deputy to four years imprisonment, and a member of the Parliament to three years imprisonment. For more details, MANS (2009b).

11. Information regarding issues within (non)reporting of assets and/or incorrect data in asset declarations have not been provided by the Commission and therefore remained unknown for the second half of 2015 and 2016.

12. 2007: 27.5 million EUR; 2008: 28.1 million EUR; 2009: 29.8 million EUR; 2010: 29.8 million EUR; 2011: 29.8 million EUR.

13. 2014: 23.2 million EUR; 2015: 26.4 million EUR; 2016: 2.5 million EUR; 2017: 20.4 million EUR

14. Svetozar Marović was sentenced to a minimum prison sentence, and in all other cases, the sentences were below the minimum MANS (2018, 8, 11).

15. For the sake of the argument, within the Law on NGO's, the Government introduced civil servants as an independent evaluators, therefore undermining the objectivity and independence of financing the projects of NGO's, particularly fight against the corruption and judicial reform which are essential for the country's completion of the accession negotiation process. For more details, see IA and CGO and CRNVO and CeMI (2018, 10).

Chapter 5

Regional Cooperation and Developing Good Bilateral Relations with the Enlargement Countries and Member States[1]

THE SAP CONDITIONS AND DOMESTIC ALIGNMENT

Pre-Negotiation Stage

Contribution to Peace and Stability in the Region through Active Participation in Regional Initiatives

On October 15, 2007, Montenegro signed the *Stabilisation and Association Agreement* (SAA) with the European Union (EU). It entered into force on May 1, 2010 (Council of the EU and European Commission, 2007, hereinafter referred to as the SAA). The SAA, as the most important instrument of the stabilization and association process (SAP), is the legal basis and first contractual agreement to establish special relations between the EU and Montenegro as a potential candidate country from the Western Balkan region (Miščević 2009, 152). The agreement placed special importance on the issue of development of regional relations among the enlargement countries and member states by devoting a whole chapter of the agreement—*Title III Regional Cooperation*—to strengthening regional cooperation and improving good bilateral relations with states included or not included in the SAA. The legal basis for developing regional cooperation and maintaining good bilateral relations was prescribed within legal provisions of the articles 14, 15, 16, and 17 of the SAA.

The legal regulations over strengthening regional cooperation required the fulfillment of certain sets of SAP conditions by Montenegro as the contracting party. Hence, *Article 14* of the SAA emphasized the need for Montenegro's active promotion of regional cooperation through its full commitment to regional peace, stability, and development of good neighborly relations and improving regional cooperation by assisting Union programs that support projects of regional or cross-border dimensions through technical assistance programs (SAA 2007, Article 14, 7). The legal provisions also influenced Montenegro as a signatory party to demonstrate additional efforts in strengthening regional cooperation and good neighborly relations not only with the remaining Western Balkan states that signed the SAA, but also with the EU member states, and with other candidate countries to the EU accession not included in the SAP. In that respect, the *Article 15—Cooperation with other countries having signed a Stabilization and Association Agreement* foresaw that Montenegro would begin negotiations after signing the Agreement with other Western Balkan states included in the SAA to conclude bilateral conventions and regional cooperation within the scope of cooperation between the countries concerned. The main areas of bilateral cooperation between the SAA countries are the following: political dialogue, establishment of free trade areas consistent with relevant WTO provisions, mutual concessions concerning the movement of workers, establishment, supply of services, appropriate payments and movement of capital, cooperation in the field of justice, freedom and security, and so on. However, Article 14 prescribed certain time limits for establishing bilateral political and economic areas of cooperation between the SAA states, as well as specified sanctions for the contracting parties if these were not delivered. Thus, the legal regulation clearly emphasized that "these conventions shall be concluded within two years after the entry into force of this Agreement," while the readiness of the SAA country to conclude those conventions would be the main conditions for further advancement of relations between Montenegro and the Union (SAA 2007, Article 15, 7–8).[2]

Also, *Article 16—Cooperation with other countries concerned by the Stabilization and Association process* and *Article 17—Cooperation with other countries candidate to EU accession not concerned by the SAP* obliged Montenegro to start pursuing regional cooperation with other states, particularly with the EU member states included in the SAP in some or in all fields of cooperation covered by this Agreement and thus in that field of common interests, but also foster regional cooperation in areas of defined conventions with other candidate countries for the EU membership such as Turkey, and in any of the fields of cooperation covered by the SAA (SAA 2007, Article 16, 8). In this sense, the Union asked Montenegro to "start negotiations with Turkey which has established a customs union with the Community, with a view to concluding, on a mutually advantageous basis, an agreement establishing a free trade area in accordance with Article XXIV of the GATT 1994 as well as liberalizing the establishment and supply of services between them at an equivalent level of this Agreement in accordance with Article V of the GATS" (SAA 2007, Article 16, 9).

As previously stated, on October 15, 2007, Montenegro signed the SAA with the EU, which came into force on May 1, 2010. After the signing of the SAA, being the initial contractual relationship agreement between the potential candidate country to join the EU and the EU itself, and the completion of its ratification in the Parliament, the *Interim Agreement between the EU and Montenegro* came into force on November 13, 2007. Based on obligations stemming from the SAA, the government introduced the *National Integration Program (NPI) 2007–2012* in June 2008 as the main strategic framework for internal democratic and economic reforms, thus highlighting the national strategy for adopting the *acquis communautaire* (Vlada Crne Gore 2008b). The NPI, as the main strategic domestic document for overall implementation and monitoring of fulfillment of the EU requirements, contained the main measures, activities, and/or plans for the implementation of the SAA. Additionally, the NPI was comprised of a number of other relevant strategic documents, namely the Action Plan for the implementation of recommendations from the European Partnership and the Action Plan for strengthening the administrative capacities for the implementation of the SAA (Vlada Crne Gore 2008b, 2–3; Đurović 2012, 447–48). Shortly after the SAA was signed, the Parliament of Montenegro adopted the *Resolution on implementation of Montenegro's obligation in the framework of the Stabilization and Association Agreement* on December 27, 2007. The resolution stressed that Montenegro's full membership in the EU remained a strategic national goal fully supported by the Parliament, hence calling for the government to submit once every three months a report on the overall activities under the SAP to the Committee for International Cooperation and European integration (Vlada Crne Gore 2008c, 201–02).

Essentially, strengthening regional cooperation and developing good bilateral relations with the enlargement countries and the EU member states by fulfilling terms of the SAA remained in this phase one of the most important political conditions for Montenegro's advancement in the accession process (Đurović 2016; Miščević 2009). Arguably, the EU did not impose any kind of adoption pressure on the state to comply with the given requirements in this particular phase. Rather, the membership in the abovementioned regional initiatives was solely the state's own decision to align with the SAP conditions although the country still did not sign the SAA with the EU. In fact, Montenegro showed already in the early stage of its European path a wish to Europeanize itself although no legal obligations were stating so. This being said, concerning the Union's demand over Montenegro's active promotion of regional cooperation through its full commitment to regional peace and stability in 2008 and 2009, the state overall saw satisfactory results. The country:

- gained membership in *South-East European Cooperation Initiative (SECI)* in June 2008, whose main aim is to foster regional cooperation in fields of fight against terrorism and organized crime;[3]
- achieved membership in *US-Adriatic Charter* on December 4, 2008, for aiding its attempts to join the NATO Alliance;

- was committed to regional activities by means of active participation in various regional initiatives, including Central European Initiative (CEI), Migration, Asylum, Refugees Regional Initiatives (MARRI), Central European Free Trade Agreement (CEFTA), Centre for Security Cooperation (RACVIAC), and *Adriatic and Ionian Initiative (AII)*, and in transformation of the Stability Pact for South-East Europe into the South-East European Cooperation Process (SEECP) and the *Regional Cooperation Council (RCC)* in 2008 (Vlada Crne Gore 2018a; European Commission 2008b, 19, 2009b, 19).

Hence, based on Montenegro's submitted application from December 15, 2008, the European Commission introduced the Opinion on Montenegro's application for membership in the EU on November 9, 2010 (European Commission 2010b). Following the progress in addressing the Copenhagen (political) criteria from 1993 as well as the SAP conditions from 1999, the Commission recommended to the Council to grant Montenegro the status of candidate country (European Council 2010, 12). It was clearly indicated that Montenegro broadly satisfied the SAP conditions by playing a constructive regional role through active participation in regional initiatives and that Podgorica maintained good neighborly relations with the regional countries. However, the Commission also underlined the need for the country to continue its constructive engagement in regional cooperation by developing good neighborly relations with the remaining regional states and to address open bilateral issues with the neighboring countries as well (European Council 2010, 10). As a result, given the positive opinion of the Commission on Montenegro's application for EU membership, the European Council in its conclusions on December 17, 2010, agreed to grant Montenegro the status of candidate country.

After gaining the candidate country status, Montenegro continued to take positive steps in promoting regional cooperation through its full commitment to regional peace and stability, and also by improving bilateral relations with the SAA countries, member states, and other candidate countries not included in the SAA during 2010 and 2011. In this respect, Montenegro continued to play a constructive role in various regional initiatives through its chairmanship of CEI (2010), SEECP (2010), AII (2010–2011), and US-Adriatic Charter (2011). In particular, under the chairmanship within the SEECP, Montenegro adopted *the Regional Strategic Document and Action Plan on Justice and Home Affairs 2011–2013* in March 2010. Also, the candidate country played a visible regional role in strengthening regional cooperation with its active participation in other regional initiatives, notably CEFTA, MARRI, RACVIAC, and RCC, and it continued to intensify its regional activities by supporting the process of reconciliation in the Igman Initiative and RECOM[4] (MVPEI 2011a, 3–4; European Commission 2012b, 22).

Reconciliation and Climate Conducive to Addressing Open Bilateral Issues and Legacies of the Past

After declaring its independence in 2006, Montenegro continued to play a constructive role in establishing good bilateral relations with the neighboring countries, member states, and other enlargement countries not included in the SAA. Overall political relations with other regional countries were good, and Montenegro continued to play a constructive role in maintaining peace and stability in the region during the pre-negotiation phase by developing cooperation with the neighboring countries in the fields of border control, environmental protection, energy supply tourism, culture, science, technology, and cross-border cooperation, and so on (European Commission 2007b, 2008b, 2009b, 2010b, 2011b).

Relations with *Albania* were developed significantly. Albania officially recognized Montenegro as an independent state on June 12, 2006, while diplomatic relations between these countries were established on August 1, 2006 (Vlada Crne Gore 2018b; European Commission 2007b, 17). Bilateral relations were improved when the prime minister of Montenegro Milo Đukanović visited Albania on November 25, 2008, and when President Sali Berisha and minister of Foreign Affairs of Albania Ilir Meta visited Montenegro in 2009, which resulted in the decision to construct a joint border crossing at Sukobin-Murićani. The common border crossing was opened on June 18, 2009, followed by a number of signed agreements on sharing practical experience in the adoption of the acquis and alignment with the EU policies in the field of judiciary, and signing agreements on cooperation in the areas of culture, education, and science (Vlada Crne Gore 2018b, European Commission 2008b, 19, 2009b, 19–20). Montenegrin-Albanian relations were further developed through political, economic, and legal cooperation, connecting the electro-energy system by linking cross border areas of Skadar (Albania) and Podgorica (Montenegro), and the signing of an agreement on reciprocal travel of citizens of both countries without a passport (Vlada Crne Gore 2018b; MVPEI 2011a, 4–5, 2011b, 4, 2012a, 5; European Commission 2011b, 22).

Bilateral relations between *BiH* and Montenegro were significantly advanced during the pre-negotiation phase. BiH officially recognized Montenegrin independence on June 21, 2006, and established diplomatic ties on September 14, 2006 (Vlada Crne Gore 2018b; European Commission 2007b, 17). As a result of good bilateral cooperation, in 2008, 2009, and 2011, President Filip Vujanović, Prime Minister Milo Đukanović, minister of Foreign Affairs Igor Lukšić, and speaker of the Parliament of Montenegro Ranko Krivokapić officially visited Sarajevo and began strengthening mutual cooperation in the fields of defense, police, cross-border cooperation, and finally civil protection (Vlada Crne Gore 2018b; European Commission 2008b, 19, 2009b, 19–20). Other agreements entered into force, namely the ones on cooperation on mutual legal assistance in civil and criminal matters, on mutual recognition of decisions in criminal matters, tourist cooperation, and exchange of data in regard to social insurance. However, open bilateral disputes between the two countries, especially the border demarcation issue, were still pending and remained unresolved (MVPEI 2011a, 4–5, 2012a, 4; European Commission 2011b, 22).

Relations with *Croatia* advanced in this period as well. Croatia officially recognized Montenegro on June 12, 2006, and established diplomatic relations on July 7, 2006. Both sides showed great willingness to resolve the issues of missing assets, persons, and refugees (Vlada Crne Gore 2018b; European Commission 2007b, 17). Bilateral relations with Croatia were intensified in mutual official visits of the prime minister and speaker of the Parliament of Montenegro to Zagreb and vice versa in 2008, which consequently resulted in enhancing further cooperation in the areas of defense and water management (Vlada Crne Gore 2018b; European Commission 2008b, 19–20). Good bilateral relations between the two countries were intensified when the prime minister of Croatia, Jadranka Kosor, visited Podgorica on June 22, 2009, and signed agreements on protection of the rights of the Montenegrin minority in the Republic of Croatia and the Croat minority in Montenegro in Zagreb on January 14, 2009, as well as an agreement on cooperation in the areas of science and technology (Vlada Crne Gore 2018b; European Commission 2009b, 19). Developments of political relations were also observable through the official visit of the president of Montenegro, Filip Vujanović, to Zagreb on October 10 and 11, 2011, and visit of the speaker of the Parliament of Croatia, Boris Šprem, to Podgorica on October 16 and 17, 2011, which resulted in intensifying relations in economic and trade relations, water management, and tourism. Also, an agreement on police cooperation was signed, while the extradition agreement with Croatia covering its citizens involved in organized crime was being implemented (Vlada Crne Gore 2018b; MVPEI 2011a, 5–7, 2011b, 4–5, 2012a, 6; European Commission 2011b, 23). However, the border demarcation dispute on the Prevlaka Peninsula remained unresolved in this period, although temporary the border regime of joint police control (of mixed Croatian and Montenegrin police forces) initiated in 2002 functioned without any obstacles. Both states agreed to settle the border demarcation dispute through international arbitration at the International Court of Justice (ICJ) by delegating their commission to set up a legal framework (Vlada Crne Gore 2018b; MVPEI 2011a, 4–5, 2011b, 4–5, 2012a, 4–6; European Commission 2007b, 17, 2008b, 19–20, 2009b, 19, 2011b, 23).

Relations with *Former Yugoslav Republic of Macedonia* (FYROM) were satisfactory as well. FYROM officially recognized Montenegro as an independent state on June 12, 2006, while diplomatic relations between these countries were established on June 14, 2006 (Vlada Crne Gore 2018b; European Commission 2007b, 17). Cooperation with *FYROM* was further improved when agreements on dual citizenship, EU affairs, air traffic, tourism, agriculture, education science, economy, and trade relations, and protection in the event of natural disasters. Also, cooperation was intensified through extradition agreements covering Montenegrin citizens having engaged in organized crime, corruption, and money laundering felonies, and through an agreement on dual citizenship (Vlada Crne Gore 2018b; MVPEI 2011a, 5–7, 2011b, 4–5, 2012a, 6; European Commission 2009b, 19–20, 2011b, 23).

Montenegro continued to have a stable relationship with *Kosovo.* Montenegro recognized Kosovo as an independent state in October 2008 following Kosovo's decision to unilaterally declare independence from Serbia in February 2008 (European Commission 2008b, 19–20). Political relations were further improved through the first official visit of the minister of Foreign Affairs of Montenegro, Milan Roćen, to Priština. A bilateral agreement related to registration of displaced persons from Kosovo living in Montenegro entered into force on June 29, 2011, and a readmission agreement was signed on the same day. However, although some progress was made in the development of trade and economic relations, the issue of border demarcation, as well as recognition of the Montenegrin minority in Kosovo, were still pending (Vlada Crne Gore 2018b; European Commission 2009b, 19–20).

The relations with *Serbia* were overall good after the dissolution of the State Union of Serbia and Montenegro in 2006. Serbia officially recognized Montenegro as an independent state on June 15, 2006, and established diplomatic relations with Podgorica on June 22, 2006. Based on the decision to establish diplomatic relations, the ambassador of Montenegro to Serbia, Anka Vojvodić, was accredited in December 2006 (European Commission 2007b, 17). However, certain downward trends between the two countries were observable following Montenegro's decision to recognize Kosovo as an independent state. Former Montenegrin ambassador to Serbia, Anka Vojvodić, was declared persona non-grata in October 2008. Despite certain political tensions, further development of political cooperation was intensified when the president of Montenegro, Filip Vujanović, officially visited Belgrade on May 18–20, 2009, as well as when the prime minister of Serbia, Mirko Cvetković, officially visited Podgorica on October 15, 2009, and signed the agreements on defense, social security, and culture (European Commission 2008b, 19–20). Additional improvements were also seen in strengthening economic relations, particularly through agreements on judiciary, joint border patrol, and joint police cooperation in fighting organized crime (European

Commission 2009b, 19–20). Political relations were strengthened through the mutual official visits of the prime minister of Montenegro, Igor Lukšić, to Belgrade, and the prime minister of Serbia, Mirko Cvetković, to Podgorica in July and December 2011, respectively, through cooperation in the fields of science, trade, economy, and education. However, although both states showed willingness to improve political relations, certain open bilateral issues between the two countries continued to exist even after the separation, particularly the issues of dual citizenship and border demarcation (Vlada Crne Gore 2018b; MVPEI 2011a, 5–7, 2011b, 4–5, 2012a, 6; European Commission 2008b, 19–20, 2009b, 19–20, 2011b, 23).

Concerning the development of bilateral relations with other candidates not included in the SAA, cooperation with *Turkey* was intensified through the official visit of President Abdullah Gül, minister of Foreign Affairs Ahmet Davutoğlu, and the speaker of the Assembly of Turkey, Mehmet Ali Şahin, to Podgorica in 2009, which resulted in two agreements on free trade and defense being signed. Cooperation was intensified through trade relations, especially through humanitarian aid provided to Montenegro following the floods that hit the state in December 2010. Finally, Montenegro was committed to developing relations with the EU member states, in particular with *Italy*. With the signing of agreements on defense, economy, and trade cooperation, the EU remained Montenegro's main trading partner. In addition to Italy, Montenegro continued to maintain friendly relations with *Slovenia* and *Romania* with the signing of an agreement on police cooperation in 2007 (Vlada Crne Gore 2018b; MVPEI 2011a, 5, 11, 2011b, 3, 7, 2012a, 6, 9; European Commission 2007b, 17, 2009b, 20, 2011b, 23).

Negotiation Stage

Contribution to Peace and Stability in the Region through Active Participation in Regional Initiatives

As an EU candidate country, Montenegro continued to demonstrate significant willingness to improve its regional cooperation through active participation in regional initiatives, maintaining regional peace, security, and stability, and developing good neighborly relations with the enlargement countries and other EU member states during the process of accession negotiations. Similarly, the Union clearly outlined the importance of addressing the SAP conditions as one of the main challenges for successful completion of the EU accession process (European Commission 2012b, 2013b, 2014b, 2015b, 2016b).

Following the Union's concerns over the state's contribution to strengthening regional cooperation, the candidate country, in the period between

2012 and 2017, played a constructive role through active participation in the regional initiatives, namely CEFTA, CEI, MARRI, RACVIAC, AII, SEECP, RCC, and US-Adriatic Charter. The state also strongly supported regional organizations reaffirming the idea of regional reconciliation, such as the Igman Initiative and RECOM (Vlada Crne Gore 2018a; MVPEI 2012b, 8, 2012c, 7–8; European Commission 2012c, 16, 2013b, 11, 2014b, 12, 2015b, 21, 2016b, 21).

The positive impetus toward strengthening regional cooperation and maintaining good neighborly relations among the countries of the region was seen in Montenegro's proposal to establish "the Western Balkan Six" regional initiative: a high-level political dialogue between regional leaders aimed at accelerating their process of European integration. This initiative of the Western Balkan Six (WB6) represented a positive step toward institutionalization of relations between non-EU member states in the process of European integration, foreseeing the establishment of a common Western Balkan Parliament,[5] formation of common Balkan police (BALPOL), establishment of a Regional Centre for the fight against corruption and organized crime, a common labor market, education, and health care. According to a working document, all actions were to be supported by Croatia and Slovenia simplifying border crossings in the region by eliminating passport requirements. As a result, the first meeting at the political directors' level took place in Budva in July 2013 (MVPEI 2013a, 47–48; European Commission 2013b, 11).

Special importance to further development of regional relations in the region was given through the "Berlin Process." It was initiated by the German chancellor Angela Merkel on August 28, 2014, and aimed at further enhancement of regional cooperation in the Western Balkans and assistance to these states in their European integration. The process has been supported by the European Commission, the EU member states—Austria, Croatia, France, Germany, Italy, Slovenia, and the United Kingdom, and various international donors. The Process's connectivity agenda refers to connecting people (social dimension), economies (economic dimension), and states (political dimension) of the region through cooperation in the areas of transport, infrastructure, economic connectivity, youth cooperation, and cooperation among businesses and civil societies. It has encouraged intergovernmental cooperation through the establishment of the Regional Youth Cooperation Office (RYCO), the Western Balkans Chambers Investment Forum, and the Western Balkans Funds, and has also inspired the meeting of regional civil society organizations (Civil Society of the Western Balkans Summit Series), youth organizations (Youth Forum), and business associations (Business Forum; Berlin Process, Civil Society Forum of the Western Balkans Summit Series 2014).

The goal of the Process was highlighted by its chair within the Final Declaration. It stated that the Conference "should provide a framework for a period of four years,[6] during which we will further our endeavours to make additional real progress in the reform process, in resolving outstanding bilateral and internal issues, and in achieving reconciliation within and between the societies in the region," as well as enhance "regional economic cooperation and laying the foundations for sustainable growth." Through the support of the Commission's IPA and the member states, the participant states agreed to further cooperate within the framework of the Energy Community for Southeast Europe, particularly in regard to energy security, energy efficiency and climate protection, and reducing youth unemployment in the region. Also, they agreed on defining and extending three Trans-European Transport Networks core corridors to the Western Balkans in April and June 2015 by determining short-term priorities, namely simplifying border crossing procedures, road safety, and maintenance schemes of these corridors, which was supposed to be achieved before the Paris summit (Berlin Process, Final Declaration by the chair of the Conference on the Western Balkans 2014).

One year after the Berlin Western Balkan Summit, high-ranking officials of the Western Balkan countries met in Vienna on August 27, 2015, for the second *Vienna Summit Meeting on the Western Balkans* in the framework of the Berlin Process. While the Western Balkans achieved sustainable progress in the areas of transport[7] and energy connectivity,[8] with an agreement on the establishment of a youth cooperation office in Tirana, the EU member states outlined the importance of strengthening regional cooperation and resolving outstanding bilateral disputes. The Western Balkan states committed themselves to resolving any open questions through bilateral negotiations or other means of peaceful dispute settlement through international arbitration. In this sense, the participating states welcomed the signing of the border agreement between BiH and Montenegro at the margins of the Vienna Summit as a positive example among the Western Balkans in resolving border demarcation disputes (Berlin Process, Final Declaration by the chair of the Vienna Western Balkans Summit 2015; Annex 2—Join Declaration on the establishment of the RYCO in the Western Balkans; Annex 3—Regional Cooperation and the Solution of Bilateral Disputes).

The positive echo of the previous Berlin 2014 and Vienna 2015 Western Balkans Summits within the framework of the Berlin Process was further strengthened through the Paris Summit on July 4, 2016, organized by France. *The Paris Western Balkan Summit* enhanced cooperation between the countries of the region in the field of youth cooperation and connectivity in the fields of transport and energy. However, although progress was made in various sectoral areas, the EU member states outlined the need to intensify regional cooperation in the Western Balkans through the process of reconciliation as an essential element for promotion of peace and stability and overcoming legacies of the past. According to the participating states, the signed agreement of establishment of the RYCO in Tirana was to provide an important contribution to the process of reconciliation within the region by enhancing exchanges and mobility of its youth (Berlin Process, Final Declaration by the chair of the Paris Western Balkan Summit 2016).

Reconciliation and Climate Conducive to Addressing Open Bilateral Issues

When it comes to the Union's demands over the state's efforts to actively promote regional cooperation through its full commitment to maintaining regional peace and stability, Montenegro continued to develop good bilateral relations with neighboring countries and other EU member states. Addressing outstanding bilateral issues between the Western Balkans before its accession into the EU, especially border demarcation problems, remained an essential element for Montenegrin advancement in and completion of the accession process (European Commission 2012b, 2013b, 2014b, 2015b, 2016b).

Bilateral relations with *Albania* were strengthened through political cooperation and official visits by the president of Albania, Bamir Topi (January 2012), the prime minister of Albania, Edi Rama, to Podgorica (November 2013), the president of Montenegro, Filip Vujanović, to Tirana (May 2012), and Prime Minister Milo Đukanović and minister of Foreign Affairs of Montenegro Igor Lukšić to Tirana (March 2013). Also, relations between the two countries were intensified by signing agreements on cooperation in the areas of defense, joint border crossing, education, recovery of Albania's debt to Montenegro, mutual protection of classified information, education and electronic exchange of customs data, and a protocol of cooperation between the police forces of the two countries during the summer tourist season (Vlada Crne Gore 2018b; European Commission 2012b, 17, 2013b, 11, 2014b, 13; MVPEI 2012b, 4, 2012c, 4, 2012d, 5, 2013b, 13–14, 2014, 10–11, 13–14). However, certain declining trends in the development of bilateral cooperation between the two countries occurred in January when Montenegro officially lodged a diplomatic demarche due to the display of the "Greater Albania" flag at prime minister of Albania Edi Rama's residence. However, shortly after, this flag incident was resolved in an official meeting of Montenegrin and Albanian high-ranking officials. There were no open bilateral issues between the two states (European Commission 2015b, 22, 2016b, 22).

Bilateral cooperation with *BiH* continued to improve on the political level through the official visit of the chairman of BiH Presidency Bakir Izetbegović and Vjekoslav Bevanda to Podgorica in October 2012 in 2013 and the president of Montenegro Filip Vujanović to Sarajevo in September

2012. Relations between the two countries were further strengthened in the fields of legal and trade affairs with the signing of agreements in the areas of legal aid and enforcement of court decisions, mutual protection of classified information, dual citizenship, international transport, and the ratification of a treaty on extradition (European Commission 2012b, 17, 2013b, 11; MVPEI 2012b, 4, 2012d, 5, 2013b, 13–14, 2014, 13–14). Montenegro maintained very close cooperation with BiH through the official visit of Prime Minister Milo Đukanović to Sarajevo in June 2014, and by signing protocols on the exchange of information and evidence on war crimes in April. Also, Montenegro, BiH, and Serbia signed a protocol to establish a joint center for police cooperation in Trebinje (BiH) in 2014, which officially opened in March of that year. However, far more importantly, additional activities to further improve good neighborly relations were being carried out, which included activities geared toward the signing of a border demarcation agreement between BiH and Montenegro in May 2015 (MVPEI 2014, 10–11; European Commission 2014b, 13, 2015b, 22). Positive impetus toward developing good neighborly relations was seen in the joint ratification of agreements on border demarcation in April 2016, where both countries demonstrated additional efforts to adopt the convention on regional cooperation under Article 15 of the SAA (Vlada Crne Gore 2018b; European Commission 2016b, 22).

Montenegro continued to strengthen its bilateral relations with *FYROM* by intensifying its political relations with this country, which was followed by the official visit of president of Montenegro Filip Vujanović in March 2012, and minister of Foreign Affairs of Montenegro Igor Lukšić to Skopje in February 2013. Ratification of signed agreements on cooperation in the fields of legal affairs, police cooperation, and mutual customs assistance soon followed; there was also economic and police cooperation, and cooperation on the EU accession process and on readmission of persons residing without authorization (MVPEI 2012b, 5–6, 2012c, 5–6, 2012d, 6, 2013b, 13–14; European Commission 2012b, 17, 2013b, 11). Both countries signed agreements on sharing diplomatic and consular services, on mutual enforcement of court decisions in criminal matters, on legal aid in civil and criminal matters, and a protocol on cooperation in the area of military training. No open bilateral issues exist between two countries (Vlada Crne Gore 2018b; MVPEI 2014, 13–17; European Commission 2014b, 13, 2015b, 22, 2016b, 22).

Relations with *Kosovo* were overall good and further intensified by the official visit of minister of Foreign Affairs of Kosovo Enver Hoxhaj to Podgorica in January 2012 and minister of Foreign Affairs of Montenegro Igor Lukšić to Priština in 2014, and the entering into force of an agreement on uniform tariffs for border insurance in July 2012 (European Commission 2012b, 17, 2014b, 13; MVPEI 2012b, 5–6, 2012c, 5–6, 2012d, 6).

Political relations were also developed through the appointment of the ambassador of Montenegro, Ferhat Dinoša, to Priština (MVPEI 2014, 13–17; European Commission 2014b, 13). As a result, cooperation with Kosovo was intensified by ratifying previously signed agreements on extradition, mutual enforcement of judicial decisions in criminal matters, and on legal assistance in criminal matters (MVPEI 2013b, 13–14; European Commission 2013b, 11). Also, both states signed agreements on the recognition of pension rights, on police cooperation, on the opening of joint border crossings, and on local border traffic in December 2013, as well as protocols on joint border patrols and border cooperation in March 2014 and on cooperation in the fight against human trafficking in April 2014. A positive impulse toward settling bilateral disputes was observed in Montenegrin ratification of the agreement on border demarcation with Kosovo in December 2015, followed by the signed border demarcation agreement between Montenegro and Kosovo at the Vienna Western Balkans Summit in August 2015 and the signed agreement on cooperation between the Commissions for Missing Persons of Montenegro and Kosovo in October 2015 (European Commission 2015b, 22, 2016b, 22). Montenegro ratified a border demarcation agreement while the same ratifying procedures are awaiting completion by Kosovo's parliamentarians. However, although there was a certain amount of progress in resolving the border demarcation issue, no further developments were detected regarding the constitutional recognition of the Montenegrin minority in Kosovo or the return of displaced persons (Vlada Crne Gore 2018b).

Bilateral relations with *Serbia* improved and remained satisfactory. Relations with *Serbia* were intensified through the official visit of President Tomislav Nikolić in January and minister of Foreign Affairs of Serbia Ivan Mrkić in April, and minister of Foreign Affairs of Montenegro Igor Lukšić to Belgrade in May 2013 (MVPEI 2013b, 13–14; European Commission 2013b, 11). Cooperation between the neighboring countries was strengthened when agreements on cooperation on air traffic control and protocol on cooperation in resolving fate of missing persons were signed (European Commission 2012b, 17; MVPEI 2012b, 5–6, 2012c, 5–6, 2012d, 6). In addition, the agreement on police cooperation between the two countries entered into force, while a joint special task force for fighting corruption and crime became operational, thus resulting in common police actions in both states becoming a reality (MVPEI 2013b, 13–14; European Commission 2013b, 11). The prime minister of Montenegro Milo Đukanović paid an official visit to Belgrade in December 2014, while further cooperation was made by signing agreements on diplomatic training and on mutual sharing of premises for diplomatic and consular offices in June, and on undertaking joint activities in arresting prominent organized crime groups and on defense. Furthermore, Montenegro, Serbia, FYROM, and BiH signed an agreement on reducing prices of roaming services on public mobile communication networks in September (MVPEI 2014, 13–17; European Commission 2014b, 13, 2016b, 22). Although both countries demonstrated progress in the development of political relations, still, there were no developments with reference to the dual citizenship issue, border demarcation problems, or disputes over the right to religious assets in Montenegro between the Montenegrin and Serbian Orthodox churches (Vlada Crne Gore 2018b; European Commission 2012b, 17, 2013b, 11, 2015b, 22, 2016b, 22).

Concerning cooperation with the candidate countries not included in the SAA, bilateral relations with *Turkey* remained traditionally good and friendly. These relations were further intensified on political and economic levels through the official visit of the prime minister of Montenegro to Ankara in March 2012 and the signing of a number of agreements on protecting and promoting investments, air transport, labor, social security, and employment, as well as a memorandum of understanding on education (MVPEI 2012b, 8–9). Further cooperation was seen in enhanced economic relations and tourism, science, health, and readmission agreements, and in a consular protection agreement (Vlada Crne Gore 2018b; MVPEI 2013b, 15–17; European Commission 2013b, 12). Montenegro aimed to strengthen bilateral relations with Turkey with agreements on cooperation on military training in October, and on health and medical sciences in December, while the agreements on mutual assistance on customs issues and on social security were ratified in 2015. Also, both countries developed even further economic cooperation through the Joint Commission for Economic Cooperation (Vlada Crne Gore 2018b; European Commission 2015b, 22). Turkey strongly supported Montenegrin accession to NATO while a cooperation agreement between the Chamber of Commerce of Montenegro and the Union of Turkish Business and Chambers of Commerce (TOBB) was signed in September (MVPEI 2013b, 12–13; Vlada Crne Gore 2018b; European Commission 2016b, 22).

Concerning the improvement of bilateral relations with the EU member states, Montenegro continued to improve relations with *Croatia*. The two states intensified bilateral cooperation on the political level through an official visit by minister of Foreign Affairs of Croatia Vesna Pusić to Podgorica in June 2012, and minister of Foreign Affairs Igor Lukšić and speaker of Assembly Ranko Krivokapić to Zagreb in February 2013, resulting in the adoption of a number of agreements in the fields of the economy and tourism. Development of cooperation was realized by signing agreements on mutual enforcement of court decisions in criminal matters, on scientific/technical and educational cooperation in the field of the sea, and a memorandum on cooperation in the field of health. This EU member state strongly advocated Montenegro's membership in the Alliance and further cooperation was seen in defense through the signed agreements on military engineering and leadership, in training of Montenegrin cadets in Croatia in 2014, and in education through already signed agreements on study programs in 2014 (Vlada Crne Gore 2018b; European Commission 2015b, 22). The temporary border agreement of joint police control functioned without any obstacles, and it remained a good example for addressing bilateral issues in a positive neighborly spirit. Despite a positive impulse, no further developments were undertaken by the two states to resolve the bilateral border demarcation dispute, although both countries showed political willingness for a peaceful settlement of the border dispute over the Prevlaka Peninsula by committing the dispute to the ICJ (European Commission 2012b, 17, 2013b, 12, 2014b, 13, 2015b, 22; MVPEI 2013b, 15–17, 2012b, 5–6, 2012c, 5–6, 2012d, 6).

By the same token, during the negotiation phase, Montenegro overall played a constructive role in developing good bilateral relations with *Italy* as an EU member state through intensified economic, trade, education, science, and service cooperation. Both countries continued to have friendly relations, signing agreements on cooperation in the field of the environment, on enhancing the applications of the European Convention on Extradition and the European Convention on Mutual Assistance in Criminal Matters, on scientific cooperation, and on cooperation in the transport of passengers and freight in the international road system (European Commission 2013b, 12; European Commission 2014b, 13). In addition, Montenegro adopted a decision to open a consulate in Trieste (European Commission 2015b, 22).

FULFILLMENT OF THE SAA CRITERIA AS ESSENTIAL FOR THE STATE'S ADVANCE IN THE ACCESSION PROCESS

Pre-Negotiation Stage

Originally, concerning the Union's requirement for the state's active involvement in regional cooperation and maintaining good neighboring relations, the empirical findings reveal two main observations during the pre-negotiation phase. First, by signing and entering into force of the SAA, the Union introduced the issues of regional cooperation and development of good bilateral relations as a legally binding provision for the potential candidate country as a key condition for further advancement in the accession process. Due to civil war consequences on the territory of former Yugoslavia (1991–1995) and internal political problems that existed in Albania and FYROM, the Commission in 1999 established an innovative relationship model with the countries in the region through the process commonly known as the SAP. The main aim of the SAP is to strengthen regional and bilateral activities to achieve regional stabilization and thereafter accession to the EU (Miščević 2009, 151–52; Đurović 2012, 343–46).

Beginning in the late 1990s, the Union developed a highly ambitious enlargement strategy commonly known as the SAP, which comprises a certain EU membership perspective and defines tools for achieving that perspective for all Western Balkan states. The SAP is the comprehensive EU Strategic Approach toward the Western Balkans states. It includes a wide range of activities between the EU and the given potential candidate country, the gradual adoption of EU laws by the candidate country, and standards in various fields, as well as defines the model of cooperation with EU institutions (Elbasani 2008). The most important instrument of the SAP is the SAA, which is the first essential contractual relationship for establishing special, high-level cooperation between the Union and the potential candidate country (Miščević 2009, 152). The SAP emerged as a consequence of the failure of the Regional Approach policy framework (1997), which aimed to strengthen regional cooperation and improve bilateral relations between post-Yugoslav countries. This innovative enlargement model remains a two-fold bilateral and regional process tailored by the EU as an enlargement tool and as an instrument of state-building and post-conflict stabilization. The EU approach has been institutionalized within the SAP based on the principle of stabilization through association tailored to assist the Western Balkans in the process of democratization and economic transformation by aligning with detailed and graduated range of conditionality (Copenhagen criteria) combined with bilateral and regional conditions (Elbasani 2013; Juncos 2018). The scope and range of conditions extends from rule of law requirements, with a special focus on independence of the judiciary and the fight against corruption and organized crime, to an alignment with economic policies, to a full commitment to the establishment of permanent peace and stability in the region (SAP 2007).

Interestingly, the SAA belongs to the type of accession agreement that was the "Europe Agreement" as signed by countries from Central and Eastern Europe in the 1990s. Moreover, the SAA can be characterized as a more advanced model of Europe Agreement (Association Agreements). The content of the SAA, and its legal provisions, goals, institutions, common bodies, mechanisms, and transit period are almost identical to the Europe Agreements (Đurović 2016). However, due to the specifics of the post-Yugoslav space and previous association experiences, the SAA did bring certain novelties. With the exception of the introduction of new chapters related to the judiciary and home affairs, and a higher number of cooperation policies, the main differences between the SAA and the Europe Agreements are related to the content of the development clause and its defined legal provisions on strengthening regional cooperation and improving bilateral relations with the enlargement countries (Čermak 2019). With the SAA entering into force, the development clause confirms the status of a potential candidate country for EU membership, but it does not define an actual date of accession to the Union. Also, legal provisions stipulated within the SAA obliged Montenegro to make additional efforts in actively promoting regional relations through its full commitment to regional peace and stability, and also in developing bilateral cooperation with neighboring countries: the signatory countries of the SAA, the EU member states, and with other candidate countries (Turkey) not included in the SAA (Đurović 2012, 345; Miščević 2009, 152).

Evidently, the Union paid significant attention to issues of strengthening regional cooperation and maintaining good neighborly relations within the SAA. Although the SAA contains other principles of development of relations with the EU on the promotion of democracy and strengthening democratic institutions, rule of law, protection of human and minority rights, and improvement of economic and trade relations, it can be assumed that fulfillment of the regional cooperation requirement represents the essence of the contractual agreement, especially because of the need for the institutionalization of this policy. This particularly means that the introduced legal provisions within the SAA aim to achieve accession of the Western Balkans to the Union, while at the same time trying to establish full and permanent stabilization of not only of the individual states but of the region as a whole. Therefore, it might be reasonable to claim that the SAA became one of the most important enlargement frameworks for Montenegro's advance in the accession process (Đurović 2012; Hughes and Sasse and Gordon 2004; Bechev 2006).

Apart from preserving regional stability, the complexity of the Western Balkan region has spawned one more important political problem primarily specific to the post-Yugoslav space—border issues. Open bilateral disputes are rooted in the geopolitics and history of the Western Balkan region, where they gained their full expression after the breakup of the former Yugoslavia. These outstanding border problems include a wide range of issues. Apart from the issue pertaining to the rights of national minorities, border and territorial disputes refer to delineations and full border demarcation and recognition of the sovereignty of the state within its border both at the local and international level (Djolai and Nechev 2018, 6). However, the border demarcation problem as an outstanding bilateral issue that exists among former Yugoslav states has had a significant impact on further development of neighborly relations and on further progress in the process of European integration of the region. Past experiences have demonstrated that the biggest problems emerge when EU member states use their power asymmetry against a candidate country to achieve certain internal and/or external foreign policy goals. Unfortunately, the Union is not able to do anything since it does not possess any kind of political, technical, or legislative mechanism to prevent blocking actions by the member state. In this particular situation, the candidate state finds itself in a certain paradox where the "negotiation option" is off the table, because it is more than obvious that the Union won't accept those states whose statehood is contested or whose borders are not recognized (Djolai and Nechev 2018, 6; Dmitrov and Djokai and Wunsch 2015, 5–6). For instance, the 2009 bilateral border disputes between Slovenia and Croatia over the territorial waters in the Piran Bay (northern part of the Adriatic Sea) consequently led to Croatia being blocked by Slovenia in the negotiating process for a year. The same bilateral border demarcation issues are observable in the case of Montenegro and its neighbors, namely with BiH, Croatia, Kosovo, and Serbia. When disputes exist among the candidate countries for EU accession, the resolution of a border issue should be pursued through the Commission's introduction of conditionality in the bilateral dispute, supported by a wide range of incentives that might help advancement in the EU integration process. If the circumstances change and if the country in dispute becomes a member state, the Commission should impose certain provisions or safeguards that will prevent the member state from using asymmetrical power mechanisms against the other candidate countries—this was the lesson learned from the Slovenia-Croatia bilateral dispute (Bechev 2011; Djolai and Nechev 2018, 12; Dmitrov and Djokai and Wunsch 2016, 8–9).

On the domestic level, Montenegro achieved overall visible progress in strengthening regional cooperation and developing bilateral relations with the enlargement countries and other member states during the pre-negotiation phase. The country had a profoundly visible role in contributing to regional peace and stability through its active participation in regional initiatives, notably MARRI, RACVIAC, RCC, thus demonstrating full commitment toward promoting the ideas of cooperation in the fields of free trade, economy, security, defense, migration, and the fight against corruption and organized crime. Additionally, Montenegro continued to play a constructive role in other regional organizations through its role as chairman in CEFTA (2009), CEI (2010), SEECP (2010), AII (2010–2011), and US-Adriatic Charter (2011). In particular, under the Montenegrin chairmanship of the SEECP, *the Regional Strategic Document and Action Plan on Justice and Home Affairs 2011–2013* in March 2010 was adopted, thus proving Montenegro's dedication to building regional stability and solving policy issues. Finally, Montenegro showed its support of various regional initiatives, namely the Igman Initiative and RECOM, by recognizing the need for reconciliation among the countries in the region that had been affected by the war (Vlada Crne Gore 2008b, 495; European Commission 2008b, 19, 2009, 19, 2012b, 22; MVPEI 2011a, 3–4).

By the same token, shortly after international recognition, Montenegro started playing a constructive role in improving bilateral relations with the enlargement states and with other member states during the pre-negotiation phase. As expected, the state devoted the most attention to developing bilateral cooperation with neighboring countries included in the SAA. The country immediately took decisive steps in improving good neighborly relations with Albania, BiH, Croatia, Kosovo, FYROM, and Serbia by intensifying cooperation in the fields of political, legal, economic, and trade relations. As a result, bilateral relations between Montenegro and Serbia, BiH, and Kosovo were substantially developed through the signed agreements on joint border control, on joint police cooperation in the fight against organized crime, on displaced persons, and on readmission (MVPEI 2011a, 4–7, 2011b, 4–5, 2012a, 5–6).[9] Positive outcomes of strengthening good neighborly bilateral relations were also seen in the construction and establishment in 2009 of the first joint border crossing in the region, the Albanian-Montenegrin Sukobin/Murićani, as well as in the signing of the first dual citizenship agreement of its kind in the region with FYROM (European Commission 2008b, 19, 2009b, 19–20). However, the most positive example of resolving outstanding bilateral disputes in the spirit of good neighborly relations was seen between Montenegro and Croatia over the border demarcation issue on the Prevlaka Peninsula. The two neighboring countries agreed to peacefully settle the border demarcation dispute through international arbitration at the ICJ, even though temporary joint border control has functioned smoothly since 2002 (European Commission 2007b, 17, 2008b, 19–20, 2009b, 19, 2011b, 23).

However, although Montenegro continued to demonstrate a proactive approach in developing good neighborly relations with the Western Balkan countries, certain declining trends were also observable. After the dissolution of the former Yugoslavia, a number of open bilateral disputes between Montenegro and other neighboring countries remained unresolved, especially in the field of border demarcation. Apart from the case with Albania and FYROM, Montenegro was faced with substantial bilateral border demarcation problems with other post-Yugoslav states—BiH, Croatia, Kosovo, and Serbia—during the pre-negotiation phase (please see Table 5.1). Moreover, with the exception of positive initiatives by the Montenegrin and Croatian Governments over peaceful settlement of the border demarcation issue of the Prevlaka Peninsula by committing the dispute to international arbitration at the ICJ, the remaining neighboring countries did not demonstrate any political will to resolve outstanding bilateral border disputes by using peaceful legal means (MVPEI 2011a, 4–7, 2011b, 4–5, 2012a, 4–6).

Therefore, based on the provided observations, the empirical evidence reveals that Montenegro achieved visible progress in the active promotion of regional cooperation through its full commitment to regional peace and stability and improvement of bilateral relations with other enlargement countries and the member states during the pre-negotiation phase, as one of

Table 5.1 Bilateral Disputes between Montenegro and Neighboring Countries during the Pre-Negotiation Phase, 2007–2012

	Albania	*BiH*	*Croatia*	*FYROM*	*Kosovo*	*Serbia*
Montenegro	**NO**	**YES**	**YES**	**NO**	**YES**	**YES**
Reasons:		Border dispute	Border dispute		Border dispute; Recognition of MNE minority	Border dispute; Issue of dual citizenship

Source: Author's own elaboration

the key conditions for the advancement in the accession process. Visibly, the state demonstrated strong commitment in providing additional contributions to security and stability in the Western Balkans through its active participation in regional initiatives, reconciliation, and building a climate conducive to addressing open bilateral issues and legacies of the past. Hence, the Union primarily had a reinforcing impact on the overall strengthening of Montenegro's regional cooperation efforts and maintaining good neighborly relations during the pre-negotiation phase. This being said, the EU external incentives had positive reinforcing effects on the empowerment of regional stability and bilateral relations with other enlargement countries and the EU member states, thus demonstrating at the same time a positive impetus for further integration reform processes. As a result, the Union's pressure on the country to fulfill the regional relations policy demands was perceived by the domestic actors as suitable and appropriate, consequently resulting in an alignment with the policy and credible results in strengthening regional cooperation and developing good neighborly relations through resolution on the issues of displaced persons, return of missing assets, war reparations, and strong cooperation with the International Criminal Tribunal for the former Yugoslavia.

Based on the research observations, it is reasonable to argue that Montenegro continued to play an active and constructive role in strengthening its regional cooperation and maintaining good neighborly relations with the Western Balkans, consequently addressing the SAP conditions during the pre-negotiation phase. A number of bilateral disputes, especially border demarcation problems, hampered further improvement of bilateral relations with neighboring countries, but overall the state demonstrated a desire to settle bilateral disputes with other regional countries through peaceful means. Therefore, the candidate country progressively assumed the obligation set out in the EU membership criteria, while at the same time creating conditions to move forward in the process of EU integration.

Negotiation Phase

In a nutshell, the empirical data on Montenegro's efforts to build regional stability during the negotiation phase reveals two main observations. First, on the EU level, the Union has demonstrated a more proactive approach in promoting regional cooperation and strengthening good bilateral relations, especially among the neighboring countries. Primarily, the Union has been committed to improving regional relations among the Western Balkans through its active promotion of regional cooperation in the fields of transport and infrastructure, economic connectivity, youth cooperation, and cooperation among businesses and civil societies of the Western Balkan states. The initiation of the Berlin (2014), Vienna (2015), and Paris Western Balkan Summits (2016) under the framework of the "Berlin Process" has substantially contributed to strengthening the regional connectivity agenda by connecting the people, economies, and states of the region (Civil Society Forum of the Western Balkan Summit Series 2014). Positive outcomes of the summit gatherings have been particularly observable in regional economic and social development, with cooperative agreements on energy efficiency targets, three Trans-European Transport Networks core corridors, and establishing a youth cooperation office in Tirana (Berlin Process, Final Declaration by the chair of the Conference on the Western Balkans; Berlin Process, Vienna Western Balkans Summit 2015, Annex 2—Joint Declaration on the establishment of the RYCO in the Western Balkans). Moreover, strengthening the regional economic and social dimensions has substantially affected the political dimension of regional relations, namely by resolving outstanding bilateral issues: that is, the goal of the process that was outlined by the then chair, German chancellor Angela Merkel, in the Final Declaration from 2014. As a result, on the margins of the Vienna Western Balkans Summit from 2015, Montenegro and BiH and Montenegro and Kosovo signed border demarcation agreements—the first legal agreements among the post-Yugoslav states aiming to resolve open bilateral disputes (Berlin Process, Final Declaration by the chair of the Vienna Western Balkans Summit 2015; Annex 3—Regional Cooperation and the Solution of Bilateral Disputes).

Second, at the domestic level, Montenegro has overall achieved significant progress in actively promoting regional cooperation through its full commitment to regional peace and stability, and also in developing good neighborly relations during the negotiation phase. More precisely, the candidate country has actively participated in regional initiatives, notably CEFTA, CEI, MARRI, RACVIAC, SEECP, AII, RCC, US-Adriatic Charter, Igman, and RECOM Initiatives (MVPEI 2012b, 8, 2012c, 7–8; European Commission 2012c, 16, 2013b, 11, 2014b, 12, 2015b, 21, 2016b, 21). Montenegro also displayed a positive impulse toward strengthening regional cooperation and improving good neighborly relations with its commitment to establishing the regional initiative called the "Western Balkans Six," a high-level political dialogue between regional leaders aiming to aid potential and candidate states in their advancement in the EU accession process (European Commission 2013b, 11). Beyond any doubt, the Western Balkan Six remains one of the rare examples of a regional organization dedicated to the EU integration process and, perhaps far more importantly, it was initiated by one of the non-EU member states. Moreover, Montenegro's steps toward the institutionalization of relations in the Western Balkans, particularly in the establishment of a joint parliament, police, and regional center for the fight against corruption and organized crime, and common labor market, education, and health care, may be interpreted as an indispensable regional willingness to overcome the war legacies of the 1990s, and therefore, to find a common ground of cooperation in the fields of rule of law, economy, and trade—all key criteria for moving forward in the EU integration process.

On the other hand, the empirical data also indicate Montenegro's serious commitment to the process of reconciliation in the post-Yugoslav space by creating a climate conducive to tackling open bilateral issues. The candidate county has continued to play a constructive role in the development of good neighborly relations during the negotiation phase by intensifying cooperation in the areas of political, economic, trade, security, defense, justice, and EU affairs. Bilateral relations between Montenegro and BiH, FYROM, and Serbia have been improved in the fields of police cooperation, fight against corruption, organized crime, terrorism, and drug trafficking (European Commission 2012b, 17, 2013b, 11, 2014b, 13, 2015b, 22, 2016b, 22). Also, cooperation between Montenegro and Kosovo has been strengthened through mutual enforcement of court decisions in civil and criminal matters and extradition, whereas relations with Albania have shown improvements in the areas of defense, border crossing, education, and mutual protection of classified information (MVPEI 2013b, 13–14, 2012b, 4, 2012c, 4, 2012d, 5). Montenegro has also demonstrated visible progress in enhancing bilateral cooperation with the countries not included in the SAA, or with other EU member states. As a result, the country has improved its bilateral relations with Turkey through constructive cooperation in the fields of protection and promotion of investments, economy, trade, and social security, while at the same time relations with Croatia and Italy have continued to advance in the areas of police cooperation and justice, economy, tourism, education, technical cooperation, and mutual assistance (MVPEI 2012b, 8–9; European Commission 2015b, 22; Vlada Crne Gore 2018b).

Moreover, positive trends in developing good neighborly relations have been particularly observable in Montenegro's true commitment to the peaceful settlement of outstanding bilateral disputes, especially border demarcation issues between the post-Yugoslav countries (please see Table 5.2). In this respect, Montenegro and BiH and Kosovo signed border demarcation agreements on the margins of the Vienna Western Balkans Summit in 2015, which resulted in joint ratification of Montenegro-BiH demarcation agreements in December 2015 and April 2016 (the first of its kind between the former Yugoslav states), and Montenegro's unilateral ratification of a demarcation agreement with Kosovo in December 2015 (European Commission 2015b, 22, 2016b, 22).[10] Furthermore, a positive desire for the peaceful settlement of open bilateral problems, including the border demarcation dispute over the Prevlaka Peninsula, was particularly observable between Montenegro and Croatia (non-EU and EU member state), who agreed to commit the dispute to the ICJ if bilateral negotiations fail. Simultaneously, the temporary border regime on joint police control has since 2002 functioned without any obstacles, and it still remains the most profound example of maintaining good neighborly relations in the region (MVPEI 2013b, 15–17, 2012b, 5–6, 2012c, 5–6, 2012d, 6).

However, certain bilateral disputes have not been resolved during the negotiation phase despite the Union's proclamation that no candidate country may join the EU unless it previously addresses border demarcation problems and legacies of the past. In line with the EU's demands as highlighted in the Berlin Process, outstanding bilateral problems between Montenegro and Serbia in the areas of border demarcation, recognition of dual citizenship, and the right to use religious assets in Montenegro (Serbian and Montenegrin Orthodox Churches' issue) have not been tackled yet. In addition, resolution of the open bilateral disputes that exist between Montenegro and Kosovo,

Table 5.2 Bilateral Disputes between Montenegro and Neighboring Countries during the Negotiation Phase, 2012–2017

	Albania	*BiH*	*Croatia*	*FYROM*	*Kosovo*	*Serbia*
Montenegro	**NO**	**NO**	**YES**	**NO**	**NO**	**YES**
Reasons:		Border dispute	Border dispute		Border dispute; Recognition of MNE minority	Border dispute; Dual citizenship; Religious assets between Orthodox Churches
Year of resolution:		**2015**	?		**2018**	?

Source: Author's own elaboration

especially when it comes to the constitutional recognition of the Montenegrin minority, has been constantly postponed.

Hence, following the above-provided discussion, the empirical evidence indicates that Montenegro has demonstrated progress in strengthening regional cooperation through its full commitment to active participation in regional initiatives, and maintaining good neighborly relations with neighboring countries and the EU member states during the negotiation phase, that is, toward one of the most essential criteria for moving forward in the European integration process. Consequently, the EU has had positively reinforcing effects on the empowerment of the country's contribution to peace and stability in the region by its active participation in various regional initiatives, and reconciliation and climate conducive to addressing open bilateral issues.

Therefore, based on the provided empirical evidence it would be grounded to claim that Montenegro has purposefully addressed the issue of strengthening regional cooperation through its active participation in regional organizations and improved bilateral relations especially with the neighboring states. Evidently, although there are a certain number of bilateral disputes preventing good bilateral relations in the region, the country has in general played a constructive role in peacefully settling outstanding bilateral issues, especially border demarcation problems. As a result, Montenegro as a candidate country has achieved considerable results in fulfilling the EU conditions related to the key criteria for completing the accession negotiation process.

EXPLAINING POSITIVE TRENDS IN ADDRESSING REGIONAL COOPERATION AND MAINTAINING BILATERAL RELATIONS REQUIREMENTS DURING THE INTEGRATION PHASE

Given these observations, the main question that arises is: How can one explain positive trends in the state's further strengthening of regional cooperation and improving bilateral relations? More precisely, what kind of external and domestic factors have influenced the state's contribution to the regional peace and stability by maintaining good bilateral cooperation with the neighboring countries through peaceful settlement of outstanding bilateral issues and legacies of the past?

Four main explanations can be provided. First, Montenegro's membership in the regional initiatives is primarily based on its willingness to participate in organizational activities, and, perhaps far more importantly, the functioning of regional initiatives largely depends on the financial support of their members and international donors. Although the enlargement country maintained relative free to choose which regional initiatives it wanted to actively participate in, the functioning of regional organizations and respective activities mainly depended on the members' financial contributions and international donor support (Vučković and Đorđević 2019, 169). Following the cases of CEFTA, CEI, MARRI, RACVIAC, and RCC, the activities of these regional initiatives were largely financed by their member states, the Union itself, and various international contributors. If one takes into account the case of Montenegro's membership in the CEI for instance, the annual financial contribution in the total amount of 3,960 EUR to maintain membership status comes to mind (Vlada Crne Gore 2018a). Apparently, it is the parties' financial contribution to the functioning of regional initiatives that substantially limits the scope of actions of these organizations. In that sense, financial support of the member states creates an interdependent relationship between participants and regional initiatives in favor of the member contributors, consequently establishing organization(s) without the ability to impose sanction mechanisms if the countries do not comply with the initiative's requirements or courses of action.

Second, building regional stability was largely achieved through the financial support and technical assistance of the EU. The legal provisions stipulated within the SAA clearly emphasized that development of regional cooperation and improving good neighborly relations was to be supported by Union assistance for programs funding regional or cross-border projects through technical assistance (SAA 2007, Article 14). The EU designed special Instruments in the Pre-Accession Assistance I and II (IPA I and II) for potential and candidate countries for EU membership to strengthen regional relations with neighboring countries, the member states, and other countries by using Regional and Cross-Border Cooperation—CBS (II IPA component). The main aim of the CBS is to further strengthen the stability, security, and prosperity of the Western Balkans region through active development of relations and cooperation between cross-border regions. Cross-border relations aim to encourage border cooperation between neighboring states in strengthening economy, efficiency, and security of borders, the prevention of and fight against organized crime, the promotion of legal and administrative cooperation, and so on (Đurović 2012, 341).

Based on the provided instruments within the pre-accession assistance, Montenegro actively participated in various cross-border cooperation programs under the CBS II IPA component during the whole integration stage:

- *10 neighbouring programs*[11]—Montenegro-Albania; Montenegro-BiH; Montenegro-Croatia; Montenegro-Serbia, and 1 program—*Adriatic Cross Border Program* (i.e., *Adriatic*)[12] including both regional countries and the member states;

- and *2 transnational programs—South East European Space* (SEES)[13] and *Mediterranean program* (MED).[14]

The EU's more proactive approach in the process of strengthening regional cooperation and developing good neighborly relations is the third explanation for positive trends in the given area. As has already been mentioned, full commitment to building regional stability and perhaps far more importantly, peaceful settlement of outstanding bilateral disputes, especially border demarcation problems between the former Yugoslav states, remain one of the most important SAP conditions for the state's further advancement in the accession process (SAP 2007). After surviving the economic and financial crisis, the Union itself has devoted more attention to strengthening regional relations in the Western Balkans by encouraging these countries to closely cooperate in the areas of economy, infrastructure, energy, transport, youth cooperation, education, and science. Correspondingly, the Berlin Process initiated by German chancellor Angela Merkel in 2014, supported by the European Commission, the EU member states of Austria, Croatia, France, Germany, Italy, Slovenia, and the United Kingdom, and various international donors, aimed to reaffirm the connection of societies (social dimension) and economies (economic dimension) of the region by providing suitable conditions for further improving regional relations (political dimension). This being said, development of the social and economic connectivity dimensions should somehow serve as the initial mechanism to peacefully settle outstanding bilateral disputes, particularly border demarcation issues (Vučković and Đorđević 2019; Juncos 2018). As a result, the effects of the Western Balkans Summits in Berlin (2014), Vienna (2015), and Paris (2016) under the framework of the Berlin Process have been reflected in the border demarcation agreements signed between Montenegro and BiH and Montenegro and Kosovo on the margins of the Vienna Summit in 2015. Peaceful settlement of border demarcation between the neighboring countries has been highlighted by the Union as a major condition to be addressed before full membership of the candidate states in the EU (Djolai and Nechev 2018, 5–12; Dmitrov and Djokai and Wunsch 2016, 5–9). Thus, following the Union's assertion that the candidate countries will not be allowed to import existing bilateral issues into the EU, Montenegro's intention to resolve its border demarcation problems with the former Yugoslav states remains a positive example of resolving this problem before the country is to assume the obligations of EU membership.

Finally, the most convincing reason for positive trends in the fulfillment of the SAP conditions lies primarily in the state's willingness to effectively align itself with the EU requirements. Evidently, Montenegro was persuaded by the EU of the usefulness and legitimacy of the EU demands and processes in the area of strengthening regional cooperation and improving good neighborly relations (Sedelmeier 2011, 15; Schimmelfennig and Sedelmeier 2005, 18–20). In other words, the usefulness of tackling regional cooperation criteria by the country did not call into question the enduring political power of the ruling elites, or its widespread political influence on all levels of governance and in legislative and judicial branches. In fact, the state's fulfillment of the SAA conditions during the integration phase did not interfere with the basic principles of established political structure in the country, nor did it jeopardize the survival of the domestic political elites, as was the case with in the previous empirical chapter regarding issues of politicization of the judiciary and political corruption. Instead, smooth fulfillment of the SAP conditions was beneficial for the domestic political elites because it substantially strengthened their political positions both at the regional and the EU level (Vachudova 2014, 122–38; Bechev 2006, 27–43).

The constructive role of Montenegro's political elites in improving bilateral relations with other Western Balkan countries produced a double effect. Primarily, Montenegro positioned itself as a positive example of maintaining good neighborly relations at the regional level (which was not the case with other countries in the region), although the state had numerous open bilateral disputes with other post-Yugoslav states, especially in border demarcation issues. Since 2006, the country has shown a continuous tendency to improve its bilateral cooperation with Albania, BiH, Croatia, and Kosovo on the one hand, while at the same time maintaining moderately good neighborly relations with Serbia (European Commission 2012b, 2013b, 2014b, 2015b, 2016b). The good neighbor role played by Montenegro created conditions for Podgorica to position itself as a kind of special peace mediator between the Western Balkan countries burdened by postwar-related problems (BiH-Croatia-Serbia; BiH-Serbia; Croatia-Serbia; Kosovo-Serbia), and it therefore benefited from the EU accession process. Moreover, Montenegro's three crucial decisions were as listed: (1) to declare independence from Serbia in 2006 (which is mainly perceived by other neighboring countries as a trouble-maker state); (2) to apologize for the aggression on the city of Dubrovnik and BiH during the 1990s and to pay war reparations to Croatia (2010) and BiH (2008);[15] (3) and finally, to recognize the independence of neighboring Kosovo in 2008, which undoubtedly influenced the reduction of regional pressure in ethnic tensions and national intolerance (Bechev and Ejdus and Taleski 2015; Vučković and Đorđević 2019). By leaving inherited postwar problems to Serbia, the country immediately started playing an active role in promoting regional cooperation through its full commitment to regional peace, stability, and developing good neighboring relations. This foreign policy decision quickly received strong support for the country's European and Euro-Atlantic ambitions, not just throughout Balkans but also from the EU itself. The Union obtained in Montenegro a reliable factor of regional stability supporting European integration, with Podgorica becoming a role model for the generally problematic Western Balkan countries (DeBardeleben 2008; Bechev 2011).

CONCLUSION

Overall, Montenegro has achieved visible progress in strengthening regional cooperation and maintaining good bilateral relations with the enlargement countries and the EU member states during the whole accession process. In particular, the candidate country has demonstrated substantial efforts in promoting regional cooperation through its active participation in regional initiatives, such as CEFTA, CEI, MARRI, RACVIAC, AII, SEECP, RCC, US-Adriatic Charter, RECOM, and Igman Initiative. Also, the state has been fully committed to developing good neighborly relations with the rest of the region by playing a constructive role in reconciliation and fostering a climate conducive to addressing open bilateral issues and legacies of the past (MVPEI 2012b, 8, 2012c, 7–8; European Commission 2012c, 16, 2013b, 11, 2014b, 12, 2015b, 21, 2016b, 21).

Based on the state's visible progress in developing regional cooperation and improving bilateral relations with the Western Balkans, this chapter has identified three main reasons why Montenegro has indeed demonstrated its willingness to functionally induce EU rules and norms. First, there is a lack of influence of domestic veto players over the issues related to building regional stability due to the lack of domestic conditions which would jeopardize their private interests. It might be grounded to assume that the fulfillment of the SAP conditions over the country's participation within regional initiatives and tackling open bilateral disputes have not resulted in welfare or power costs for public and private actors (Cebelis 2016, 20; Elbasani 2019, 190–92). The content of the legal provisions stipulated within the SAA is more oriented toward development of regional relations among the enlargement countries and the EU member states and the establishment of stronger economic and trade contractual bonds between the Union and contracting parties, therefore not calling into question existence of veto players. Hence, change in the current status quo in improving regional policies does not limit the widespread influence of veto players, nor does it increase their opportunity costs, welfare, or power losses from compliance (Schimmelfennig and Sedelmeier 2005; Schimmelfennig and Engert and Knobel 2006; Sedelmeier 2011). In addition, active participation of facilitating actors, notably regional CSOs, in the promotion of reconciliation has indubitably played a constructive role in strengthening regional cooperation and developing good neighborly relations in the region. Several regional nongovernmental organizations, notably RECOM and Igman Initiative, have substantially contributed to maintaining peace and stability in the region through their full commitment to regional reconciliation in the countries affected by the postwar transition (RECOM; Igman Initiative).[16] Those regional NGOs, as EU domestic allies, have devoted substantial efforts to strengthening the process of transitional justice within the post-Yugoslav space by connecting high-level regional political representatives to overcome this issue, and in directing various national and ethnic individuals and groups toward the process of reconciliation and resolving post-conflict traumatic experiences.

Second, the domestic ruling elites have demonstrated visible political will to align with the EU requirements. Given the fact that strengthening regional cooperation and improving bilateral relations with the neighboring countries do not call into question the political survival of the ruling elites, it might be grounded to assume that the fulfillment of the SAP conditions has been rather beneficial for the domestic actors. Apparently, it is Montenegro's commitment to developing good neighborly relations through the initiation of the Western Balkans Six initiative and active participation in peaceful settlement of open bilateral disputes between the post-Yugoslav states that has had a substantial effect on strengthening the position of the domestic ruling elites as a factor of stability in the region (European Commission 2013b, 11; MVPEI 2013a, 47–48). Consequently, by using the current political particularities of the region, Montenegro's political elites have presented themselves as indispensable in regional changes on the regional level, as well as on the EU level, which requires the Union's support to solve regional political problems (Bieber 2020; Kmezić 2020; Bechev and Ejdus and Taleski 2015; Bechev 2011).

Third, one can witness the more active role of the Union and its member states in the process of promoting regional cooperation through the development of good bilateral relations. The Western Balkans Summits, under the framework of the Berlin Process, has substantially contributed to strengthening regional relations by establishing a clear road map of development in the areas of infrastructure, energy, transport, youth cooperation, education, and science. Moreover, the establishment of this multilateral cooperation has provided a double effect (Civil Society Forum of the Western Balkan Summit Series 2014). Originally, by supporting and strengthening the regional political, economic, and trade cooperation, the Union primarily sought to strengthen its relations with the Western Balkans by positioning itself as a reliable economic and trade partner and active promoter of the European integration process. On the other hand, joint regional dedication to the EU accession process has created conditions for the development of political relations in the region and, therefore, consequently has resolved more sensitive and complex open bilateral issues, namely border demarcations, recognition of minority rights, displaced and missing persons, return of assets, and recognition of Kosovo, and so on (Vučković and Đorđević 2019, 174–76).

Nevertheless, based on the previous discussion, this chapter has argued that the EU has managed to Europeanize Montenegro by building regional stability through its active participation in regional initiatives and reconciliation and fostering a climate conducive to addressing open bilateral issues during the entire integration phase. Visibly, the Union has had positively reinforcing effects in empowering the state's efforts in strengthening regional cooperation and improving good neighborly relations. The positive reinforcing impact is primarily a product of corelations between the Union and favorable domestic conditions. This research has proposed the main argument that strengthening regional cooperation and developing good neighborly relations remains an interdependent process dependent on various factors, primarily the effectiveness of the EU external incentives and the willingness of the domestic ruling elites to comply with the SAP conditions. Given the fact that fulfilling the regional cooperation criteria does not require the state's adoption of the EU acquis, the state's active participation in the regional initiatives, as well as the peaceful settlement of outstanding bilateral disputes depend largely on the Union's external pressure and the willingness of the political elites to address those requirements.

In line with the given empirical elaborations, the question that is being raised is whether the interdependency of both external and internal factors is sufficient for obtaining complete insights into why the Union has succeeded in Europeanizing Montenegro in the fields of strengthening regional cooperation and developing good bilateral relations.

This particular issue is addressed in the conclusion of this book.

NOTES

1. This chapter does not contain an Appendix due to the state's fulfillment of the SAP conditions.

2. The Union highlighted that the same convection activities will be conducted with the remaining countries of the region once these states have signed the SAA. For more details, see SAA (2007, Article 15: 7–8).

3. Prior to signing the SAA and the adopted resolution by the Parliament, the country during 2006 and 2007 conducted certain activities in strengthening regional cooperation through acquisition of full membership in regional initiatives:

- *Organization for Security and Cooperation in Europe (OSCE)* on June 22, 2006, whose range of activities covers three dimensions of security—military-political, economic-ecological, and human;

- *Central European Initiative (CEI)* on August 1, 2006, whose main goals are related to improvement of cooperation between the countries of Central, East, and Southeast Europe through establishment of stable democracies and market economies, and providing assistance to the enlargement countries for EU membership;
- *Migration, Asylum, Refugees Regional Initiatives (MARRI)* on October 2, 2006, whose main aims are to address issues of human movement in the Western Balkans through promotion of closer regional cooperation and a comprehensive, common, and harmonized approach to asylum, migration, border control, visa regimes, and displaced persons;
- *Central European Free Trade Agreement (CEFTA)* on January 1, 2007, whose main goal is establishment of a zone of free trade between non-EU member states;
- *Centre for Security Cooperation (RACVIAC)* on March 21, 2007, whose main aim is related to strengthening stability and security in Southeast Europe;
- *Council of Europe (CoE)* on May 11, 2007: one of the oldest and most important regional organizations promoting democracy, protection, and promotion of human rights and ensuring rule of law within its member states;
- *South-East European Cooperation Process (SEECP)* on May 11, 2007, whose main goals are to promote and strengthen good neighborly relations between the countries of Southeast Europe, and to transform the region in the zone of peace, security, stability, and cooperation;
- *Adriatic and Ionian Initiative (AII)* on June 1, 2007, which represents a forum for exchanging political opinions and conducting multilateral cooperation in many fields, including transport, maritime affairs, tourism, education, environmental protection, cultural heritage protection, and fight against organized crime (Vlada Crne Gore 2018a).

4. The mission of the NGO Igman Initiative is to promote and facilitate regional cooperation among signatory parties to the Dayton Agreement and to influence their governments to resolve key issues related to citizens of the four countries—BiH, Croatia, Montenegro, and Serbia. For more details, http://www.igman-initiative.org/. NGO RECOM—Coalition for Reconciliation Commission is a regional commission for establishing facts about war crimes and other serious violations of human rights committed in former Yugoslavia from January 1, 1991, until December 31, 2011. For more details, http://recom.link/.

5. According to Montenegro's proposal, each state would delegate ten representatives.

6. 2014–2018.

7. The Western Balkan six Prime Ministers agreed in Brussels in April 2015 and then in Riga in June 2015 on the regional core transport network corridors, with projects to be implemented by 2020 and the appointment of corridor coordinators. Also, they agreed on a list of six transport infrastructure investment projects, including an intermodal terminal, two bridges, and three railway projects reflecting core priorities,

and necessary maturity for imminent implementation to be proposed for inclusion in the IPA 2015 multicountry program.

8. The Western Balkans agreed on a shortlist of four investment projects to be proposed for inclusion in the IPA 2015 multicountry program. They include power interconnectors and reinforcement to the region's electricity transmission system. Additional Projects of Energy Community Interest (PECI), whether electricity or gas, were to be proposed for funding in subsequent years. Also, they decided to establish the regional energy market by establishing power exchanges and the regional balancing market, as well as making the best use of already-existing Coordinated Auction Office. For more details, see Final Declaration by the chair of the Vienna Western Balkans Summit on August 27, 2015.

9. Montenegro signed bilateral agreements with Serbia on joint border patrol and joint police cooperation in the fight against organized crime, with BiH on joint border patrol, and with Kosovo on displaced persons and readmission.

10. Less than three years after the agreement was signed, the Parliament of Kosovo ratified the border demarcation agreement on March 21, 2018. Reasons for stagnation over ratification of the agreement were the lack of two-third of the majority in the Parliament to vote for this proposal and strong opposition from Kosovo's right-wing nationalist political party Vetëvendosje (Self-determination).

11. For more details, Đurović (2012, 493).

12. IPA Adriatic CBC Programs includes Albania, BiH and BiH institutional cooperation; preserving national and cultural cooperation, including prevention of risk; availability and networking, and technical cooperation. Montenegro participated in seventeen projects. For more details, see https://www.eu.me/mn/ipa/ipa-i-2007-2013/ii-komponenta-prekogranicna-saradnja.

13. IPA SEES Programs includes the following: Albania, Austria, BiH, Bulgaria, Croatia, FYROM, Greece, Hungary, Italy, Montenegro, Moldavia, Slovakia, Slovenia, Serbia, Romania, Turkey, and Ukraine. Priorities of the programs were the following: innovation and development of entrepreneurship, protection and development of environment, development of transnational synergy for sustainable growth of the region. The EU provided Montenegro with 2,300,000 EUR for conducting projects in the period 2007/2009. For more details, see Đurović (2012, 492).

14. IPA MED Programs includes Albania, BiH, Britain, Cyprus, Croatia, Greece, France, Italy, Malta, Montenegro, Portugal, Slovenia, and Spain. Priorities of the programs were the following: building of innovation capacities, protection of environment and promotion of sustainable territorial development, enhancement of mobility and territorial connections in area of the Mediterranean region. The MED program was supported by the EU with 256 million EUR for the period of 2007/2013. For more details, see Đurović (2012, 492–93).

15. Since 2010, Montenegro started paying war reparations to citizens of Dubrovnik. Also, the government in 2008 signed a court settlement with Bošniak families deported and killed in 1992. Victims and their relatives, 247 individuals in total, received the amount of 5 million dollars for compensation.

16. BiH, Croatia, Montenegro, Kosovo, Serbia.

Chapter 6

Discussion on Mechanisms of Europeanization Presented in the Case Study of Montenegro

Evidently, the European Union (EU) had, as mentioned in the previous empirical chapters, positive reinforcing effects on improving regional cooperation and maintaining good bilateral relations, and negative reinforcing effects on strengthening the judicial system and anti-corruption policy during the first decade of the Montenegrin integration phase. The given deficiency of judicial reforms and combating corruption in Montenegro is, on the one hand, primarily the result of inconsistent and inefficient EU conditional policy, and on the other hand, the result of domestic factors that are unfavorable for properly facilitating reform activities, thus resulting in an overall weak and mitigating reform progress. This being said, the insufficiently active role of the EU in imposing judicial and anti-corruption criteria over independence and accountability, and prevention and repression of corruption, combined with the lack of political will to reduce political influence over the judiciary and in anti-corruption bodies, have subsequently resulted in the adoption of a selective approach by the domestic elites in charge of fulfilling those conditions/dimensions, that is, regional cooperation and improving good bilateral relations, areas that do not jeopardize their political control over the Montenegrin judicial sector and anti-corruption supervisory institutions (Mendelski 2015; Kmezić 2017; CGO 2019; IA and CGO and CRNVO and CeMI 2018).

Thus, if one acknowledges that judicial independence/accountability, and prevention/suppression of corruption measures are more important dimensions than contributions to the peace and stability in the region through active participation in the regional initiatives and building a climate conducive to addressing open bilateral disputes of the political accession criteria, then one may claim that the process of judicial reform and the fight against corruption in Montenegro during the integration phase has failed to achieve positive reinforcing effects in the given transformation process. This assertion is based on the view that it is more demanding to address the criteria of judicial reform and fight against the corruption, as the process requires full state commitment, than is to align with SAP conditions of active participation in regional initiatives and maintaining good neighborly relations (Džankić and Keil and Kmezić 2019; Đurović 2016; Gateva 2015; Laursen 2013). As a result, the Union has had negative (deficient) reinforcing effects which systematically undermine the process of fostering judicial and prosecutorial impartiality and accountability and the independence of law enforcement anti-corruption bodies.

Based on the results within the policy fields, this research confirms that Brussels has thus far failed to Europeanize Montenegro in the process of European integration, particularly in the areas of judiciary reform and the fight against corruption. I argue that the Union has either had a throughout negatively reinforcing influence or no impact at all on strengthening the rule of law policy framework. This is a product of the relationship between the Union and unfavorable domestic conditions, and has consequently resulted in the illusion of domestic changes. Although the Union's active role in promoting the rule of law cannot be ignored, this chapter has also highlighted that the quality of judicial reform and anti-corruption processes largely depends on the relationship between domestic conditions and the modes of conducting reforms in the given area (Mendelski 2015; Elbasani and Šelo Šabić 2018; Keil 2018; Džankić 2018). Therefore, based on the claim that the Union's efforts have failed to positively impact judicial reform and the fight against corruption, this book argues that the current EU enlargement policy is merely a charade, not only in the process of European integration of Montenegro but also in Western Balkan region as a whole (Börzel and Risse 2012; Börzel 2011; Elbasani 2013; Sedelmeier 2011; Frayburg and Richter 2010; Keil 2013; Noutcheva 2009; Noutcheva and Aydin-Düzgit 2012; Kmezić 2020).

Following the EU's insufficient conditional policy approach, it makes sense to elaborate the current hollow trends in the Montenegrin accession process. Although the EU has outlined visible inconsistencies regarding constant conditional pressure, one may witness Montenegro continuing to move forward in the EU integration process while at the same time showing political unwillingness to reduce politicization of the judiciary, political corruption, or to achieve concrete and sustainable results in prosecution and final conviction of high-level cases (MANS 2017, 2018, 2019). Consequently, the state's judicial system and anti-corruption institutional framework are still under political influence although more than ten years have passed since the beginning of the accession process (CGO 2019). Also, the EU's strategy for promoting of rule of law reform in the judiciary and in the fight against corruption has been permissive during the whole integration phase, while at the same time allowing the candidate country to select and tackle certain political criteria based on which it can advance in the integration process (IA and CGO and CRNVO and CeMI 2018). It is rather paradoxical that a candidate state may resort to a selective approach in fulfilling regional cooperation conditions by addressing easier political demands rather than harder ones. Therefore, one might observe the tendency of a state to tackle simpler regional cooperation requirements, namely active participation in regional initiatives and addressing open bilateral issues, instead of more demanding ones, such as judiciary reform and combating corruption, or the independence and impartiality of judges, prosecutors, and law enforcement authorities. This in essence means tackling those regional cooperation dimensions while not addressing the issue of political influence over the judiciary or anti-corruption bodies. In situations in which a state needs to reduce the political influence in the judiciary and provide concrete and sustainable results in the area of prosecution and final conviction of high-level corruption, a candidate state instead chooses to hide behind the relatively solid results achieved in improving its regional cooperation and bilateral relations, therefore addressing politicization dimensions only in superficial terms (Vučković and Đorđević 2019). In the state's logic of calculations, it is possible to continue to advance in the accession process even while failing to achieve measurable results in empowering judges, prosecutors, and anti-corruption law enforcement bodies.

The EU, by positioning itself merely as a monitoring agent, shows its lack of interest in guiding the Montenegrin reform process, resulting in what can be seen as an EU enlargement charade. This undoubtedly raises questions as to the actual range of results achieved in the EU integration process and further problematizes the possibility of Montenegro effectively aligning with the EU policies and implementing acquis (Džankić and Keil and Kmezić 2019; Gateva 2015; BiEPAG 2016). Consequently, the EU's reluctance in supervising the rule of law requirements as a key condition for EU membership calls into question the Union's commitment to seeing sociopolitical transformation of Montenegro, and, perhaps far more importantly, it opens the space for a legitimate debate on whether the EU is ready for new enlargement (Kmezić 2017; Börzel 2016; Belloni 2016). Arguably, inconsistent fulfillment of judicial reform and combating corruption conditions by Montenegro, on the one hand, and noticeable permissiveness by or lack of interest on the part of the EU, on the other, invites deliberations on the effectiveness of the Europeanization of Montenegro and its true ability to assume the obligations of EU membership toward the end of the accession negotiation process.

There is no doubt that the obtained empirical findings on the existence of interdependent relations of the EU and domestic factors have a stronghold in the applied theoretical concept. Unequivocally, the Europeanization process of Montenegro has remained an EU-driven process during the whole integration process. However, the conditions under which the candidate country tries to align with the EU acquis and uses different logics of rule adoption mainly depend on given policy areas. Following the logic of Europeanization through externally driven compliance by conditionality, the state has not adopted the EU rules and norms in the areas of judicial reform and combating corruption mostly because the benefits of the given EU rewards do not exceed domestic adoption costs. Rather, Montenegro's decision to not comply with the EU's demands has primarily been the result of domestic cost-benefit calculations and the influence of a number of external and internal factors, namely: (1) the lack of credible membership perspective along with the Union's reluctance to provide any commitment toward a precise timetable for the accession; (2) damaged credibility of the EU conditional policy by subordinating it to other geopolitical and geostrategic aspects and international relations perspectives perceived by Montenegro as a politically motivated decision and a clear signal for advancement in the accession process without having to address membership conditions; (3) the strong role of various domestic individual and collective veto players in maintaining the status quo over implementation and enforcement of legal and institutional changes due to high domestic rule adoption costs. By the same token, the clear mechanisms of the Union's socially driven learning model for imparting rules and norms have worked well at both the EU and the domestic level in developing regional cooperation and maintaining good bilateral relations. Under the strategy, Montenegro has aligned with the EU conditions on strengthening regional cooperation because it has been persuaded: (1) by the appropriateness and legitimacy of the EU rules and procedures, that is, the rules are clearly determined and result from a legitimate rule-making process that is perceived by the target country as the Union's creation and under its ownership; (2) by the state's identification with the EU values and norms; (3) and by the positive normative resonance with domestic rules, that is, the state's openness to fulfilling the SAP conditions as a result of a long-lasting political crisis in the region (Schimmelfenning and Sedelmeier 2005, 8–18; Sedelmeier 2011, 15; Cebelis 2016, 20).

In light of the theoretical perspectives within the Europeanization literature, it can be inferred that the EU's impact on domestic changes have depended primarily on the compatibility of the EU's externally driven compliance through conditionality/persuasion and the domestic response through the socialization of norms. In other words, given Schimmelfennig and Sedelmeier's theoretical perspective on the Union's influence on domestic changes in Montenegro, the interplay of domestic and external factors in judicial reform and the fight against corruption has resulted in the politicization of the judiciary and of law enforcement anti-corruption authorities, Brussel's inconsistency, and the low quality of legal and institutional changes. Therefore, one may conclude that the EU-driven rule of law reform has been deficient in reforming the judiciary and combating corruption, consequently strengthening the domestic political elites and their positions by helping to introduce an ineffective legal and institutional framework.

APPLICABILITY OF THE THEORETICAL FRAMEWORK TO THE WESTERN BALKANS COMPLEXITY AND INFLUENCE OF INTERNATIONAL FACTORS

Although this theoretical concept has largely explained the process of adopting EU standards, the question that is being raised at this point is whether the interdependency of both external and internal factors is sufficient to explain the complex process of Europeanization of Montenegro and the entire Western Balkans region. More specifically, whether the interplay between the EU and domestic actors provides satisfactory insights into the Union's negatively reinforcing effects on empowering judicial reform and the fight against corruption.

To provide an explanation to the questions at hand, it is first necessary to answer a specific question of crucial importance: Can the theoretical concept that was fully applicable to the logic of Europeanization of Central and Eastern Europe (CEE) also be applied to the logic of Western Balkans (after more than thirteen years since its introduction)? This being said, is there any influence of other factors, apart from the overlapping impact of the EU and domestic factors, which can also explain why the EU has failed to Europeanize Montenegro even though more than ten years have passed since the beginning of the accession process?

It seems that the Western Balkan countries are currently facing political realities and a security environment that differ from those of the early 1990s in the CEE region. While both regions (have) demonstrated the same aspiration to join the EU after the collapse of communism, both of these areas (have) faced substantially different political issues and international relations security challenges (Grimm and Mathis 2018, 163–84; Ginsberg and Penksa 2012; Elbasani 2013). The concepts of the New World Order (Duffield 2001; Krauthammer 1990; Huntington 2004) and "the end of history" (Fukuyama 1992) were primarily characterized by the victory of the United States in the Cold War confrontation and the consequent dissolution of the Soviet Union and the disappearance of the bipolar system of international relations. The end of the Cold War Era and the disappearance of communism brought to the CEE countries not just freedom from the totalitarian regime, but also a different international relations environment, which was reflected in the further strengthening of the EC/EU integration processes (Vachudova 2005; Grabbe 2006; Pridham 2005). Those past circumstances in international politics after the end of the Cold War were largely suitable for the CEE countries to accelerate the process of EU integration, not just because of the credible membership perspective given to this region by the Union, but primarily due to the establishment of a new multilateral system of international relations and the lack of influence of great (regional) powers in the new international politics.

However, unlike the accession momentum of the CEE countries, the current political and security situation in the Western Balkans does not show any main features of a peaceful and secure region in which powers cooperate to preserve regional stability. Rather, following the past decade, the territory of the Western Balkan states has become once again the scene of animosity between great powers and confrontation over their geopolitical and geostrategic ambitions. The great powers once again have started using the tools of military and security competition, aiming to maximize their power at the expense of other states in the Western Balkan region as a consequence of the given situation in the multilateral system of international relations. Certainly, the current political and security environment in the Western Balkan region displays all of the characteristics of a powerful rivalry of great powers, strongly grounded in the theoretical approach of neorealism. Mearsheimer's (2001) theory of neorealism based on the concept of "offensive realism" claims that the multipolar system is more inclined to war than the bipolar system of international relations due to the existence of several powerful states, potential hegemons, who are the most dangerous actors within the system. This approach argues that states fear each other and therefore constantly compete for gaining more power because the main goal of each country is to maximize its share of world power at the expense of other countries. According to the theory of offensive realism, the ultimate goal of all great powers is primarily to obtain the status of hegemon and to be the only great power in the system of international relations. Indeed, this theoretical interpretation is primarily observable in the Western Balkans region, where competitiveness, as a pattern of behavior in the international sphere, exists between various great powers, namely the EU (US), Russia, China, and Turkey (Naj 2004; Layne 1993; Pollak 2006).

Following this theoretical conception, these actors are not satisfied with the current distribution of power in the region, and therefore all their actions are based on shifting the power in their favor. The countries have continuously demonstrated revisionist ambitions over the current distribution of power in the region by using both hard and soft power tools to change the balance of power if served at a reasonable price. Obviously, the pursuit of power remains the main driving force of the great powers in the Western Balkans. This, however, does not mean that these powers merely seek to gain power at the expense of others, but rather that they prevent others from such gains as well. In the case of the given region, the great powers primarily behave in this manner because they fear each other and are never certain of each other's ambitions or intentions. To maximize their power in the region, great powers such as the EU, Russia, China (and Turkey) are trying to alter the balance of power by constantly looking for opportunities at the expense of their rivals (Peral 2009; Wohlforth 2010; Denmark and Mulvenon 2010). Given the fact that the main goal of these states is to achieve the status of hegemon in the system of international relations, the great powers have shown great interest in engaging in the given region in recent years for various geopolitical reasons and regional geostrategic importance. They have used a wide range of positive and negative means—economic, trade, diplomatic, and military actions—to shift the balance of power. Thus, it might be grounded to claim that the rivals have at their disposal various means by which to secure their supremacy in the region, and therefore, achieve the hegemon status by removing all potential internal or external threats challenging their power and influence (Mearsheimer 2001; Mearsheimer 2018; Burchill 2005; Little 2007).

RUSSIA

The inability to be actively involved in new international politics, especially over the advancement of the CEE states in the EU accession process at the end of the twentieth century, was particularly noticeable in the then-transitional and newly redefined Russia (Radeljić 2017a; Braun 1997). The loss of vast territories, the lack of access to warm seas and ports, the absence of a corridor linking Russia with the West, and more than 23 million Russians living outside its borders were clear signs that the postcommunist giant was facing negative political and strategic post-Cold War consequences. If one considers the fact that Russia's military forces were significantly weakened, reduced, and pulled back some 1,500 km to the east while its planned economy experienced a complete collapse, then it might be reasonable to conclude that disintegration processes hit Russia so hard that it was impossible to compete or to challenge the EU on either the political or economic level (Bžežinski 2001, 40; Lane 2007, 461–77). Indeed, Russian internal political and economic crises lasted for more than a decade, and when combined with profound geostrategic problems they had a significant impact on Russia and its active participation in international relations (Hill 2015; Kisindžer 2015).

However, after the election of Vladimir Putin for president in 2000, primarily through the definition and adoption of the Russian Foreign Policy Concept, Russia became more active in its external engagement in the Balkans, and began its active commitment to the peaceful resolution of open disputes between former Yugoslav states. The first tangible Russian foreign policy actions in the Balkans were seen in the early 1990s with the country's support of the creation of the Federal Republic of Yugoslavia (consisting of Serbia and Montenegro) in 1992. However, as a member of the Contact Group, Russia advocated an end to violence in the civil war in BiH, and opposed Western powers who were determined to use military force against the Serbian leadership. Later, during the Kosovo crisis and the escalation of NATO intervention on the Milošević regime in 1998 and 1999, Russia insisted on applying an internal issue approach, leaving Serbian sovereignty and territorial integrity untouched in accordance with UN Security Council Resolution 1160, adopted in March 1998 (Radeljić 2017b, 273–74; Horvath 2014, 2–5; Fabrykant and Magun 2019, 20–24).

In line with the concept of offensive realism, the Western Balkan states have emerged at the top of the Russian foreign policy agenda during the past decade as a form of geopolitical confrontation with the EU and the United States (Bechev 2017). The Russian strategy of competition reemerged quickly after the adoption of the Foreign Policy Concept in 2013. The policy clearly defined Russia's three crucial foreign policy goals for achieving supremacy at the international level: remaining a nuclear power, remaining a great power, and remaining a regional hegemon. This sort of zero-sum approach has been of utmost importance in Moscow's foreign policy toward the Balkans, as the region is important for maintaining Russian influence and serving as a buffer zone in which Russia is given a dominant position (Aron 2016; Petrillo 2013, 2–3).

Russia has profound relationships with many Western Balkan states, including Montenegro, through strong historical, cultural, and political ties (Šekularac 2017). Strong political and historical connections between the two Slavic countries have been further strengthened since Montenegrin independence, when many Russians invested their funds in developing the post-transition Montenegrin economy (Anderson 2019, 4; Conley and Melino 2019, 4). Consequently, Russia has positioned itself as one of the largest economic investors in Montenegro, in the total amount of 1.3 billion EUR, while around 460 million EUR were invested in fields of metallurgy and services[1] (CSD 2018a, 4; Conley and Melino 2019, 4). Russian influence in this small Adriatic country has also increased through the Russians' purchase of real estate, which has increased property prices on the Montenegrin coast. In fact, Russia has strongly supported Montenegrin tourism, and Russian citizens have become one of the largest groups of travelers to visit Montenegro[2] (CSD 2018a, 1). Russia, however, also took advantage of the Montenegrin state capture. The commercial sectors, such as metallurgy and tourism, dominated by state-owned companies and owned by domestic ruling elites, were susceptible to rent. A number of controversial Russian oligarchs and investors played a major role in purchasing low-level state companies and factories (such was the case with Oleg Deripaska and his plans to invest in the Montenegrin aluminum plant, Kombinat aluminijuma Podgorica). And although profit may have been their primary motive, their investments have also provided Russia with a mechanism of influence (Bechev 2018; CSD 2018a).

Russia uses the opportunities of uneven soft and hard power within broad policy areas to take advantage of the Balkans' political and economic difficulties to expand its influence and potentially diminish regional stability. By using various opportunities, such as the Euro and migration crises, Brexit, and high internal unemployment (consequently tarnishing the Union's image), Russia continuously seeks to leverage its substantial influence by undermining the values of the EU and NATO and their achievements in the Western Balkans (Galeotti 2018; Mujanović 2018; House of Lords of the United Kingdom 2018). The Russian opinion on the Western Balkans is predominately determined by its relations with the West. During the time of the Medvedev presidency, Moscow showed no objections to the NATO enlargement of Albania and Croatia in 2009, while post-Crimea Russia has started observing the region from a zero-sum perspective where a Western gain is a Russian loss (Bechev 2017). Many scholars agree that Russia bears the features of an "opportunistic spoiler." By using the rhetoric of maintaining supposed brotherhood, coupled with a shared sense of victimhood, Russia has underpinned its foreign policy actions and initiatives through strong interference in the regional internal political process and changes. At the same time, it has been reluctant to provide the region an alternative perspective for achieving stability and prosperity compared to Western models (Bechev 2018). Notably, Russia does not have a long-term strategy over the development of relations with the Western Balkans, but its advantages are primarily seen in swift decisions and flexible actions (House of Lords of the United Kingdom 2018). To gain supremacy in the Western Balkan space, and therefore to undermine the credibility of the Alliance and the EU, Russia has used both soft and hard power mechanisms in the form of supporting religious groups, financing political parties and individuals, establishing anti-western media outlets, strengthening political corruption and clientelism, inspiring coups, and so on (Mujanović 2018; Galeotti 2017; European Parliament 2017a; European Western Balkans 2017). At present, Moscow has changed its Western Balkan strategy from a policy-based initiative to taking advantage of divisions within the states (Bechev 2018). Even before the Montenegrin accession to NATO, Russia was reluctant to abandon its plan to revive a Pan-Slavism and unify once again all Slavic countries under its influence. To expand its influence on internal political processes and changes in Montenegro, Russia has predominately supported the actions of the Serbian Orthodox Church in denying Montenegrin statehood and advocated for the campaigns of the opposition party Democratic Front in opposing Montenegrin accession to NATO in 2015 (Coney and Melino 2019; Anderson 2019). In addition, the weak state of the media, where the quality of reporting is low and exposure to political manipulation, fake news, and disinformation are becoming standard, has helped strengthen the Russian propaganda narrative among citizens (Bechev 2017).

In viewing the Western Balkans as its traditional sphere of influence, Russia has strongly opposed NATO enlargement and, in recent years, has opposed the EU integration process as well (Bieber and Tzifakis 2019; House of Lords of the United Kingdom 2018). The relationship between Montenegro and Russia worsened with the Montenegrin decision to align with EU sanctions against Russia following the annexation of Crimea in 2014, and to join NATO on June 5, 2017 (Morrison 2018). As a result, Montenegrin foreign policy acts have been perceived by the Kremlin as hostile and this has been reflected in continuing declining trends in the fields of political and economic cooperation. Prior to NATO admission, Russia continuously and strongly sought to thwart Montenegro's ambitions to join the Alliance. At first, Russia primarily used soft power tools to prevent the state from joining the Alliance. These ranged from (1) strong political accusations disseminated by high-ranking political officials, such as when Russian Deputy Prime Minister Dmitry Rogozin said that Montenegro was going to regret joining NATO, and, surprisingly, from Russian Foreign Minister, Sergey Lavrov, who in March 2017 stated that Montenegro had sacrificed its economic relations with Russia by joining NATO; (2) the Russian Foreign Ministry's warning not to travel to Montenegro, after which Russian state media immediately began running a negative campaign portraying Montenegro as corrupt and insecure (although it's a highly popular holiday destination among Russians); and (3) the banning of Montenegrin wines over alleged hygiene concerns (Coney and Melino 2019; Anderson 2019; CSD 2018a).

The Russian ruling political elite was not reluctant to use hard power means against the small Adriatic state in its efforts to thwart the accession to NATO. The latest in a series of confrontations between two countries occurred in 2016, just a few months before Montenegrin acquisition of full membership in the Alliance, when Montenegro accused Russia of meddling in the 2016 parliamentary election by attempting to overthrow the prime minister and most prominent political figure Milo Đukanović by financially supporting the strongest opposition political party, the Democratic Front (DF) (Bieber 2020; Morrison 2018). Consequently, the Special Prosecutor's Office opened a court case on the coup attempt against some of the DF leaders, several Serbian nationalists, and two Russian military intelligence officers. Based on the testimony of former policeman Mirko Velimirović (who allegedly entered a police station in Podgorica two days before an election) and Aleksandar Sinđelić (a Serbian citizen who allegedly fought for Novorossiya

(New Russia) forces in Eastern Ukraine), a plot was organized to disrupt the elections and to install a pro-Russian government. As a result of their testimony, the police arrested Branislav Dikić, a former member of the Serbian Gendarmerie, nineteen other Serbian citizens, and two high party opposition members of the center-right party Democratic Front, Andrija Mandić and Milan Knežević. They were accused of organizing a criminal terrorist organization in the attempt to stage a coup d'état in which Prime Minister Milo Đukanović would be overthrown from power by an assassination attempt (Morrison 2018, 162–67). The State Prosecutor's Office also filed an indictment against two Russian military intelligence members, Eduard Šišmakov and Vladimir Popov, who were accused of providing operational services for launching a state of coup on polling day. The government held the stance that Russia had been meddling not only in the 2016 election process but also in anti-NATO protests a year before (2015), organized by the pro-Serbian coalition block Democratic Front, calling into question the development of bilateral relations between two states. Although the two Russian and nine Serbian citizens, and two high-ranking party officials of the opposition Democratic Front, were found guilty, little evidence has been provided of Russian meddling in the parliamentary election or its attempt to stage a coup d'état (Gadzo 2019).

Nevertheless, despite the alleged coup initiated by the Russian Government and its use of hard and soft power in undermining security and stability in the country, Montenegro succeeded in joining NATO. While current political tensions exist on both sides, Montenegrin politicians continue to emphasize that they want the best possible relations with Russia, even after the alleged coup orchestrated by Russia (Bieber and Tzifakis 2019). Although the number of investments has halved since the period of gaining independence, the fact remains that Montenegro continues to be dependent on Russian economic support. Montenegro's economic dependency on Russian investments in real estate and tourism opens the real question of the possibility of reducing Russian influence in the country, bearing in mind, of course, the fact that there are more than 250,000 Russian Federation citizens who visit Montenegro each year and a significant number of them own property in the country (Uljarević and Vučković 2014).[3] Meanwhile, Russia continues to strengthen its influence in the country by establishing political party ties with pro-nationalist opposition political parties and by supporting the active involvement of the Serbian Orthodox Church in social conditions and internal political affairs. The strategic presence of Russia and its further influence in the region cannot be ignored, and it might be reasonable to assume, based on past soft and hard power actions, that this great power will continue to undermine the stability of Montenegro during the EU integration process. After all, Montenegro has aligned with the EU's foreign policy actions on imposing sanctions on

Russia since 2014. Objectively speaking, Russian interference in the state's internal political affairs is now only possible through the accession negotiation process, and it represents a good way to destabilize not just Montenegro and the region, but also to produce a spillover effect toward the EU member states (Bechev 2017; Mujanović 2018; Galeotti 2017). Therefore, it might be grounded to expect that further Russian meddling activities will be directed toward strengthening an anti-regime block through providing more financial support to opposition party activities to discredit Montenegro's progress in the accession process, particularly over the rule of law reforms, lobbying, and presenting the state to European institutions as an entity with deeply rooted problems of corruption, organized crime, and politicized judiciary. One must not neglect the fact that Russia was accused by the West of initiating the alleged coup in Montenegro because of its activity in undermining the EU's effort to strengthen peace, security, and stability in the region.

CHINA

Unlike Russia, China relies more on soft power use to increase its influence in Montenegro and in the Balkans. During the past decade, China has managed to strengthen its regional cooperation with the Western Balkans by means of the sub-regional initiative "16+1," consisting of eleven EU member states and five candidate countries. Under the "One belt, One road" initiative (OBOR), China's interests in the Balkans substantially differ from those of Russia. China is not opposed to the EU and NATO enlargement of the Western Balkans, and it mainly uses its economic leverage to enhance its regional influence (Turcsányi 2018; Kavalski 2019; Vangeli 2018; Pavlicevic 2018).

Even before Montenegro held a referendum on independence in 2006, the government decided to carry out the plan to build a 165 km long highway that would connect Montenegro's Port of Bar with Belgrade and then with Budapest and beyond. The "project of the century," as it was often called by high-ranking Montenegrin officials, or more precisely, the highway project Bar-Boljare, including the construction of 41km of the most difficult priority section Smokovac-Uvač-Mataševo, has remained the one and only major Chinese investment project in Montenegro. Due to highly inaccessible hilly terrain, the whole highway route is estimated to cost €2.7 billion, and remains one of the most demanding infrastructure projects in Europe (Grgić 2017, 1).

In terms of the legal aspects of the contract, the Ministry of Transport and Maritime Affairs of Montenegro (MTMAM) and the Embassy of the People's Republic of China signed the *Amendments to the Agreement on Improvement of Cooperation in Infrastructure Construction* on February 14, 2014.[4] The government evaluated an offer by the China Communications Construction Company (CCCC) and its subsidiary the China Road and Bridge Cooperation (CRBS) as highly ranked, thus opening the door for signing the *Contract for Bar-Boljare Highway Section* on February 26, 2014. Shortly after, the government and CRBC signed the *Preferential Buyer Credit Loan Agreement on Bar-Boljare Highway Section Smokovac-Matašević Construction Project* on October 30, 2014, and the *Law on Highway Bar-Boljare* on December 12, 2014, consequently creating conditions to further intensify economic cooperation between the two parties. Based on the loan agreement, CHEXIM Bank provided a loan of US $943,991 million (or €688.16 million) to MTMAM to construct a highway priority section; this represents 85% of the highway's value. Out of the total amount of €809.58 million, the remaining 15% (around €120) million is to be provided from the state budget. The repayment period is set at twenty years with an interest rate of 2% and with a six-year grace period. The construction period would take four years, and the contractor agreed that 30% of the sub-contractors employed in the construction areas would be domestic (Zakon o autoputu Bar-Boljare 2014; Ugovor o preferencijalnom zajmu za kupca za Projekat izgradnje autoputa Bar-Boljare, dionica Smokovac-Mateševo 2014; Ugovor o projektovanju i izgradnji autoputa Bar-Boljare dionica Smokovac-Uvač-Mateševo 2014).

The whole infrastructure project, especially the signed arrangements regarding the construction of the highway priority section, remains controversial. Primarily, the credit agreement contains legal provisions which oblige the government to provide financial guarantees for compulsory repayment of loans in the event they are not paid on time. In the case of nonfulfillment of financial obligations by the state, an arbitration procedure is foreseen. This being said, potential disputes between creditor and borrower open the clear possibility for both parties to submit the "dispute to arbitration to the China International Economic and Trade Arbitration Commission (CIETAC)" in Beijing, agreeing that any "arbitration decision will be final and binding on both sides" (Zakon o autoputu Bar-Boljare 2014, Article 8.5). Moreover, in the event of a potential dispute, the government agreed to relinquish its immunity in regards to its sovereignty or in any other way for itself or its property, with the exception of diplomatic and consular representations and military properties, while the rights and obligations of the parties to the contract would be governed and interpreted in accordance with the laws of China (Zakon o autoputu Bar-Boljare 2014, Article 8.1).

For the sake of argument, the defined credit conditions to a greater extent satisfy the financial needs of CHEXIM Bank and the Chinese state-run company CRBS, consequently allowing them full financial protection of debt repayment throughout state guarantees. The arbitration process remains highly controversial primarily in the context of the manner and place of arbitration proceedings. Obviously, the legal provision clearly emphasized the fact that the potential inability of the borrower to repay the debt defines a plausible possibility for an arbitration procedure in China and based on the Chinese legal system. Therefore, hypothetically speaking, if CIETAC makes a binding decision not in favor of the borrower, Montenegro will, to satisfy the state guarantees, abandon its own sovereignty on property in parts of its own territory, except foreign diplomatic, consular, and military properties. However, it remains unclear whether CIETAC can freely and independently make a decision that will not (potentially) favor China? In addition to the major problem of the recklessness of state guarantees regarding debt payments, the government pledged to return the loan in US dollars and not in euros. The state also failed to establish a set currency exchange rate between the US dollar and the euro, which created the possibility that Montenegrin citizens would have to repay even greater debt if the US dollar changed its monetary value in the future (Zakon o autoputu Bar-Boljare 2014, Article 2.1). In hindsight, the government did not protect itself and its citizens from currency risk when it "hedged" its foreign currency debt (and signed the loan in US dollars), that is, it failed to lock in the currency rate on the day of signing the loan agreement (Vijesti 2015). As a consequence, the problem of exchange rates is already increasing the cost of the highway. In February 2019, after almost three and a half years since the beginning of the highway construction, the drop in the value of the euro against the dollar has increased the highway debt by €57 million (RTCG 2014). This credit arrangement places increased pressure on public finances, increasing public debt to more than 75% of the GDP. Perhaps far more importantly, the arrangement jeopardizes Montenegro's main foreign policy priority: accession to the EU.

International financial experts have warned that China has a clear strategy for how to make poor and insufficiently economically developed countries dependent on Chinese credit loans, drawing them into a debt relationship that is very difficult to get out of. The fact that Montenegro is not a solitary case (although it is the only European state that agreed to the abovementioned loan conditions), indeed there are other Asian and African countries that have signed similar infrastructure loan arrangements with China in the past, makes the problem of high public debt even more worrisome. Washington's Center for Global Development identified eight countries of particular concern that could suffer from debt distress due to One Road-One Belt-related financing, namely Djibouti, Kyrgyzstan, Laos, the Maldives, Mongolia, Pakistan, Tajikistan, and Montenegro. Interestingly, these experts in economic opportunity claim that CHEXIM Bank is a common creditor to all of the abovementioned countries, consequently resulting in a high risk of debt distress due to additional One Road-One Belt credit financing (CSD 2018b). However, the proposed Chinese credit arrangements are not a novelty in international politics. At the outset, those loans which seem to be very easy to return as so-called "soft credits" actually present a hazard for the countries that take them out. Some states have even lost their main strategic positions due to their inability to repay loans provided by CHEXIM Bank. The cases of Kenya, which lost its harbors, DR Congo, which lost its cobalt mines, and Uganda, which built 51 km of highway (much like the case of Montenegro) and was not able to repay the loans to the creditor, confirm that Montenegro may be faced with a similar confiscation of its valuable properties by China if the state is not able to pay off its debts (TV Vijesti 2019).

The Chinese state-run companies (CCCC and CRBC) seem to be ruthless in detecting the weaknesses of the infrastructure contract(s), thereby further raising the amount of the debt foreseen in the original loan agreement. This being said, according to official state data, the state has already lost around €27 million over the past three years due to tax benefits for the main contractor, CBRC, especially in tax exemptions and payroll contributions, customs duties on imports of goods, and a refund of part of the excise duty paid (Vijesti 2018). Also, due to the state's failure to properly outline its "main infrastructure project" (it forgot to include the construction of Smokovac loop, electricity and water supply networks, and removal of transmission lines) in the official highway agreement, the government agreed to provide an additional €30 million (by signing an annexation agreement), and at the same time refused to start an arbitration process as originally announced (FOS Media 2019). And finally, if we include the costs arising from the lack of a fixed exchange rate and the decline in the value of the euro (estimated at around €57 million and which come into play in July 2021), it is very easy to calculate that the Montenegrin debt will increase by an additional €100 million.

For the very same reasons, this highway project has been the subject of interest and debate in the EU for last couple of years, primarily due to China's intentions to strengthen their influence in the Western Balkan region through the OBOR initiative, especially in Montenegro (and Serbia)—a regional front-runner in the EU accession process with a credible membership perspective to join the Union by 2025. Data reveals that the public debt will increase to a staggering 74% of Montenegro's GDP by the end of construction of the highway priority section. The International Monetary Fund (IMF) noted clearly that the state's "decision to build the first highway phase and the approval in 2016 of an ill targeted and costly mothers' benefit and large public-sector wage increases increased the deficit, and government debt reached 74 percent of GDP in 2016" (IMF 2018, 13). The EU in its annual progress report emphasizes that "given the high levels of public debt, its repayment profile and the tightening of global financial conditions, it is essential to rebalance the budget structure towards growth-enhancing spending and to continue fiscal consolidation efforts (European Commission 2018b, 42)." As a result, there is a clear risk of Montenegro not being able to align with the EU standards of an acceptable level of public debt before joining the Union, forcing the government to increase taxes, freeze the public sector, and seize the social benefits for mothers with three or more children to strengthen its financial position (European Commission 2019, 5). Montenegro's debt has created an asymmetrical relationship between the state and China, and it has consequently positioned itself in a subordinate role, being significantly dependent on Chinese loans and their willingness to finish the remaining highway sections. "There is a big question about how they complete it," said an EU official who wanted to remain anonymous "Their fiscal space has shrunk enormously. They have strangled themselves. And for the time being this is a highway to nowhere" (Noah and Vasovic 2018).

Nevertheless, Chinese investments are more than welcome in the Western Balkans, including in Montenegro. By providing loans to the Western Balkan countries, Chinese companies are visibly present on the Montenegrin market and are competitive with domestic firms in reconstructing and building highways, roads, tunnels, and bridges (Benner and Gaspers and Ohlberg and Poggetti, and Shi-Kupfer 2018; Hurley and Morris and Portelance 2018). Hence, it is not surprising that Sino-Montenegrin relations have been substantially emphasized as "traditionally good and brotherly," and the construction of highways is seen as a "symbol of friendship" (FOS Media 2017). Obviously, improvement in the bilateral relations between the two states remains a consequence of Chinese involvement in the CEE through its regional "16+1" initiative, which shows Montenegro to be a reliable partner within the area of regional economic cooperation development. Moreover, such extraordinary bilateral political relations have also had a visible impact on Montenegro's outlook on the issue of Chinese sovereignty, principally supporting the politics of "One China." Still, it is no wonder why Milo Đukanović quite clearly expressed the possibility to support a policy of alternatives (instead of opportunities), and therefore cooperation with China, by noting that if the EU "wants to be faster than China, and be faster than the others, she has to provide her offer package, and to be consistent in realization and vision of United Europe and not debating as we have witnessed in previous years" (RTCG 2018). This statement from the president of Montenegro is not surprising at all, as the choice of policy of alternatives has been beneficial for the semi-authoritarian ruling elites. China's commercial involvement in Montenegro has been appreciated by domestic ruling elites because it has provided a substantial infrastructure loan despite rejections of credit from the West, and, perhaps far more importantly, those policies do not interfere in internal political processes nor do they threaten the political legitimacy of the domestic ruling elites. This kind of Montenegrin economic development policy is of special importance to China, because the latter is aware that the former will join EU one day, and it will be in a position to lobby for Chinese political interests.

In the end, it is important to highlight that the economic and political consequences of the infrastructure "project of the century" are enormous. The state still has not issued the "main project of the priority section Smokovac-Matešević" almost 45 months since the official start of the highway construction (Monitor 2019). Additionally, the highway is already two years late and, according to state official statements, the 41 km priority section won't be officially opened until the end of September 2021.[5] Regardless of the highway building dynamics, loan installments are slowly coming due, which means that Montenegro will begin repaying €66.4 million monthly for the next fourteen years, beginning in July 2021. The open question still remains how Montenegro will repay its obligation to China due to high public debt, but perhaps far more importantly, whether the (potential) Chinese seizure of strategic state property, such as Port of Bar, hydroelectric and thermal power plants, attractive coastal areas, and so on, will satisfy Beijing's current foreign policy appetites. Finally, with an additional debt of around €100 million merely for a short section of highway, it remains unclear whether and when the government will finish the remaining 126 km of the highway connecting northern Montenegro with the border of Serbia. Hence, the question remains how the state will get the remainder of funds needed to complete the remaining highway sections. One solution could be another Chinese loan. Another solution is seen in building the highway through a public-private partnership. Regardless of the final outcome, one thing is more than clear. Montenegro has entered into a "highway adventure" without much knowledge or thoughtfulness about the feasibility of the project, leaving their citizens to pay the price.

INSUFFICIENT INTERPLAY OF THE EU-DOMESTIC FACTORS AND THE INFLUENCE OF RUSSIA AND CHINA AS UNDERMINING ACTORS

Based on the provided theoretical argumentations and empirical explanations, it might be grounded to conclude that the interplay of domestic and EU factors in addressing political accession criteria is not sufficient to fully explain why the Union has failed to Europeanize Montenegro in the EU integration process. Without question, Schimmelfennig and Sedelmeier's theoretical concept has provided valuable and credible insights on the process of adopting EU rules and norms by the nonmember states by focusing on two levels of interaction—the EU externally driven pressure and the domestic response. In particular, it has revealed that the Union's impact on domestic changes in

Montenegro has resulted in the country's lack of willingness to align with the EU's demands, Brussel's inconsistency and ineffectiveness, and the low quality of legal and institutional changes introduced.

However, Schimmelfennig and Sedelmeier's theoretical framework has a limited explanatory scope on the question of why the EU has had a negative reinforcing impact on empowering judicial reform and combating corruption and a positive reinforcing impact on empowering regional cooperation in Montenegro. Obviously, the current theoretical framework contains visible loopholes in the existing argumentation through the lack of applicability of logic of Europeanization of the CEE countries to the Western Balkans case, by failing to address the existence and influence of other international factors in undermining the process of adoption of the EU acquis and policy alignment. It particularly omits the very important argument that the effective fulfillment of the EU political accession criteria does not solely depend on the interdependency of the EU and domestic factors, but it also depends in large part on other international factors, specifically the influence of other great powers. Moreover, based on Mearsheimer's theory of offensive realism and its concept of competition between great powers in the desire for hegemony, the Russian and Chinese attempts to maintain geopolitical influence in the Western Balkans region, including Montenegro, at the expense of other states, can be seen as an important contribution to the scientific literature on Europeanization and further development of the existing theoretical framework. It is quite clear that the profound influence Russia has had on the internal political affairs in Montenegro and the entire region can be seen as another valuable empirical explanation for why the state has failed to effectively comply with the EU requirements. The impact of Russia in the region, seeing as its traditionally sphere of influence is undoubtedly powerful, combined with the effects of using both hard and soft power mechanisms, have undermined regional stability and therefore the stability of the EU itself. At the same time, it has consequently affected Montenegro's ability to assume the obligation of EU membership in the near future. On the other hand, Chinese influence in Montenegro in recent years has been leveraged through the use of economic soft power and its continuous investments in infrastructure projects, keeping the state's doors open to further economic growth. However, this format has been criticized by the Union, which emphasizes that economic cooperation remains controversial due to conflicts with EU law and erosion of EU norms and values.

Although the EU has not effectively imposed overall domestic changes, it is quite clear that the Union's externally driven initiatives have led to some visible results in judicial reform, particularly in judicial effectiveness and efficiency, during the integration phase. Additionally, externally driven pressure has convinced the candidate country to align itself with the SAP conditions by actively promoting regional cooperation through its full commitment to regional peace and stability and development of good neighborly relations. Compared to other international factors, the EU has continued to be a major driving force in the overall reform process in Montenegro, thus resulting in positive changes in rule of law, human and minority rights, regional cooperation, and the market economy. Therefore, it might be reasonable to conclude that the state has shifted in its approach to adopting the acquis and aligning with the EU policies primarily due to the fact that Montenegro and its society now identify with EU values and norms, as well as due to a lack of alternatives in the form of external incentives provided by other international factors.

CONCLUSION

The research outcomes over the presented theoretical and empirical discussions have revealed three major conclusions that serve as valuable starting points for further developments of Europeanization research area. First, based on the empirical results, this study has argued that the EU has failed to Europeanize Montenegro, especially in the fields of judicial reform and the fight against corruption during the whole integration phase. The Union has particularly had a negatively reinforcing impact on strengthening the Montenegrin judiciary and the corresponding anti-corruption policy framework. This is a product of the interplay between the Union and unfavorable domestic conditions, and results in overall negative reinforcing effects.

Second, the study has concluded that the effective adoption and alignment with the EU accession demands does not solely depend on the interdependency of the EU and domestic factors, but rather it also substantially depends on the influence of other international factors, namely the influence of Russia and China in the Western Balkans. Following the improved theoretical argumentation, the empirical findings have shown that the strong influence of Russia in Montenegro and in the whole region, through its interference into internal political affairs, remains one of the most important factors that substantially undermines the state's compliance with the EU requirements. By using various soft and hard power means, Russia seeks to destabilize the states of the region by producing the same spillover destabilizing effects aimed at the EU member states as well. The case of Montenegro and Russian active involvement in the process of undermining the stability of the country, which is the front-runner in the EU accession process, has proved this claim. On the other hand, it might be grounded to argue that Montenegro's opportunity to cooperate with other international actors such as China, a power in the region that does not threaten the political legitimacy of the domestic ruling elites or interfere in internal political affairs, has significantly dampened the enthusiasm for advancement in the EU accession process among the domestic political leaders. Thus, the state's ability to choose between the policies of alternatives and of opportunities may be one of the explanatory factors for why the domestic political elites have demonstrated continuous unwillingness to effectively address the Copenhagen political criteria. As a result, the EU has been faced with highly problematic Europeanization of Montenegro during the entire accession process.

The third and last conclusion stems from the applied theoretical approach. It reveals that the Europeanization theory as presented by Schimmelfennig and Sedelmeier is not fully applicable to the complex processes in the Western Balkans. It requires additional academic attention in redefining current theoretical concepts so as to be properly adjusted to specific Western Balkans circumstances and conditions. Therefore, new theoretical concepts assume that the interplay between the EU, domestic and international factors for adopting the EU acquis and alignment with the EU policies by nonmember states represents an important contribution in regards to filling the existing research gap in the appropriate academic scholarship, particularly in the fields of European integration and EU studies alike. Also, it may serve as a solid starting point regarding the theoretical basis for redefining the existing framework and developing new scientific knowledge in the area of Western Balkan politics.

NOTES

1. For the sake of the argument, controversial Russian businessman Oleg Deripaska bought Aluminum Plant in Podgorica (AKP) in 2005, a biggest state-owned company in Montenegro which provided around 15% of Montenegrin GDP. For more details, Conley and Melino (2019).
2. Representing around 25% of total Montenegrin tourism.
3. Russian investments in the Montenegrin economy have been significantly reduced in recent years from 29.4% of total revenue in 2006 to 5.5% in 2015. For more details: http://www.csd.bg/artShow.php?id=18131.
4. This Agreement was considered as a starting point for the legalization of activities regarding the realization of the highway priority section.
5. The highway project started on May 11, 2015, and was supposed to be finished on May 11, 2019.

Appendix 1

Judicial Reform in Montenegro

Normative and empirical analysis of EU—Montenegro documents for the 2006–2017 period

Top-down Approach					*Bottom-up Approach*		
Date	*Body/Document*	*Recommendation(s)*	*Deadline*	*Final Realization*	*Measure(s)/Activity*	*Government`s Evaluation*[1]	*Researcher`s Evaluation*[2]
8.11.2006	**2006 MNE Progress Report**	1-Establishment of strategy of judicial reform	2007	June 2007	1.1-Judicial Reform Strategy 2007-2012 (JRS)	Realized	Realized
	2006-2007 EU enlargement strategy -	2-Political influence of Parliament in judiciary	2007	27.12.2007	2.1-Action Plan for Implementation of the Justice Reform Strategy 2007–2012		
			2008	27.3.2008	2.2-Commission for the Implementation of the Action Plan		
	European Commission	3-Strengthening legislative and institutional framework of judicial efficiency and effectiveness		27.4.2006	3.1-Law on Judicial Education	Realized	Realized
17.1.2007	Council of the EU	**European Partnership**		17.5.2007	**Action Plan for Implementation of the European Partnership**	Realized	Partly Realized
		Short-term priorities: 1.1-Adoption of new Constitution	2007–2009	19.10.2007	1.1.1-Constitution	Realized	Partly Realized
		1.2-Finalize plans to reform the judicial system	2007–2009	June 2007 27.12.2007 28.3.2008	1.2.1-JRS 1.2.2-Action Plan for Implementation of the JRS 1.2.3-Commission for the Implementation of the Action Plan	Realized	Realized

1.3-Remove control of recruitment and career management from Parliament and establish transparent procedures	2007–2009		1.3.1-Measure has not been achieved		Unrealized
1.4-Sustainable financing for judicial system	2007–2009	2.4.2008	1.4.1-Amendments on the Law on Courts	Realized	Realized
		27.6.2008	-Amendments on the Law on State Prosecutors	Realized	Realized
		15.6.2007	-Law on salaries and other income of judicial office holders and the rules and procedure for the State Prosecutor`s Office	Realized	Realized
1.5-Provide guarantees to strengthen the autonomy and efficiency of the prosecution system, including budget issues	2007–2009	27.6.2008	1.5.1-Amendments on the Law on State Prosecutors	Realized	Realized
		15.6.2007	-Law on salaries and other income of judicial office holders and the rules and procedure for the State Prosecutor`s Office	Realized	Realized

(Continued)

Top-down Approach			Bottom-up Approach				
Date	*Body/Document*	*Recommendation(s)*	*Deadline*	*Final Realization*	*Measure(s)/Activity*	*Government`s Evaluation*[1]	*Researcher`s Evaluation*[2]
		2.1-Rationalization and modernization of court system	2007–2009	2.4.2008	2.1.1-Amendments to the Law on Courts	Realized	Partly Realized
				27.06.2008	-Amendments on the Law on State Prosecutors	Realized	Realized
				18.8.2009	-Criminal Procedure Code (CPC)	Realized	Realized
				13.12.2007	-Law on protection of the right to a trial within a reasonable time	Realized	Realized
	Medium-term priorities	3.1-Training of judges, prosecutors, and court staff and strengthening JTC	2007–2009	IQ2007	3.1.1-Published the brochure "Law on Judicial Education"	Realized	Realized
				IQ2007	-Adoption of the Training Program for Judges and Prosecutors and Associates for 2007	Realized	Realized
				IVQ2007	-Implementation of the Training Program for Judges and Prosecutors and Associates for 2007	Realized	Realized
		1.1-Completion of strategic framework of judiciary	2012	2012	1.1.1-Implementation of JRS	Realized	Partly Realized

1.2-Implementation of reform plans	2012	2012	1.2.1-Implementation of JRS	Realized	Partly Realized
	2009	1.9.2011	1.2.2-Implementation of CPC	Realized	Realized
1.3-Implementation of transparent recruitment and career management procedures	IV 2008	2.4.2008	1.3.1-Amendments to the Law on Courts	Partly Realized	Partly Realized
	V 2008	27.6.2008	1.3.2-Amendments to the Law on State Prosecutors	Partly Realized	Partly Realized
2.1-Upgrading the sources of prosecutor system	IIIQ 2008	27.6.2008	2.1.1-Amendments to Law on State Prosecutors	Realized	Realized
	2012	2011	-Implementation of CPC	Realized	Realized
	2012	2012	2.1.2-Implementation of JRS	Realized	Partly Realized
3.1-Functioning of JTC and implementation of IT strategy	Continuous	Continuous	3.1.1-Engagement of foreign experts in education of judges and prosecutors	Realized	Realized
	2012	2012	3.1.2-Implementation of Judicial Strategy Reform which contains special IT strategy	Realized	Partly Realized
3.2-Upgrading the source of judicial system	2012	2012	3.2.1- Implementation of JRS	Realized	Partly Realized
	2010	2011	3.2.2-Establishment of an audio-video recording of court proceedings in all courts	Partly Realized	Partly Realized

(Continued)

Top-down Approach					Bottom-up Approach		
Date	Body/Document	Recommendation(s)	Deadline	Final Realization	Measure(s)/Activity	Government`s Evaluation[1]	Researcher`s Evaluation[2]
6.11.2007	**2007 MNE Progress Report 2007–2008 EU Enlargement Strategy** - European Commission	1.1-Political influence of the Parliament over judiciary through the appointment of Judicial Council	2007	19.10.2007	1.1.1-Constitution	Realized	Partly Realized
			IQ 2008		-Law on Judicial Council		
		1.2-Appointment of Prosecutorial Council by parliament	I-IIIQ 2008	28.2.2008	1.1.2-Establishment of Judicial and Prosecutorial Councils	Realized	Partly Realized
			IQ 2008	19.4.2008	1.2.1-Amendments to the Law on State Prosecutors	Partly Realized	Partly Realized
		1.3-Appointments, promotions, disciplinary proceedings and dismissal of judges and prosecutors	2007	30.8.2008	1.3.1-Adoption of Constitution	Realized	Unrealized
			IQ 2008	27.6.2008	1.3.2-Law on Judicial Council	Realized	Realized
			IIIQ 2008		-Amendments to the Law on Courts		
			I-IIIQ 2008		-Rules of Procedure of the Judicial Council		
			IQ 2008		-Commission for appointment, and 36 judges elected		
			I-IIIQ 2008	19.10.2007	1.3.3-Amendments the Law on State Prosecutors	Realized	Partly Realized
			IIQ 2008		-Rules of Procedure of the Prosecutorial Council		
					-Commission for appointment elected		
		2.1-Serious concern over backlog in both civil and criminal cases	Continuous	28.2.2008	2.1.1-Law on Obligations	Realized	Partly Realized

IQ 2008	2.4.2008	2.1.2-Implementation of the Law on protection of the right to a trial within a reasonable time	Realized	Partly Realized
		-Establishment of records of claims for fair satisfaction in the Supreme Court provided special provision in budget for paying a fair amount of satisfaction	Realized	Partly Realized
IQ 2008	29.3.2008	2.1.3-Draft on Amendments to the Law on Notaries	Realized	Partly Realized
	27.6.2008 1.9.2009	-Rulebook on the number of places and offices of the notaries	Realized	Realized
	7.8.2008 Continuous	-Rulebook on the method and program for the notary examination	Realized	Realized
IQ 2008 and continuously	20082008	2.1.4-Establishment of the Mediation Centre	Realized	Unrealized
	Continuous	2.1.5-Annual framework for dealing with backlog cases established	Realized	Realized
	28.2.2008 27.6.2008 2.4.2008	-1,500 cases from the Basic Court in Podgorica were delegated to other courts that are less burdened with a backlog of cases	Realized	Realized

(*Continued*)

Top-down Approach			*Bottom-up Approach*				
Date	*Body/Document*	*Recommendation(s)*	*Deadline*	*Final Realization*	*Measure(s)/Activity*	*Government`s Evaluation*[1]	*Researcher`s Evaluation*[2]
		2.2-Insufficient career development rules	IQ 2008	29.3.2008	2.2.1-Law on Judicial Council	Partly Realized	Unrealized
			I Q 2008 III Q 2008		-Amendments on the State Prosecutors	Partly Realized	Unrealized
			I-IIIQ 2008		-Amendments to the Law on Courts	Partly Realized	Unrealized
					-Rule of Procedures of the Judicial Council	Partly Realized	Unrealized
		2.3-Prosecutors realized in representing the state in property and legal matters	IQ 2008	20.3.2009	2.3.1-Law on State Property	Partly Realized	Partly Realized
5.11.2008	**2008 MNE Progress Report 2008-2009 EU Enlargement Strategy** -European Commission	1.1-Political influence of the Parliament through the appointment of Prosecutorial Council			1.1.1-Measure has not been achieved		Unrealized
		1.2-Risk of judicial independence through the participation of the Ministry of Justice as voting member in the Judicial Council			1.2.1-Measure has not been achieved		Unrealized
		2.1-Improvement Code of Ethnic			2.1.1-Code of Ethics of Judges		
			IVQ 2008	26.7.2008	2.1.2-Commission for monitoring the implementation of the Judicial Code of Ethics within the Judicial Council	Realized	Realized
			IVQ 2009 Continuous	2009 Continuous	2.1.3-No violation of the Code of Ethics by the judges and prosecutors and deputy prosecutors in 2008 and 2009	Realized	Realized

		3.1-High number of pending cases and excessively lengthy procedures	IQ 2008	15.8.2008	3.1.1-Amendments to the Law on Notaries	Realized	Realized
			Continuous	Continuous	3.1.2-Annual framework programs of backlog cases	Realized	Realized
			IVQ 2008	December 2008	3.1.3-Analysis of implementation of the Law on Enforcement Procedure	Realized	Realized
		4.1- Properly conducting initial and continuous training programs	Continuous	Continuous	4.1.1-Focus on continuous trainings on CPC and European Convention of Human Rights	Realized Realized	Partly Realized Realized
14.10.2009	**2009 MNE Progress Report 2009-2010 EU Enlargement Strategy** -European Commission	1.1-Appointment of Prosecutorial Council and appointment and dismissal of State Prosecutor by parliament			1.1.1-Measure has not been achieved		Unrealized
		1.2-Unclear division of responsibility for supervision of the courts between the Ministry of Justice and Judicial Counci			1.2.1-Measure has not been achieved		Unrealized
		1.3-Participation of the Minister of Justice as a member of the Judicial Council			1.3.1-Measure has not been achieved		Unrealized
					1.4.1-Measure has not been achieved		Unrealized

(Continued)

Top-down Approach			*Bottom-up Approach*				
Date	*Body/Document*	*Recommendation(s)*	*Deadline*	*Final Realization*	*Measure(s)/Activity*	*Government`s Evaluation*[1]	*Researcher`s Evaluation*[2]
		1.4-Election and dismissal of the president of the Judicial Council by parliament 2.1-Inefficient judicial enforcement procedures and lengthy court procedures	2009	2010	2.1.1-Law on Enforcement and Security of Claims is in the parliamentary procedure	Partly Realized	Unrealized
		2.2-Allocation of cases in courts that needs to be implemented and computerized	Continuous	Continuous	2.2.1-PRIS was introduced in 2010 as a complete and functional information system within the judicial bodies	Realized	Realized
		2.3-Improvement of reliability of court data as well as the introduction of a computerized case management system in all courts	IQ 2010	17.3.2010	2.3.1-Law on Information Security	Realized	Realized
			IIQ I-IIQ 2008	2010	2.3.2-Introduction of PRIS in the state prosecutor's offices	Realized	Partly Realized
			Continuous	Continuous	2.3.3-Centralization of data, the entry of existing data, and their regular update	Realized	Partly Realized
			Continuous	Continuous	2.3.4-Reduction of backlog of cases in the State Prosecutor's offices	Partly Realized	Partly Realized
		3.1-Conducting training programs to prepare the prosecution service for its role in the pre-trial procedure under the new CPC	Continuous	13-14.9.2010	3.1.1-Organized topic entitled "Implementation of the new CPC, amendments to CPC and challenges in practice"	Realized	Realized

9.11.2010	**Commission Opinion on Montenegro`s application for membership of the EU** **2010–2011 EU Enlargement Strategy** -European Commission			17.2.2011	**1.Action Plan of Monitoring Recommendations from the Opinion of the European Commission** - Ministry of Foreign Affairs and European Integration		
				1.3.2012	**2.Annual Report on Realization of Measures from the Action Plan for the Implementation of the Judicial Reform Strategy 2007–2012 for 2011-** Government of Montenegro		
		1.1-Appointments of members of the judicial and prosecutorial councils and of state prosecutors, and reinforcement of the independence, autonomy of judges and prosecutors	IIQ 2011	3.6.2011	1.1.1-Draft amendments to the Constitution 1.1.2-Amendments to the Law on Judicial Council -Rules of Procedures of the Judicial Council	Realized	Unrealized

(Continued)

Top-down Approach			*Bottom-up Approach*				
Date	*Body/Document*	*Recommendation(s)*	*Deadline*	*Final Realization*	*Measure(s)/Activity*	*Government`s Evaluation*[1]	*Researcher`s Evaluation*[2]
			IQ 2011	4.8.2011 30.11.2011 15.7.2011	-Commission for appointment of judges	Realized	Realized
					1.1.3-Amendments to the Law on State Prosecution Office	Realized	Realized
					-Rules of Procedure of the Prosecutorial Council	Realized	Realized
		2.1-Reinforcement of the accountability of judges and prosecutors	IIQ 2011	4.8.2011	2.1.1-Amendments to the Law on Judicial Council	Realized	Realized
			IIQ 2011	4.11.2011	-Disciplinary Commission	Realized	Realized
				4.8.2011	-Commission for monitoring implementation of the code of ethics for judges	Realized	Realized
			IIQ 2011	28.4.2011	2.1.2-Amendments to the Law on Courts	Realized	Realized
			IIQ 2011	10.10.2011	2.1.3-Amendments to the Law on State Prosecution Office	Realized	Realized
				4.8.2011	-Disciplinary Commission	Realized	Realized
				22.7.2011 2011 2011	-Commission for monitoring implementation of the code of ethics for prosecutors	Realized Realized Realized	Realized Realized Realized

3.1-Reinforcement of the effectiveness of judges and prosecutors	IIQ 2011	27.7.2011	3.1.1-Law on Enforcement and Security of Claims	Realized	Realized
			-Amendments to the CPC	Realized	Realized
	IIQ 2011	22.06.2011	3.1.2-Appointement of notaries and establishment of Notary Chamber	Realized	Realized
	IVQ 2008	29.04.2011	3.1.3-Effective alternative settlement of disputes	Realized	Realized
	Continuous	Continuous	3.1.4-Annual programs for solving backlog of cases	Realized	Partly Realized
4.1-Reinforcement of the efficiency of judges and prosecutors	Continuous	Continuous	4.1.1-Judicial Information System (PRIS) started being operational	Realized	Partly Realized
	Continuous	1.1.2010	4.1.2-Established the web portal of courts: www .sudovi.me	Realized	Realized
	Continuous	Continuous	4.1.3-Annual training program of continuous education of judges and prosecutors	Realized	Partly Realized
	Continuous	Continuous			

(Continued)

Top-down Approach				Bottom-up Approach			
Date	Body/Document	Recommendation(s)	Deadline	Final Realization	Measure(s)/Activity	Government`s Evaluation[1]	Researcher`s Evaluation[2]
12.10.2011	**2011 MNE Progress Report 2011–2012 EU Enlargement Strategy** - European Commission			25.4.2012	**1.1-Annex to Report to European Commission on Montenegro's Progress for 2012—for a period of September 1, 2011–April 25, 2012**		
29.06.2012	**Resolution which refers to 2011 Progress Report on Montenegro** -European Parliament			6.9.2012.	**1.2-Annex to Report to European Commission on Montenegro`s Progress for 2012—for the period of April 25, 2012–September 1, 2012** - Ministry of Foreign Affairs and European Integration		
		1.1-Appointment of the Supreme Court President and the Supreme State of the Prosecutor by the parliament by simple majority -Appointment of the judges Constitutional Court in line with European standards -Limited mandates of the Supreme State Prosecutor and the Heads of Prosecutors` Offices remain problematic		28.5.2012	1.1.1-Draft Amendments to the Constitution of Montenegro -Draft of Constitutional Law for the Implementation of the Amendments to the Constitution of Montenegro	Realized	Unrealized

1.2-Merit-based elements of the career system need to be substantially strengthened and a country-wide single recruitment system remains to be established	IIQ 2011	30.11.2011	1.2.1-Rules of Procedure of the Judicial Council	Realized	Partly Realized
		19.9.2011	-Commission for the written test for the candidates who have been appointed as judges for the first time - Judicial Council on 21 February 2012 appointed 1 judge in Constitutional Court, 4 judges of Higher Courts, and 1 judge in Basic Court	Realized	Partly Realized
	IIQ 2011	4.11.2011	1.2.2-Rules of Procedure of the Prosecutorial Council -Introduced the proposal for the appointment of 3 state prosecutors and 9 deputy state prosecutors in 2012 based on new criteria within the recruitment system	Realized	Partly Realized

(Continued)

Top-down Approach					*Bottom-up Approach*		
Date	*Body/Document*	*Recommendation(s)*	*Deadline*	*Final Realization*	*Measure(s)/Activity*	*Government`s Evaluation*[1]	*Researcher`s Evaluation*[2]
		2.1-Insufficient monitoring of judiciary in corruption and conflict of interest	Continuous	2012	2.1.1-Disciplinary Commission launched a disciplinary procedure against 1 judge, and only 1 disciplinary measure/warning was imposed -No disciplinary procedures have been launched against prosecutors	Realized	Partly Realized
		2.2-Comprehensive protection of judges and prosecutors within the functional immunity	Continuous	Continuous	2.2.1-Measure has not been achieved	Realized	Unrealized
		2.3-Devoting more attention to the issue of publicity of court rulings			2.3.1-Introduction of the website: www.sudovi.me		Realized
		3.1-Weak enforcement of civil decision and long duration of court proceedings	IIQ 2009	23.11.2011	3.1.1-Law on Public Bailiffs; -Rules of Procedure on number of seats and official headquarters of public bailiff -Rules of Procedure of the form and content of official legitimation of public bailiffs and deputy public bailiffs		Realized

		3.2-Streamlining the courts system 4.1-Training of judges and prosecutors, i.e., the lack of permanent mandatory courses and set curricula		- Rule of Procedure on the work of public bailiff 3.2.1-Measure has not been achieved 4.1.1-Measure has not been achieved	Realized	Unrealized Unrealized
22.5.2012	**Report from the Commission to the European Parliament and the Council on Montenegro`s Progress in the Implementation of Reforms** -European Commission	1.1-De-politicised and merit-based appointments of members of the judicial and prosecutorial councils and of state prosecutors as well as the independence and autonomy of judges and prosecutors 1.2-Reinforcement of accountability of judges and prosecutors 1.3-Reinforcement of effectiveness of judges and prosecutors	8.3.2012	**1.1-Annex to the European Commission’s Spring Report on meeting the 7 key priorities for the period September 1, 2011–March 1, 2012** -Ministry of Foreign Affairs and European Integration Note: all the reform activities conducted by the Montenegrin state bodies in 2012 are presented in documents: -Annex to Report to European Commission on Montenegro`s Progress for 2012—for		

(*Continued*)

Top-down Approach					Bottom-up Approach		
Date	Body/Document	Recommendation(s)	Deadline	Final Realization	Measure(s)/Activity	Government`s Evaluation[1]	Researcher`s Evaluation[2]
		1.4.-Reinforcement of efficiency of judges and prosecutors			the period of September 1, 2011–April 25, 2012 -Annex to Report to European Commission on Montenegro`s Progress for 2012—for the period of April 25, 2012–September 1, 2012		
12.11. 2012 10.10.2012	-European Parliament **2013 Progress Report on Montenegro** **The EU Enlargement Strategy 2013–2014** -	1.1-Montenegro should amend its Constitution ensuring independence and accountability of the judiciary -The Judicial Council and the Prosecutorial Council should be composed by at least 50% of members stemming from the judiciary and selected by the Councils -Prosecutors should not be appointed by the Parliament -Reasons for dismissal of judges and prosecutors should be included in the Constitution	July 2013	27.6.2013	**1. Action Plan for Chapter 23 Judiciary and Fundamental Rights**	Realized	Partly Realized
				31.7.2013	1.1.1-Amendments from I to XVI to the Constitution of Montenegro and the Constitutional Law for the enforcement of the Amendments to the Constitution	Realized	Partly Realized
28.04.2013	European Commission **2014 Progress Report on Montenegro** **The EU Enlargement Strategy 2014–2015-**	1.2-The recruitment process needs to be transparent and merit based, and introduction of a single, nationwide recruitment system	September 2013–October 2014	12.3.2015	1.2.1-Law on the Judicial Council and Rights and Duties of Judges	Realized	Unrealized

16.10.2013	European Commission **Resolution on the 2014 Progress Report on Montenegro** -European Parliament		November–December 2014		1.2.2-Law on Courts	Realized	Unrealized
					1.2.3-Law on State Prosecutor`s Office	Realized	Realized
					1.2.4-Law on Constitutional Court	Realized	Realized
			September 2013–October 2014	20.10.2015	1.2.5-Rules of Procedure of the Judicial Council	Realized	Realized
8.10.2014			2015 and continuously	12.11.2015	1.2.6-Rules of Procedure of Prosecutorial Council	Realized	Partly Realized
		1.3-A fair and transparent system of promoting judges and prosecutors needs to be established together with a periodical professional assessment of judges and prosecutors' performance	IQ 2015 and continuously	12.3.2015	1.3.1-Law on the Judicial Council and Rights and Duties of Judges -Law on Courts -Law on State Prosecutor`s Office	Realized	Partly Realized
11.03.2015	**2015 Progress Report on Montenegro The EU Enlargement Strategy 2015–2015**		September 2013	9.12.2015	1.3.2-Rulebook for the evaluation of judges and presidents of courts	Realized	Partly Realized
	-			23.12.2015	1.3.3-Rulebook for evaluation of state prosecutors and heads of state prosecutor`s office	Partly Realized	Partly Realized
	European Commission	1.4-Ensure internal independence of judges and review the system of orders within the prosecution system	IQ 2015	13.8.2013	1.4.1-Amendments to the Criminal Procedure Code	Partly Realized	Partly Realized
10.11.2015		1.5-Sufficient administrative capacities and financial means need to be ensured to the Judicial and the Prosecutorial Councils to effectively perform their tasks	IQ 2015	1.7.2014	1.5.1-Composition of the Judicial Council	Realized	Realized

(*Continued*)

Top-down Approach			Bottom-up Approach				
Date	*Body/Document*	*Recommendation(s)*	*Deadline*	*Final Realization*	*Measure(s)/Activity*	*Government`s Evaluation*[1]	*Researcher`s Evaluation*[2]
10.03.2016	**Resolution on the 2015 Progress Report on Montenegro** -European Parliament		IIIQ 2014	21.1.2014	1.5.2-Composition of the Prosecutorial Council	Realized	Realized
			July 2013	16.9.2013	1.5.3-Rulebook on internal organization and systematization of the Judicial Council Secretariat; -Employment of 3 officials	Realized	Realized
			September 2014 and continuously	January 2013–June 2016	1.5.4-Secretary, 6 officials and 1 probationer were appointed within the Secretariat of the Prosecutorial Council	Continuous	Partly Realized
		2.1-Amend "conflict of interest" rules, ensuring that there is an effective monitoring of asset declarations and cross-checking with other relevant information	Continuous	Continuous	2.1.1-Declaration of assets of the presidents of courts, judges, public prosecutors, and deputy public prosecutors declare in accordance with the Law on Prevention of Conflict of Interest	Realized	Realized
		2.2-Ensure effective monitoring of compliance with the code of ethics	March 2014	22.3.2014	2.2.1-Code of Ethics of Judges	Realized	Realized

9.11.2016	**2016 Progress Report on Montenegro The EU Enlargement Strategy 2016–2017** - European Commission		March 2014	20.5.2014	2.2.2-Amendments to the Code of Ethics of Public Prosecutors -Commission for monitoring of Code of Ethics was appointed	Continuous Realization	Realized
			Continuous	Continuous	2.2.3-Commissions for monitoring compliance with the Codes of Ethics of Judges and Public Prosecutors, and the Commission`s submission of the semi-annual or annual reports on compliance with the Codes of Ethics to the Judicial and the Prosecutorial Councils	Realized	Realized
		2.3-Review rules on disciplinary and dismissal procedures and their implementatior and amend where necessary	July 2013	31.7.2013	2.3.1-Amendments from I to XVI to the Constitution of Montenegro	Realized	Partly Realized
			September 2013-October 2014	12.3.2015	2.3.2-Law on the Judicial Council and Rights and Duties of Judges -Law on State Prosecutor`s Office	Continuous realization	Unrealized

(Continued)

Top-down Approach			Bottom-up Approach				
Date	Body/Document	Recommendation(s)	Deadline	Final Realization	Measure(s)/Activity	Government`s Evaluation[1]	Researcher`s Evaluation[2]
			IQ 2015	26.5.2015	2.3.3-Disciplinary Council within the Judicial Council -Disciplinary Council within the Prosecutorial Council	Realized	Realized
			January 2014	14.5.2015	2.3.4-Databases on procedures conducted regarding the accountability of judges and public prosecutors within the PRIS	Realized	Realized
		2.4-Review the system of functional immunity for judges and prosecutors	September 2013-October 2014	2014	2.4.1-Law on Judicial Council and Rights and Duties of Judges and Law on the State Prosecutor's Office	Realized	Realized
			Continuous	12.3.2015	2.4.2-Annual report on performances of the Judicial Council and overall conditions within the judiciary for 2015	Realized	Realized
		3.1-Ensure reliable and consistent judicial statistics and introduce a system to monitor the length of trials	September 2013-IIQ 2015	March 2016	3.1.1-Instructions on the preparation of statistical reports on the work of the courts	Realized	Realized

		September 2013-IIQ 2016	15.1.2015	3.1.2-Amendments to the Rulebook on orientation measures presented by the Working Group which foreseen establishment of appropriate standards for the workload of judges and standard timeframes for proceedings for specific types of cases and/or in specific courts	Continuous realization	Partly Realized
		Continuous	26.2.2015	3.1.43-Three officers employed in the IT department of the Secretariat of the Judicial Council	Continuous realization	Unrealized
	3.2-Review and rationalise the court network and ensure sufficient funding for the efficient functioning of the entire court system. Further reduce the existing backlog, especially as regard civil cases	June 2013	Continuous	3.2.1-Plan of rationalization of judicial network for a period 2013–2015	Continuous realization	Partly Realized
		2013-2015	27.6.2013	3.2.2-Realization of measures from Plan of rationalization of judicial network for a period 2013-2015	Partly Realized	Unrealized
		Continuous	2013-2015	3.2.3-Monitoring backlog of cases within PRIS and establishing Annual programs for resolving backlog of cases at the level of all courts	Partly Realized	Partly Realized

(Continued)

Top-down Approach			Bottom-up Approach				
Date	*Body/Document*	*Recommendation(s)*	*Deadline*	*Final Realization*	*Measure(s)/Activity*	*Government`s Evaluation*[1]	*Researcher`s Evaluation*[2]
			Continuous	Continuous	3.2.4-Activities towards reducing existing backlog of cases (voluntary secondment of judges, delegating cases, improving and controlling the work of delivery and enforcement service, and alternative dispute resolution, etc.	Partly Realized	Realized
			Continuous	Continuous	3.2.5-Amendments to the Law on Mediation	Realized	Realized
		3.3-Strengthen the enforcement of judgments in civil cases	October 2013	6.6.2012	3.3.1-Analysis of the bailiffs in relation to judicial enforcement in terms of efficiency and costs of enforcement proceeding	Realized	Realized
			January 2014	Nov 2013	3.3.2-Conducted practical actions in accordance with the Law on Enforcement and Security of Claims and the Law on Bailiffs in order to start operating of	Continuous realization	Partly Realized

			bailiffs and take enforcement cases from the jurisdiction of courts	Continuous realization	Realized
		2014	-Regulation on tariff of bailiffs	Realized	Realized
		22.06.2013	-Regulation on amendments of the regulation on the tariff of bailiffs	Realized	Realized
	IVQ 2015	January 2016	3.3.3-Introduced Analysis of functionality and basic software design for the work of bailiffs with the possibility of sending electronic reports to Ministry of Justice and Notary Chambers	Realized	Realized
4.1-Ensure effective functioning of the Judicial Training Centre	IVQ 2013	30.9.2015 15.10.2015	4.1.1-Established Analysis of the institutional needs of the Centre for education of holders of judicial functions and Proposal of job description for existing and future personnel of the Centre	Realized Realized	Realized

(*Continued*)

Top-down Approach			*Bottom-up Approach*				
Date	*Body/Document*	*Recommendation(s)*	*Deadline*	*Final Realization*	*Measure(s)/Activity*	*Government`s Evaluation*[1]	*Researcher`s Evaluation*[2]
			Continuous	Continuous	4.1.2-Organized training programs on implementation of CPC, Law on Civil Procedure, Law on Obligations, Law on Property Relations, Law on Enforcement and Security of Claims, etc.	Continuous realization	Realized
			2014–2015	23.9.2015	4.1.3-Law on the Training Centre in the Judiciary and the State Prosecutor's Office	Realized	Realized

[1] In accordance with defined methodological framework, based on the normative analysis the evaluation of the state bodies' work is divided in three categories: realized, semi-realized and unrealized measures and/or activities.

[2] In accordance with defined methodological framework, based on the empirical analysis the evaluation of the state bodies` work is divided in three categories: realized, semi-realized and unrealized measures and/or activities.

Appendix 2

Anti-Corruption Policy in Montenegro

Normative and empirical analysis of EU—Montenegro documents for the 2006–2017 period

Top-down approach			*Bottom-up approach*				
Date	*Body/Document*	*Recommendation(s)*	*Deadline*	*Final realization*	*Measure(s)/Activity*	*Government`s evaluation*[1]	*Researcher`s evaluation*[2]
8.11.2006	**2006 MNE Progress Report 2006–2007 EU enlargement strategy** - European Commission	1.1-Strengthen the legal and institutional framework in achieving visible results in preventing and prosecuting corruption	2006	28.6.2005	1.1.1-Program against the Corruption and Organized Crime	Realized	Realized
				24.8.2006	1.1.2-Action Plan for implementation of the Program against the Corruption and Organized Crime		
				15.2. 2007	1.1.3-Commission for monitoring of implementation of Action Plan for implementation of the Program against the Corruption and Organized Crime		
		1.2.-Amend Law on Conflict of Interest	2006		1.2.1-Measure has not been achieved	Unrealized	Unrealized
		1.3-Effective implementation of the Law on Political Parties	2007		1.3.1-Measure has not been achieved	Unrealized	Unrealized
		1.4-Development of state capacities	Continuous		1.4.1-Measure has not been achieved	Continuously	Partly Realized
		1.5-Providing credible track-record of investigation, prosecution, and final conviction of high-level corruption	Continuous		1.5.1-Measure has not been achieved	Continuously	Unrealized
17.1.2007	Council of the EU	**European Partnership**		17.5.2007	**Action Plan for Implementation of the European Partnership**	Realized	Partly Realized

Short-term priorities	1.1-Amend and fully implement current law on conflict of interest	2007–2009	27.12. 2008	1.1.1-Law on Conflict of Interests of Public Servants	Realized	Partly Realized
	1.2-Strengthening and implementing the Law on Political Parties	2007–2009	18.7.2008	1.2.1-Law on Financing of Political Parties	Realized	Partly Realized
Medium-term priorities	2.1-Setting up efficient institutional mechanisms for inter-agency cooperation and enhancing the operational capacity of law enforcement	2007–2009	Continuous	2.1.1-Inter-institutional cooperation between the judiciary and the Customs Directorate and Tax Administration	Unrealized	Unrealized
			Continuous	2.1.2-Strengthening of DACI	Partly Realized	Partly Realized
	2.2-Implementation of the anti-corruption strategy through ensuring financial and human resources to law enforcement bodies	2007–2009	28.6.2005	2.2.1-Program against the Corruption and Organized Crime	Realized	Realized
			24.8.2006	2.2.2-Action Plan for implementation of the Program against the Corruption and Organized Crime	Realized	Realized
			15.2. 2007	2.2.3-Commission for monitoring of implementation of Action Plan for implementation of the Program	Realized	Realized

(Continued)

Top-down approach			Bottom-up approach				
Date	*Body/Document*	*Recommendation(s)*	*Deadline*	*Final realization*	*Measure(s)/Activity*	*Government`s evaluation*[1]	*Researcher`s evaluation*[2]
					against the Corruption and Organized Crime		
				15.6.2007	1.2.4-Law on salaries and other income of holders of judicial office and the rules and procedure of the state prosecutor`s office	Realized	Partly Realized
		1.1-Prevention of and fight against the corruption at all level	2009–2012	2009–2012	1.1.1-Strengthening the capacities of SEC	Unrealized	Unrealized
					1.1.2-Strengthening the capacities of CPCI	Partly Realized	Partly Realized
					1.1.3-Strengthening of technical and material capacities of judicial holders	Partly Realized	Partly Realized
					1.1.4-Strengthening administrative, technical and material capacities of bodies that deals with prevention of corruption	Realized	Realized
					1.1.5-Creation of condition and capacities for performance of SIM	Partly Realized	Unrealized

1.2-Full alignment with the UN Convention on the fight against corruption and other relevant Council of Europe Conventions	2009–2012	19.1.2006	1.2.1-UN Convention against corruption	Realized	Realized
	2009–2012	6.6.2006	1.2.2-Criminal-law Conventions of the Council of Europe on Corruption	Realized	Realized
		22.6.2011	-Amendments to the Criminal Code	Realized	Realized
		26.8.2010	-Amendments to Criminal Procedure Code	Realized	Realized
		26.7.2011	-Amendments to the Law on Prevention of Conflict of Interest	Realized	Partly Realized
		29.7.2011	-Law on Public Procurement	Realized	Partly Realized
		9.8.2012	-Law on Free Access to Information	Realized	Partly Realized
2.1-Provide convincing results through establishment `effective procedures for the detection, treatment, and follow-up of cases cf—suspected fraud including EU funds	2009–2012	2009–2012	2.1.1-Strengthening the capacities in detection and conduction of financial investigations	Partly Realized	Partly Realized

(Continued)

Top-down approach			*Bottom-up approach*				
Date	*Body/Document*	*Recommendation(s)*	*Deadline*	*Final realization*	*Measure(s)/Activity*	*Government`s evaluation*[1]	*Researcher`s evaluation*[2]
6.11.2007	**2007 MNE Progress Report 2007-2008 EU Enlargement Strategy** - European Commission	1.1-Full implementation of the action plan			1.1.1-Program against the Corruption and Organized Crime	Realized	Partly Realized
		1.2-Amend the Law on Conflict of Interest	2006		1.2.2-Action Plan for implementation of the Program against the Corruption and Organized Crime	Realized	Partly Realized
		1.3-Lack transparency of financing political parties and election campaigns			1.2.3-Commission for monitoring of implementation of Action Plan for implementation of the Program against the Corruption and Organized Crime	Realized	Partly Realized
					1.2.1-Measure has not been achieved		Unrealized
					1.2.2-Law on Financing of Political Parties	Realized	Partly Realized
		2.1-Monitoring, prosecution and try corruption cases of high-level	2007	18.7.2008	2.1.1-Measure has not been achieved		Unrealized

5.11.2008	**2008 MNE Progress Report 2008-2009 EU Enlargement Strategy** - European Commission	1.1-Strengthening the legal framework		2008	1.1.1-Innovative Action Plan for implementation of the Program against the corruption and organized crime for 2008-2009	Realized	Realized
			2006	27.12.2008	1.1.2-Law on Prevention of Conflicts of Interest in Performing Public Functions	Realized	Partly Realized
			2006	18.8.2009	1.1.3-Criminal Procedure Code	Realized	Realized
				21.1.2009	1.1.4-Law on Financing the Election Campaigns for the President, Mayors and Presidents of Municipalities of Montenegro	Realized	Partly Realized
		1.2-Ensuring independert supervisory and auditing authorities` which will enforce assess declaration of assets and funding of political parties 1.3-Enhancing protection of whistleblowers in practice 2.1-Credible track-record in investigation, prosecution, and final conviction of high-level corruption		Continuous	1.2.1-SAI conducts revision of legality and successfulness of management of state property and obligations, budgets, and financial affairs	Realized	Partly Realized

(Continued)

Top-down approach			Bottom-up approach				
Date	Body/Document	Recommendation(s)	Deadline	Final realization	Measure(s)/Activity	Government`s evaluation[1]	Researcher`s evaluation[2]
		2.2-Investigate capacities of the law enforcement bodies remain very limited and there is significant lack of expertise in financial investigation			1.3.1-Measure has not been achieved		Unrealized
					2.1.1-Measure has not been achieved		Unrealized
		2.3-Insufficiently developed capacities within the Special Prosecutor Office and special anti-corruption police task force			2.2.1-Measure has not been achieved		Unrealized
					2.3.1-Measure has not been achieved		Unrealized
14.10.2009	**2009 MNE Progress Report 2009-2010 EU Enlargement Strategy** - European Commission		2010	29.7.2010	**1.Strategy for fight against the corruption and organize crime 2010-2014**	Realized	Realized
		1.1-Improvement current action plan against organized crime		29.7.2010	1.1.1-Action Plan for Implementation 2010–2012	Realized	Realized
		1.2-Introduction of independent supervisory authorities evaluates asset declarations and financing of political parties			1.1.2-National Commission for implementation of Strategy for fight against the Corruption and Organize Crime		Realized
		1.3-Adoption of the new Law on Conflict of Interests	2010		1.2.1-Measure has not been achieved	Realized	Unrealized
					1.3.1-Draft amendments on Law on Prevention		Unrealized

			of Conflicts of Interest in Performing Public Functions		Unrealized
2.1-Lack of staff and skills in administrative bodies for detecting and investigating corruption (performance of Police Directorate's internal control unit, Unit for combating organised crime and corruption, and the prosecution office)			2.1.1-Measure has not been achieved	Unrealized	Partly Realized
2.2-Improvement of the investigative capacities of law enforcement bodies	Continuous	Continuous	2.2.1-Organizing 3 seminars by the JTC and Police Academy for state bodies that deals with financial investigation, detecting, freezing, confiscating, and managing assets acquired by criminal offenses	Partly Realized	Partly Realized
2.3-Inter-agency cooperation needs to be further strengthened and significant lack of expertise in modern financial investigation needs to be improved	Continuous	Continuous	2.3.1-Employing 16 officials of Police Directorate that work on conduction of financial investigation -Enhancing the capacity of SIT	Partly Realized	Partly Realized
2.4-Establishment of solid track record of conviction of high-level corruption cases			2.4.1-Measure has not been achieved	Partly Realized	Unrealized

(Continued)

Top-down approach			Bottom-up approach				
Date	*Body/Document*	*Recommendation(s)*	*Deadline*	*Final realization*	*Measure(s)/Activity*	*Government`s evaluation*[1]	*Researcher`s evaluation*[2]
9.11.2010	**Commission Opinion on Montenegro`s application for membership of the EU 2010-2011 EU Enlargement Strategy** -European Commission	1.1-Improvement of the anti-corruption legal framework and implementation of the government's anti-corruption strategy and action plan establishment of a solid track record of proactive investigations, prosecutions, and convictions on the high-level corruption		17.2.2011	**1.Action Plan of Monitoring Recommendations from the Opinion of the European Commission** -Ministry of Foreign Affairs and European Integration		
				21.7.2011	**2.Innovative Action Plan for implementation of the Strategy against the Corruption and organize crime 2011–2012 -** Government of Montenegro		
			IQ 2011	22.6.2011	1.1.1-Amendments to the Criminal Code	Realized	Realized
			IIQ 2011	22.7.2011 26.07.2011	1.1.2- Law on Civil Servants and State Employees	Realized	Realized
			IIQ 2011		1.1.3-Amendments on the Law on Prevention of Conflicts of Interest in Performing Public Functions	Realized	Partly Realized

IIIQ 2011	29.7.2011	1.1.4-Law on Financing Political Parties	Realized	Partly Realized
IQ 2011	21.7.2011	1.1.5-Innovated Action Plan 2011-2012 for implementation of Strategy for fight against the corruption and organized crime	Partly Realized	Unrealized
2011	2011	2.1.1-Department for fight against organized crime, corruption, terrorism and war crimes -SIT	Realized	Partly Realized
IV 2011	7.11.2011	2.1.2-Investigation against 2 communal officials in case "Komunalni redari"	Realized	Partly Realized
	21.3. 2011	-Prosecution against 12 persons, out of which 3 persons are high officials of ruling party due to in case "Zavala"		
	14.5.2011 11.3.2011 9.3.2011	-Prosecution against 2 persons in case "Šarić"		
	23.8.2010 27.10.2011	-Prosecution against the individuals in cases: "Auto moto društvo Budva," "Mikulić," "Signal," and "Zeta"		

(Continued)

Top-down approach			*Bottom-up approach*				
Date	*Body/Document*	*Recommendation(s)*	*Deadline*	*Final realization*	*Measure(s)/Activity*	*Government`s evaluation*[1]	*Researcher`s evaluation*[2]
12.10.2011	**2011 MNE Progress Report 2011–2012 EU Enlargement Strategy** - European Commission	1.1-Further trainings of judges due to entry into force the new provisions of the CPC and the Criminal Code	Continuous	25.4.2012	**1.1-Annex to Report to European Commission on Montenegro`s Progress for 2012—for a period of September 1, 2011–April 25, 2012**	Realized	Realized
		1.2-Limited implementation of new legislation on financing of political parties and election campaigns which does not provide fully effectiveness of SEC to conduct independent oversight and disciplinary measures towards the civil servants	Continuous	6.9.2012.	**1.2-Annex to Report to European Commission on Montenegro`s Progress for 2012 – for a period of April 25, 2012–September 1, 2012**		
			2011	25.4-15.12.2012	-Ministry of Foreign Affairs and European Integration		
29.06.2012	**Resolution which refers to 2011 Progress Report on Montenegro** - European Parliament			Continuous 15.6.2012	2.1.2-Amendments to the Law on Temporary Seized Assets	Realized	Partly Realized

			1.1.1-12 activities of continuous education and 4 activities of initial education for 62 representatives of judiciary in area of implementation of the new criminal legislations 1.2.1-Measure has not been achieved		
2.1-Convincing number of final conviction, in particular for high-level cases as well as number of corruption cases in which the seizure or confiscation of assets is ordered	Continuous	Continuous	2.1.1-Under the plea agreement, Major of municipality Ulcinj was obliged to pay 10,000 euros to charity - Final conviction was issued in case 'Zavala'- the Mayor of municipality of Budva is convicted to 5 years, his deputy to 4 years of imprisonment, and MP to 3 years of imprisonment -Procedures for temporary seized assets were carried out in 3 cases	Realized	Partly Realized

(Continued)

Top-down approach					Bottom-up approach		
Date	Body/Document	Recommendation(s)	Deadline	Final realization	Measure(s)/Activity	Government`s evaluation[1]	Researcher`s evaluation[2]
		2.2-Enhancing the institutional and administrative capacity of law enforcement bodies			2.2.1-10 police officers are employed in the Police Directorate in order to prevent corruption criminal offenses -24 trainings of financial investigation provided	Realized	Partly Realized
		2.3-Improvement the inter-agency cooperation and exchange information between law enforcement bodies			2.3.1-Analysis of anti-corruptive institutional framework and Analysis of effects of establishment of the Agency for fight against the corruption	Realized	Partly Realized
22.5.2012	**Report from the Commission to the European Parliament and the Council on Montenegro`s Progress in the Implementation of Reforms**	1.1-Improvement of the anti-corruption legal framework and implementation of the government's anti-corruption strategy and action plan		8.3.2012	**1.1-Annex to the European Commission's Spring Report on meeting the 7 key priorities for the period September 1, 2011–March 1, 2012**		

-European Commission	2.1-Establishment of a solid track record of proactive investigations, prosecutions, and convictions in corruption of high-level cases	-Ministry of Foreign Affairs and European Integration Note: all the reform activities conducted by the Montenegrin state bodies in 2012 are presented in documents: -Annex to Report to European Commission on Montenegro`s Progress for 2012—for a period of September 1, 2011–April 25, 2012 -Annex to Report to European Commission on Montenegro`s Progress for 2012—for a period of April 25, 2012–September 1, 2012

(Continued)

Top-down approach			Bottom-up approach				
Date	*Body/Document*	*Recommendation(s)*	*Deadline*	*Final realization*	*Measure(s)/Activity*	*Government`s evaluation*[1]	*Researcher`s evaluation*[2]
12.11.2012	**Screening Report Montenegro Chapter 23—Judiciary and fundamental right**	1.1-Strengthen and possibly review the institutional framework for the fight against corruption of DACI	June 2014	27.6.2013	**1.Action Plan for Chapter 23 Judiciary and Fundamental Rights**	Realized	Partly Realized
	- European Commission		December 2015	9.12.2014	1.1.1-Law on Agency for Anti-Corruption -Established Agency for preventing corruption	Partly Realized	Partly Realized
10.10.2012	**2012 Progress Report on Montenegro** **The EU Enlargement Strategy 2012–2013** -European Commission **Resolution on the 2012**		June 2014	1.1.2016	1.1.2-Adoption of the new Rules of procedures on organization and systematization of working places by increasing the number of working positions from 55 to 60	Realized	Partly Realized
28.04.2013	**Progress Report on Montenegro** -European Parliament	1.2-Improve the system of asset declarations, strengthening in particular the supervisory competencies and the professional capacity of the Commission for prevention of conflict of interest to ensure effective and substantial checks on assets, and introduce measures preventing conflicts of interest going beyond holding double public offices	March 2014–March 2015	16.12.2014	1.2.1-Amendments of the Law on the Prevention of Conflict of Interest	Realized	Partly Realized
	2013 Progress Report on Montenegro **The EU Enlargement Strategy 2013–2014**		September 2014	March 2015	1.2.2-Improve system for efficient checks of data accuracy provided from the reports of the public officials through the new form of checks of data assets	Realized	Partly Realized

16.10.2013	-European Commission **2014 Progress Report on Montenegro**		December 2013–January/December 2014	Continuous	1.2.3-Establishment of the Commission`s software which provides automatic networking and access to databases of bodies and institutions on assets and incomes of public officials	Realized	Realized
8.10.2014	**The EU Enlargement Strategy 2014–2015** -European Commission **Resolution on the 2014 Progress Report on Montenegro** -European Parliament		September 2013	Continuous	1.2.4-Provided trainings for the employees in the Commission and Agency for Anti-Corruption Initiative in terms of control competences and use of databases prescribed within the Law	Realized	Partly Realized
11.03.2015	**2015 Progress Report on Montenegro** **The EU Enlargement Strategy 2015–2015**	1.3-Improve the system of political party funding, ensuring reliable reporting as well as effective supervision and sanctioning powers by an independent authority. Strengthen the capacities of the monitoring bodies—SAI and SEC and ensure a clear division of tasks and cooperation framework. The recommendations of GRECO should be followed-up	December 2013	16.12. 2014	1.3.1-Law on Financing Political Entities and Election Campaigns	Realized	Partly Realized
10.11.2015	-European Commission		June 2014	February 2015	1.3.2-Agency adopted Rules, Guidelines, Instruction.	Realized	Partly Realized

(*Continued*)

Top-down approach			Bottom-up approach				
Date	Body/Document	Recommendation(s)	Deadline	Final realization	Measure(s)/Activity	Government`s evaluation[1]	Researcher`s evaluation[2]
10.03.2016	**Resolution on the 2015 Progress Report on Montenegro**- European Parliament		Since July 2013 two times per year	26.2.2015	1.3.3-Strengthening the administrative capacities of the SAI and SEC: -Adopted Rulebook on internal organization and systematization based by which 1 person in SEC and 8 persons in SAI was employed -SAI employed 10 out of 13 persons for controlling the political parties -Ensuring accommodation capacities, financial needs, and forming expert service of SAI	Partly Realized	Partly Realized
9.11.2016							
		1.4-Ensure that NGOs are involved in the anticorruption agenda	November 2014	7.7. 2015	1.4.1-Anti-Corruption Committee held 11 sessions in 2015 in which attended 3 NGO`s representatives	Realized	Realized

				-In the period between January 1 and June 30, 2016, the Anti-corruption committee held 3 sessions in which attended 2 NGO`s representatives		
2016 Progress Report on Montenegro The EU Enlargement Strategy 2016–2017 -European Commission	2.1-Ensure independent, effective specialized investigation/prosecution bodies in repressing corruption	October 2014	9.11.2015	2.1.1-Law on Special Prosecutor`s Office -Special Prosecutor's Office for fight against organized crime, corruption, terrorism, and war crimes	Realized	Partly Realized
	2.2-Amend the Criminal Procedure Code where needed and ensure its effective implementation	October 2014	2014	2.2.1-Amendments to the Criminal Procedure Code	Realized	Partly Realized
		February–December 2014	Continuous	2.3.1-Law on Confiscation of Asset Benefits Acquired by the Criminal Activities	Realized	Partly Realized
	2.3-Improve the use of financial investigations, possibly through establishing a team of highly qualified investigators for this purpose	May 2014	9.4.2014	2.3.2-Established specialized organizational units within the Criminal Investigation Police through changes in organization and job description:	Realized	Realized

(Continued)

Top-down approach			*Bottom-up approach*				
Date	*Body/Document*	*Recommendation(s)*	*Deadline*	*Final realization*	*Measure(s)/Activity*	*Government`s evaluation*[1]	*Researcher`s evaluation*[2]
					-Group for conducting financial investigations, highly-technical criminal, human trafficking was established with 5 employees -Group for prevention of smuggling, human trafficking, and illegal migrations with 3 employees -Group for prevention of high-tech crime with 1 employee -Group for prevention of terrorism, weapon smuggling, and explosive materials with 3 employees		
			Continuous	1.6.2015	2.3.3-Trainings for the employees in the special unit of the Police Administration for implementation of financial	Realized	Realized

				investigations, as well as the multidisciplinary team and prosecutors and judges in combating corruption by the JTC		
	2.4-Improve the cooperation and information exchange between authorities involved in the fight against corruption, including also tax and other only indirectly linked authorities	January 2014, and continuously	2015	2.4.1-Protocol on Cooperation of the Supreme State Prosecutor's Office, Ministry of Interior and Police Directorate in the pre-trial and criminal procedures	Realized	Unrealized
		October 2014	2015	2.4.2-Agreement on standard operative procedures between the Tax Administration and Police Directorate -Agreement between Ministry of Interior, Police Directorate, and Supreme State Prosecutor's Office on securing	Realized	Partly Realized

(Continued)

Top-down approach			Bottom-up approach				
Date	*Body/Document*	*Recommendation(s)*	*Deadline*	*Final realization*	*Measure(s)/Activity*	*Government`s evaluation*[1]	*Researcher`s evaluation*[2]
					conditions on providing conditions for the smooth operation of the State Prosecutor's Office by the Police Administration -Agreement between Ministry of Interior, Police Directorate, and Supreme State Prosecutor's Office for the smooth operation of the courts and maintaining order		
			December 2014	9.11.2015	2.5.1-Law on Confiscation of Asset Benefits Acquired by the Criminal Activities	Realized	Realized
			December 2013	2014-2015	2.5.2-Recruitment of two civil servants in the Public Property Administration		
			2015	2013	2.5.3-Established the electronic register of seized property which	Realized	Realized

			contains information on the number of decisions, the name of the court or body responsible for conducting the proceedings, the type and the estimated value of the property and the person from whom the property has been seized		
2.5-Procedures for seizure, confiscation, and management of proceeds of crime need to be further regulated and the professional capacity of the relevant State Agency strengthened	September 2013	8.3.2016.	2.5.4-Establishment of the Directorate of assets	Realized	Realized
2.6-Take the necessary steps to make the system of whistle-blower protection more effective in practice		30.7.2013	2.6.1-Amendments to the Criminal Code	Realized	Partly Realized

[1] In accordance with defined methodological framework, based on the normative analysis the evaluation of the state bodies` work is divided in three categories: realized, partly-realized and unrealized measures and/or activities.

[2] In accordance with defined methodological framework, based on the empirical analysis the evaluation of the state bodies` work is divided in three categories: realized, partly-realized and unrealized measures and/or activities.

Bibliography

PRIMARY SOURCES

Berlin Process. 2014a. "Civil Society Forum of the Western Balkans Summit Series." Accessed April 14, 2018. http://wb-csf.eu/about/#wbs-berlin-2014

———. 2014b. "Final Declaration by the Chair of the Conference on the Western Balkans." Accessed April 16, 2018. http://wb-csf.eu/wp-content/uploads/2017/11/Final-Declaration-by-the-Chair-of-the-Conference-on-the-Western-Balkans.pdf

———. 2015a. "Annex 2—Join Declaration on the Establishment of the Regional Youth Cooperation Office in the Western Balkans." Accessed April 16, 2018. http://wb-csf.eu/wp-content/uploads/2017/11/Joint-Declaration-on-the-establishment-of-the-Regional-Youth-Cooperation-Office-of-the-Western-Balkans.pdf

———. 2015b. "Annex 3—Regional Cooperation and the Solution of Bilateral Disputes." *Western Balkans Summit*. Accessed April 16, 2018. http://wb-csf.eu/wp-content/uploads/2017/11/Regional-Cooperation-and-the-Solution-of-Bilateral-Disputes.pdf

———. 2015c. "Final Declaration by the Chair of the Vienna Western Balkans Summit." Accessed April 16, 2018. http://wb-csf.eu/wp-content/uploads/2017/11/Final-Declaration-by-the-Chair-of-the-Vienna-Western-Balkans-Summit.pdf

———. 2016. "Final Declaration by the Chair of the Paris Western Balkan Summit." Accessed April 16, 2018. http://wb-csf.eu/wp-content/uploads/2017/11/Final-Declaration-by-the-Chair-of-the-Paris-Western-Balkans-Summit.pdf

Constitution of Montenegro. 2007. "Articles 123, 126, 127, 128." Accessed April 17, 2018. http://www.skupstina.me/images/dokumenti/ustav-crne-gore.pdf

———. 2013. "Amendments IX, X, XI." Accessed August 18, 2020. http://www.skupstina.me/index.php/me/ustav-crne-gore

Council of the European Union. 2007. "European Partnership with Montenegro." Accessed April 15, 2018. https://eur-lex.europa.eu/legalcontent/EN/TXT/?uri=LEGISSUM%3Ar18014

Council of the European Union and European Commission. 2007. "Stabilization and Association Agreement between the European Communities and their Member States and the Republic of Montenegro." Accessed April 15, 2018. https://ec.europa.eu/neighbourhood-enlargement/sites/near/files/lexuriserv2nd_en.pdf

European Commission. 1997. "Agenda 2000: For Stronger and Wider Europe." Accessed May 17, 2018. http://ec.europa.eu/agriculture/sites/agriculture/files/caphistory/agenda2000/com972000_en.pdf

———. 1999. "Stabilization and Association Process." Accessed April 14, 2018. https://ec.europa.eu/neighbourhood-enlargement/policy/glossary/terms/sap_en

———. 2000. "Zagreb Summit Declaration." Accessed April 14, 2018. http://www.esiweb.org/pdf/bridges/bosnia/ZagrebSummit24Nov2000.pdf

———. 2006. "Renewed Consensus on Enlargement." Accessed April 14, 2018. https://ec.europa.eu/commission/presscorner/detail/en/IP_06_1523

———. 2007a. "Communication from the Commission to the European Parliament and the Council: Enlargement Strategy and Main Challenges 2007—2008." *European Commission*. Accessed April 16, 2018. https://ec.europa.eu/neighbourhoodenlargement/sites/near/files/pdf/key_documents/2007/nov/strategy_paper_en.pdf

———. 2007b. "Montenegro Report 2007." Accessed April 15, 2018. https://ec.europa.eu/neighbourhoodenlargement/sites/near/files/pdf/key_documents/2007/nov/montenegro_progress_reports_en.pdf

———. 2008a. "Communication from the Commission to the European Parliament and the Council: Enlargement Strategy and Main Challenges 2008—2009." Accessed April 15, 2018. https://ec.europa.eu/neighbourhoodenlargement/sites/near/files/pdf/press_corner/key-documents/reports_nov_2008/strategy_paper_incl_country_conclu_en.pdf

———. 2008b. "Montenegro Report 2008." Accessed April 15, 2018. https://ec.europa.eu/neighbourhoodenlargement/sites/near/files/pdf/key_documents/2009/mn_rapport_2009_en.pdf

———. 2009a. "Communication from the Commission to the European Parliament and the Council: Enlargement Strategy and Main Challenges 2009—2010." Accessed April 15, 2018. https://ec.europa.eu/neighbourhoodenlargement/sites/near/files/pdf/key_documents/2009/strategy_paper_2009_en.pdf

———. 2009b. "Montenegro Report 2009." Accessed April 15, 2018. https://ec.europa.eu/neighbourhoodenlargement/sites/near/files/pdf/key_documents/2009/mn_rapport_2009_en.pdf

———. 2010a. "Communication from the Commission to the European Parliament and the Council: Enlargement Strategy and Main Challenges 2010–2011." Accessed April 15, 2018. https://ec.europa.eu/neighbourhoodenlargement/sites/near/files/pdf/key_documents/2010/package/strategy_paper_2010_en.pdf

———. 2010b. "Commission Opinion on Montenegro's Application for Membership of the European Union." Accessed April 15, 2018. https://ec.europa.eu/neighbourhoodenlargement/sites/near/files/pdf/key_documents/2010/package/mn_opinion_2010_en.pdf

———. 2011a. "Communication from the Commission to the European Parliament and the Council: Enlargement Strategy and Main Challenges 2011–2012." Accessed April 15, 2018. https://ec.europa.eu/neighbourhoodenlargement/sites/near/files/pdf/key_documents/2011/package/strategy_paper_2011_en.pdf

———. 2011b. "Montenegro Report 2011." Accessed April 15, 2018. https://ec.europa.eu/neighbourhoodenlargement/sites/near/files/pdf/key_documents/2011/package/mn_rapport_2011_en.pdf

———. 2012a. "Report from the Commission to the European Parliament and the Council on Montenegro's Progress in the Implementation of Reforms." Accessed April 15, 2018. https://ec.europa.eu/neighbourhoodenlargement/sites/near/files/pdf/key_documents/2012/montenegro_spring_report_en.pdf

———. 2012b. "Communication from the Commission to the European Parliament and the Council: Enlargement Strategy and Main Challenges 2012—2013." Accessed April 15, 2018. https://ec.europa.eu/neighbourhoodenlargement/sites/near/files/pdf/key_documents/2012/package/strategy_paper_2012_en.pdf

———. 2012c. "Montenegro Report 2012." Accessed April 14, 2018. https://ec.europa.eu/neighbourhoodenlargement/sites/near/files/pdf/key_documents/2012/package/mn_rapport_2012_en.pdf

———. 2012d. "Screening Report Montenegro on Chapter 23—Judiciary and Fundamental Rights." Accessed April 16, 2018. https://ec.europa.eu/neighbourhoodenlargement/sites/near/files/pdf/montenegro/screening_reports/20130218_screening_report_montenegro_ch23.pdf

———. 2013. "Montenegro Report 2013." Accessed April 14, 2018. https://ec.europa.eu/neighbourhoodenlargement/sites/near/files/pdf/key_documents/2013/package/brochures/montenegro_2013.pdf

———. 2014a. "Communication from the Commission to the European Parliament and the Council: Enlargement Strategy and Main Challenges 2014—2015." Accessed April 16, 2018. https://www.ab.gov.tr/files/000etkinlikler/2014_enlargement_strategy_paper.pdf

———. 2014b. "Montenegro Report 2014." Accessed April 14, 2018. https://ec.europa.eu/neighbourhoodenlargement/sites/near/files/pdf/key_documents/2014/20141008-montenegro-progress-report_en.pdf

———. 2015a. "Communication from the Commission to the European Parliament and the Council: Enlargement Strategy and Main Challenges 2015—2016." *European Commission*. Accessed April 14, 2018. https://ec.europa.eu/neighbourhoodenlargement/sites/near/files/20151110_strategy_paper_en.pdf

———. 2015b. "Montenegro Report 2015." Accessed April 14, 2018. https://ec.europa.eu/neighbourhoodenlargement/sites/near/files/pdf/key_documents/2015/20151110_report_montenegro.pdf

———. 2016. "Montenegro Report 2016." Accessed April 14, 2018. https://ec.europa.eu/neighbourhoodenlargement/sites/near/files/pdf/key_documents/2016/20161109_report_montenegro.pdf

———. 2017a. "Eurobarometer 87."

———. 2017b. "Eurobarometer 88."

———. 2018a. "A Credible Membership Perspective for and Enhanced EU Engagement with the Western Balkans." Accessed April 14, 2018. https://ec.europa.eu/neighbourhood-enlargement/policy/eu-and-western-balkans_en

———. 2018b. "Eurobarometer 89."

———. 2018c. "Montenegro Report 2018." Accessed March 27, 2019. https://ec.europa.eu/neighbourhood-enlargement/sites/near/files/20180417-montenegro-report.pdf

———. 2019a. "Eurobarometer 90."

———. 2019b. "Montenegro Report 2019." Accessed August 6, 2020. https://ec.europa.eu/neighbourhood-enlargement/sites/near/files/20190529-montenegro-report.pdf

European Council. 1997. "Conclusions." Accessed April 14, 2018. http://www.europarl.europa.eu/summits/lux1_en.htm

———. 2010. "Conclusions." Accessed April 17, 2018. http://data.consilium.europa.eu/doc/document/ST-30–2010-INIT/en/pdf/

———. 2011. "Conclusions." Accessed April 17, 2018. http://europa.eu/rapid/press-release_DOC-11–8_en.htm

———. 2012."Conclusions." Accessed April 17, 2018. http://data.consilium.europa.eu/doc/document/ST-76–2012-INIT/en/pdf/

European Neighbourhood Policy and Enlargement Negotiations. 2020. "Montenegro—Financial Assistance under IPA II." Accessed August 23, 2020. https://ec.europa.eu/neighbourhood-enlargement/instruments/funding-by-country/montenegro_en

European Parliament. 2013. "Resolution on the 2012 Montenegro Progress Report." Accessed April 17, 2018. http://www.europarl.europa.eu/sides/getDoc.do?pubRef=%2f%2fEP%2f%2fTEXT%2bTA%2bP7-TA-2012 0117%2b0%2bDOC%2bXML%2bV0%2f%2fEN&language=EN

———. 2015. "Resolution on the 2014 Montenegro Progress Report." Accessed April 17, 2018. http://www.europarl.europa.eu/sides/getDoc.do?pubRef=%2f%2fEP%2f%2fTEXT%2bTA%2bP7-TA-2014 0104%2b0%2bDOC%2bXML%2bV0%2f%2fEN&language=EN

European Union. 2009. "Lisbon Treaty." Accessed April 17, 2018. http://eur-lex.europa.eu/legal-content/EN/TXT/PDF/?uri=CELEX:12012E/TXT&from=EN

European Union External Action. 2017. "Speech by the High Representative/Vice-President Federica Mogherini at the Parliament of Montenegro." Accessed April 14, 2018. https://eeas.europa.eu/headquarters/headquarters-homepage/21734/high-representativevice-president-federica-mogherini-parliament-montenegro_de

EU-Western Balkans Summit. 2003. "Thessaloniki Agenda for the Western Balkans: Moving towards the European Integration." Accessed April 19, 2018. http://europa.eu/rapid/press-release_PRES-03–163_en.htm

Ministarstvo unutrašnjih poslova i javne uprave Crne Gore. 2010. *Strategija za borbu protiv korupcije i organizovanog kriminala za period 2010–2014*. Podgorica: MUPJU.

Ministarstvo vanjskih poslova i evropskih integracija (MVPEI). 2011a. "Treći izvještaj o realizaciji obaveza iz Sporazuma o stabilizaciji i pridruživanju u periodu od 1. april-30. jun 2011. godine." Accessed April 2018. http://www.skupstina.me

/index.php/me/pristupanje-eu/parlamentarni-odbor-za-stabilizaciju-i-pridruzivanje /dokumenta

———. 2011b. "Četvrti izvještaj o realizaciji obaveza iz Sporazuma o stabilizaciji i pridruživanju, jul-septembar 2011. godine." Accessed April 17, 2018. http://www.skupstina.me/index.php/me/pristupanje-eu/parlamentarni-odbor-za-stabilizaciju-i-pridruzivanje/dokumenta

———. 2012a. "Peti izvještaj o realizaciji obaveza iz Sporazuma o stabilizaciji i pridruživanju, oktobar-decembar 2011. godine." Accessed May 3, 2018. http://www.skupstina.me/index.php/me/pristupanje-eu/parlamentarni-odbor-za-stabilizaciju-i-pridruzivanje/dokumenta

———. 2012b. "Šesti izvještaj o realizaciji obaveza iz Sporazuma o stabilizaciji i pridruživanju, januar-mart 2012. godine." Accessed May 5, 2018. http://www.skupstina.me/index.php/me/pristupanje-eu/parlamentarni-odbor-za-stabilizaciju-i-pridruzivanje/dokumenta

———. 2012c. "Sedmi izvještaj o realizaciji obaveza iz Sporazuma o stabilizaciji i pridruživanju, april-jun 2012. godine." Accessed May 5, 2018. http://www.skupstina.me/index.php/me/pristupanje-eu/parlamentarni-odbor-za-stabilizaciju-i-pridruzivanje/dokumenta

———. 2012d. "Osmi izvještaj o realizaciji obaveza iz Sporazuma o stabilizaciji i pridruživanju, jul-septembar 2012. godine." Accessed May 5, 2018. http://www.skupstina.me/index.php/me/pristupanje-eu/parlamentarni-odbor-za-stabilizaciju-i-pridruzivanje/dokumenta

———. 2013. *Prvi izvještaj o realizaciji obaveza iz Sporazuma o stabilizaciji i pridruživanju januar—jun 2013*. Podgorica: MVPEI: 13–17.

———. 2014. *Drugi izvještaj o realizaciji obaveza iz Sporazuma o stabilizaciji i pridruživanju septembar 2013—septembar 2014*. Podgorica: MVPEI: 10–17.

Odluka o proglašenju Amandmana I do XVI na Ustav Crne Gore. 2013. "Skupština Crne Gore." Accessed April 17, 2018. http://www.skupstina.me/images/dokumenti/ustav/AMANDMANI_I_DO_XVI_NA_USTAV_CRNE_GORE.pdf

Skupština Crne Gore. 2013. "Rezolucija o nacinu, kvalitetu i dinamici procesa integracija." Accessed July 12, 2020. http://skupstina.me/index.php/me/pristupanjc-cu/parlamentarni-odbor-za-stabilizaciju-i-pridruzivanje/dokumenta

Službeni list Crne Gore. 2014a. "Ugovor o preferencijalnom zajmu za kupca za Projekat izgradnje autoputa Bar-Boljare, dionica Smokovac-Mateševo." broj 54/2014. Accessed July 23, 2020. http://www.sluzbenilist.me/pregled-dokumenta-2/?id={934EB0DD-DADC-40CE-950F-7B1E0BA00D9E}

———. 2014b. "Ugovor o projektovanju i izgradnji autoputa Bar - Boljare dionica Smokovac—Uvač—Mateševo." broj 54/2014. Accessed July 23, 2020. http://www.sluzbenilist.me/pregled-dokumenta-2/?id={588F6BC9–789D-4D9E-B4DE-0103A1C82CB8}

———. 2014c. "Zakon o autoputu Bar-Boljare." broj 52/2014. Accessed July 23, 2020. http://www.sluzbenilist.me/pregled-dokumenta-2/?id={35AE72ED-429E-4726-B9B9–7FA4D39DC32F}

Sudski Savjet Crne Gore. 2008. "Izvještaj o radu 2008." Accessed April 15, 2018. http://sudovi.me/podaci/sscg/dokumenta/43.pdf

———. 2012. "Godišnji izvještaj 2012." Accessed April 15, 2018. http://sudovi.me/podaci/sscg/dokumenta/5109.pdf

———. 2013. "Godišnji izvještaj 2013." Accessed April 17, 2018. http://sudovi.me/podaci/sscg/dokumenta/5107.pdf

———. 2014. "Godišnji izvještaj 2014." Accessed April 18, 2018. http://sudovi.me/podaci/sscg/dokumenta/5105.pdf

———. 2015. "Godišnji izvještaj 2015." Accessed Aprl 21, 2018. http://sudovi.me/podaci/sscg/dokumenta/5103.pdf

———. 2016. "Godišnji izvještaj o radu Sudskog savjeta i ukupnom stanju u sudstvu za 2016. godinu." Accessed April 22, 2018. http://sudovi.me/podaci/sscg/dokumenta/5136.pdf

Tužilački savjet Crne Gore. 2014. "Izvještaj o radu Tužilačkog savjeta za 2013. godinu." Accessed August 6, 2019. http://tuzilastvocg.me/media/files/Izvjestaj%20o%20radu%20Drzavnog%20tuzilastva%20za%202013(1).pdf

———. 2015a. "Izvještaj o radu Tužilačkog savjeta za 2014. godinu." Accessed August 7, 2019. http://tuzilastvocg.me/media/files/Izvjestaj%20Tuzilackog%20savjeta%20za%202014%20god.pdf

———. 2015b. "Izvještaj o radu Tužilačkog savjeta za 2014. godinu." Accessed August 7, 2019. http://tuzilastvocg.me/media/files/Izvjestaj%20Tuzilackog%20savjeta%20za%202014%20god.pdf

———. 2016. "Izvještaj o radu Tužilačkog savjeta i državnog tužilaštva za 2015. godinu." Accessed August 8, 2019. http://tuzilastvocg.me/media/files/izvjestaj%20o%20radu%20vdt%20za%202015-compressed.pdf

Vlada Crne Gore. 2007a. *Akcioni plan za implementaciju preporuka Evropskog partnerstva*. Podgorica: Vlada Crne Gore.

———. 2007b. *Prvi izvještaj o relizaciji mjera iz Akcionog plana za sprovođenje Programa borbe protiv korupcije i organizovanog kriminala—1.9.2006—1.5.2007.* Podgorica: Vlada Crne Gore.

———. 2007c. *Akcioni plan za implementaciju Reforme sistema pravosuđa 2007–2012*. Podgorica: Vlada Crne Gore. Accessed March 13, 2018. http://www.skupstina.me/index.php/me/pristupanje-eu/parlamentarni-odbor-za-stabilizaciju-i-pridruzivanje/dokumenta

———. 2008a. "Izvještaj o realizaciji mjera iz Akcionog plana za implementaciju Strategije reforme pravosuđa 2007–2012. godine za prvi polugodišnji period decembar 2007—jul 2008. godine." Accessed April 15, 2018. http://www.pravda.gov.me/biblioteka/izvjestaji?pagerIndex=4

———. 2008b. "Nacionalni program za integraciju (NPI) za period 2008–2012." Accessed April 23, 2018. http://www.mep.gov.me/organizacija/dep/Vaznidokumenti/Nacionalni_program_za_integraciju_Crne_Gore_u_EU

———. 2008c. *Prvih deset kvartalnih izvještaja Vlade Crne Gore posvećenih ostvarivanju prosecu stabilizacije i pridruživanja: od skupštinske Deklaracije o pridruživanju Evropskoj uniji, juna 2005. godine, do skupštinske Rezolucije o ispunjavanju obaveza Crne Gore u okviru Sporazuma o stabilizaciji i pridruživanju decembra 2007. Godine*. Podgorica: Vlada Crne Gore.

———. 2009. "Izvještaj o realizaciji mjera iz Akcionog plana za implementaciju Strategije reforme pravosuđa 2007–2012. godine za prvi polugodišnji period jul 2008—januar 2009." Accessed February 22, 2018. http://www.pravda.gov.me/biblioteka/izvjestaji?pagerIndex=3

———. 2010. "Izvještaj o realizaciji mjera iz Akcionog Plana za implementaciju Strategije reforme pravosuđa za 2009. godinu." Accessed February 26, 2018. http://www.pravda.gov.me/biblioteka/izvjestaji?pagerIndex=3

———. 2011a. *Inovirani Akcioni plan 2012–2012 za implementaciju Strategije borbe protiv korupcije i organizovanog kriminala*. Podgorica: Vlada Crne Gore.

———. 2011b. *Akcioni plan praćenja sprovođenja preporuka iz mišljenja Evropske komisije*. Podgorica: Vlada Crne Gore.

———. 2011c. "Informacija o realizaciji ključnih aktivnosti iz Akcionog plana sprovođenja preporuka iz mišljenja Evropske komisije." Accessed April 15, 2018. http://www.skupstina.me/index.php/me/pristupanje-eu/parlamentarni-odbor-za-stabilizaciju-i-pridruzivanje/dokumenta

———. 2011d. "Peti mjesečni izvještaj o realizaciji ključnih aktivnosti iz Akcionog plana sprovođenja preporuka iz mišljenja Evropske komisije." Accessed April 18, 2018. http://www.skupstina.me/index.php/me/pristupanje-eu/parlamentarni-odbor-za-stabilizaciju-i-pridruzivanje/dokumenta

———. 2011e. "Izvještaj o realizaciji mjera iz Akcionog plana za implementaciju Strategije reforme sistema pravosuđa 2007–2012 za 2010 godinu." Accessed April 18, 2018. http://www.pravda.gov.me/biblioteka/izvjestaji?pagerIndex=3

———. 2011f. *Prvi izvještaj o realizaciji mjera iz Akcionog plana za sprovođenje strategije za borbu protiv korupcije i organizovanog kriminala*. Podgorica: Vlada Crne Gore.

———. 2012a. "Prilog izvještaju Evropske komisije o napretku Crne Gore za 2012.—za period 1. septembra 2011—25. aprila 2012, Podgorica." Accessed April 17, 2018. http://www.skupstina.me/index.php/me/pristupanje-eu/parlamentarni-odbor-za-stabilizaciju-i-pridruzivanje/dokumenta

———. 2012b. "Prilog izvještaju Evropske komisije o napretku Crne Gore za 2012.—za period 25. aprila 2012.—1. septembra 2012." Accessed April 17, 2018. http://www.skupstina.me/index.php/me/pristupanje-eu/parlamentarni-odbor-za-stabilizaciju-i-pridruzivanje/dokumenta

———. 2012c. "Izvještaj o realizaciji mjera iz Akcionog plana za implementaciju Strategije reforme sistema pravosuđa 2007–2012 za 2011 godinu." Accessed April 17, 2018. http://www.pravda.gov.me/biblioteka/izvjestaji?pagerIndex=3

———. 2012d. *Četvrti izvještaj o realizaciji mjera iz Inoviranog Akcionog Plana za sprovođenje Strategije za borbu protiv korupcije i organizovanog kriminala*. Podgorica: Vlada Crne Gore.

———. 2012e. *Treći izvještaj o realizaciji mjera iz Inoviranog Akcionog Plana za sprovođenje Strategije za borbu protiv korupcije i organizovanog kriminala*. Podgorica: Vlada Crne Gore.

———. 2012f. *Peti izvještaj o realizaciji mjera iz Inoviranog Akcionog Plana za sprovođenje Strategije za borbu protiv korupcije i organizovanog kriminala*. Podgorica: Vlada Crne Gore.

———. 2013 “Akcioni plan za Poglavlje 23. pravosuđe i temeljna prava.” Accessed April 17, 2018. http://www.eu.me/mn/23/23-dokumenti

———. 2014. “Akcioni plan za poglavlje 23. pravosuđe i temeljna prava, izvještaj broj 5.” Accessed May 24, 2018. http://www.gov.me/biblioteka/izvjestaji?pagerIndex=29

———. 2015. “Akcioni plan za poglavlje 23. pravosuđe i temeljna prava—polugodišnji izvještaj januar—jun 2015.” Accessed May 26, 2018. http://www.gov.me/biblioteka/izvjestaji?pagerIndex=24

———. 2016a. “Akcioni plan za poglavlje 23. pravosuđe i temeljna prava—polugodišnji izvještaj jul—decembar 2015.” http://www.gov.me/biblioteka/izvjestaji?pagerIndex=21

———. 2016b. “Akcioni plan za poglavlje 23. pravosuđe i temeljna prava—polugodišnji izvještaj—januar—jun 2016.” Accessed April 17, 2018. http://www.gov.me/biblioteka/izvjestaji?pagerIndex=15

———. 2017. “Akcioni plan za poglavlje 23. pravosuđe i temeljna prava—polugodišnji izvještaj—jul—decembar 2016.” Accessed April 17, 2018. http://www.eu.me/mn/23/23-dokumenti

SECONDARY SOURCES

Ahram, I. Ariel and Paul J. Goode. 2016. “Researching Authoritarianism in the Discipline of Democracy.” *Social Science Quarterly* (97) 4: 834–49.

Anastasakis, Othon. 2008. “The EU’s Political Conditionality in the Western Balkans: Towards a More Pragmatic Approach.” *Southeast European and Black Sea Studies* (8) 4: 365–77.

Anderson, Liz. 2019. “Vulnerabilities to Russian Influence in Montenegro.” *Kremlin Watch Report. European Values: Protecting Freedom.* Accessed July 25, 2020. https://www.kremlinwatch.eu/userfiles/vulnerabilities-to-russian-influence-inmontenegro.pdf.

Appicciafuoco, Lara. 2010. “The Promotion of Rule of Law in the Western Balkans: The European Union Role.” *German Law Journal* (11) 7–8: 741–68.

Aron, Leon. 2016. “Drivers of Putin’s Foreign Policy.” *American Enterprise Institute for Public Policy Research.* (June): 1–6. Accessed July 7, 2020. https://www.jstor.org/stable/resrep03253?seq=1#metadata_info_tab_contents.

Balkan Insight (BIRN). 2013. “Montenegro Probes Alleged Ruling Party Corruption.” Accessed August 23, 2020. https://balkaninsight.com/2013/06/03/montenegro-launches-probe-into-the-audio-recording-affair/

Barkin, Noah and Aleksandar Vasovic. 2018. “Chinese ‘Highway to Nowhere’ Haunts Montenegro.” *Reuters.* Accessed August 13, 2020. https://www.reuters.com/article/us-china-silkroad-europe-montenegro-insi-idUSKBN1K60QX

Bastian, Jens. 2019. “The Embrace between Russian Bear and Panda Bear an Emerging Sino-Russian Axis.” *ELIAMEP.* Accessed February 23, 2020. https://www.eliamep.gr/wp-content/uploads/2019/06/WORKING-PAPER-_Jens-Bastian_Revised_18-June-2019-Eliamep-108_2019-converted.pdf

Bechev, Dimitar. 2006. "Carrots, Sticks and Norms: The EU and Regional Cooperation in Southeast Europe." *Journal of Southern Europe and the Balkans* (8) 1: 27–43.

———. 2011. *Constructing South East Europe: The Politics of Balkan Regional Cooperation*. Basingstoke: Palgrave Macmillan.

———. 2017. *Rival Power: Russia's Influence in Southeast Europe*. Cornwall: Yale University Press.

———. 2018. "Understanding Russia's Influence in the Western Balkans." *Hybrid CoE* (September): 1–8. Accessed August 1, 2020. https://www.hybridcoe.fi/wp-content/uploads/2018/10/Strategic-Analysis-2018–9-Beshev-.pdf

Bechev, Dmitar, Filip Ejdus and Dane Taleski. 2015. "Culture of Regional Cooperation in Southeast." *BiEPAG*, Policy Brief (August): 3–35.

Belloni, Roberto. 2008. "European Integration and the Western Balkans: Lessons, Prospects and Obstacles." *Journal of Balkan and Near Eastern Studies* (11) 3: 313–31.

———. 2016. "The European Union Blowback? Euroscepticism and Its Consequences in the Western Balkans." *Journal of Intervention and State Building* (10) 4: 530–47.

Benner, Thorsten, Jan Gaspers, Mareike Ohlberg, Lucrezia Poggetti and Kristin Shi-Kupfer. 2018. *Authoritarian Advance. Responding to China's Growing Political Influence in Europe*. Berlin: GPPI-MERICS. Accessed July 21, 2020. https://merics.org/sites/default/files/202004/GPPi_MERICS_Authoritarian_Advance_2018_1.pdf

Bieber, Florian. 2011. "Building Impossible States? State Building Strategies and EU Membership in the Western Balkans." *Europe-Asia Studies* (63) 10: 1783–800.

———. 2020. *The Rise of Authoritarianism in the Western Balkans*. Cham: Palgrave Macmillan.

Bieber, Florian and Nikolaos Tzifakis, ed. 2019. *The Western Balkans in the World: Linkages and Relations with Non-Western Countries*. Oxon: Routledge.

BiEPAG. 2015. "Western Balkans and the EU: Beyond the Autopilot Mode." *BiEPAG*, Policy Brief: 3–16.

———. 2016. "EU Enlargement in the Western Balkans in a Time of Uncertainty." *BiEPAG*, Policy Brief (September): 3–12.

———. 2017. "The Crisis of Democracy in the Western Balkans: Authoritarianism and Stabilitocracy." *BiEPAG*, Policy Brief (March): 3–15.

Bojicic-Dzelilovic, Vesna, James Ker-Lindsay and Denisa Kostovicova. 2013. *Civil Society and Transitions in the Western Balkans*. Basingstoke: Palgrave Macmillan.

Börzel, Tanja. 2011. "When Europeanization Hits Limited Statehood. The Western Balkans as a Test Case for the Transformative Power of Europe." *The Freie Universität Berlin* (30) September: 3–15.

———. 2016. "From EU Governance of Crisis to Crisis of EU Governance: Regulatory Failure, Redistributive Conflict and Eurosceptic Publics." *Journal of Common Market Studies* (54): 8–26.

Börzel, Tanja and Sonja Grimm. 2018. "Building Good (Enough) Governance in Post Conflict Societies & Areas of Limited Statehood: The European Union & the Western Balkans." *The Journal of American Academy of Arts & Science* (147) 1: 116–25.

Börzel, Tanja and Thomas Risse. 2012. "When Europeanisation Meets Diffusion: Exploring New Territory." *West European Politics* (35) 1: 192–204.

Braun, Aurel 1997. "Russian Policy towards Central Europe and the Balkans." In *The Foreign Policy of the Russian Federation*, edited by Kanet, E. Roger and Alexander V. Kozhemiakin. Basingstoke, Hampshire and London: Macmillan Press Ltd.

Burchill, Scott, ed. 2005. *Theories of International Relations*. Basingstoke, NY: Palgrave Macmillan.

Burnham, Peter, Karin Gillard Lutz and Wyn Grant, ed. 2008. *Research Methods in Politics*. New York: Palgrave MacMillan.

Bžežinski, Zbinjev. 2001. *Velika šakovska tabla*. Podgorica: CID.

Cebelis, Džordž. 2016. *Veto igrači: Kako rade političke institucije*. Beograd: Službeni Glasnik.

Centar za Gradansko obrazovanje (CGO). 2019. *Prvih sedam godina crnogorskih pregovora sa EU*. Podgorica: CGO: 3–22.

Centar za monitoring (CeMI). 2010. *Reforma anti-korupcjskih institucija u Crnoj Gori*. Podgorica: CeMI: 5–54.

———. 2011. *Analiza efekata anti-korupcijskih politika u Crnoj Gori o prijedlozi za njihovo unaprijedjenje*. Podgorica: CeMI: 7–58.

———. 2013. *Administrativna istraga u borbi protiv korupcije*. Podgorica: CeMI.

———. 2014. *Dvodisnji izvjestaj o sprovodjenju antikorupcijskih politika u Crnoj Gori*. Podgorica: CeMI: 5–59.

Centar za monitoring (CeMI) and Human Rights Action Montenegro (HRA). Survey. 2016. *Stavovi gradjana o pravosudnom sistemu u Crnoj Gori*. Podgorica: CeMI and HRA.

———. 2017. *Ka efikasnosti pravosudja—unapredjenje razvoja profesija u vezi crnogorskog pravosudja*. Podgorica: CeMI and HRA.

Center for Democracy and Human Rights (CEDEM). 2012. *Nezavisno i nepristrasno pravosudje—izazovi i prepreke*. CEDEM: 3–19.

———. 2019. "Političko javno mnjenje Crne Gore." *CEDEM* (December): 18. Accessed April 15, 2018. http://www.cedem.me/me/programi/istraivanja-javnog-mnjenja/politiko-javno-mnjenje.

Center for the Study of Democracy (CSD). 2018a. "Assessing Russia's Economic Footprint in Montenegro." *CSD*, Policy Brief no. 73. Accessed August 16, 2020. https://csd.bg/publications/publication/policy-brief-no-73-assessing-russias-economic-footprint-in-montenegro/

———. 2018b. *Examining the Debt Implications of the Belt and Road Initiative from a Policy Perspective*. Washington, DC: Center for Global Development. Accessed April 22, 2020. https://www.cgdev.org/sites/default/files/examining-debt-implications-belt-and-road-initiative-policy-perspective.pdf

Čermak, Petr. 2019. "The Stabilization and Association Process as a Strategic Framework for the Europeanization of the Western Balkans." In *Balkanizing Europeanization: Fight against Corruption and Regional Relation in the Western Balkans*, edited by Vučković, Vladimir and Vladimir Đorđević. Berlin: Peter Lang.

Conley, A. Heather and Matthew Melino. 2019. "Russian Influence in Montenegro: The Weaponization and Exploitation of History, Religion and Economics." *Center for Strategic & International Studies* (May): 1–5.

Dallara, Christina. 2014. *Democracy and Judicial Reforms in South-East Europe: Between the EU and the Legacies of the Past.* New York, London: Springer.

DAN. 2014. "Afera Snimak—Kupovina glasova." Accessed August 23, 2020. https://www.youtube.com/watch?v=0brKMe9j4UI

DeBardeleben, Joan, ed. 2008. *The Boundaries of EU Enlargement: Finding a Place for Neighbours.* Basingstoke, Hampshire: Palgrave Macmillan.

Delegation of the European Union to Montenegro. 2020a. "The European Union in Montenegro." Accessed April 18, 2020. http://www.delmne.ec.europa.eu/code/navigate.php?Id=56

Delegation of the European Union to Montenegro. 2018b. "European Commission President Jean-Claude Juncker visits Montenegro." Accessed April 14, 2018. http://www.delmne.ec.europa.eu/code/navigate.php?Id=3991

Democracy Index. 2019. "2019 Rankings." Accessed August 2, 2020. https://www.eiu.com/topic/democracy-index

Denmark, Abraham M. and James Mulvenon. 2010. *Contested Commons: The Future of American Power in a Multipolar World.* Center for a New American Security.

Dimitrov, Nikola, Marika Djolai and Natasha Wunsch. 2015. "Removing Obstacles to EU Accession: Bilateral Disputes in the Western Balkans." *BiEPAG*, Policy Brief (August): 3–17.

Djolai, Marika and Zoran Nechev. 2018. "Bilateral Disputes Conundrum: Accepting the Past and Finding Solutions for the Western Balkans." *BiEPAG*, Policy Brief (April): 3–17.

Dolenec, Danijela. 2013. *Democratic Institutions and Authoritarian Rule in Southeast Europe*. Colchester: ECPR Press.

Donno, Danijela. 2013. "Elections and Democratization in Authoritarian Regimes." *American Journal of Political Science* (57) 3: 703–16.

Duffield, Mark R. 2001. *Global Governance and the New Wars: The Merging of Development and Security*. London and New York: Zed Books.

Đurović, Gordana. 2012. *Evropska unija Crna Gora: Politika proširenja*. Podgorica: Univerzitet Crne Gore—Ekonomski fakultet.

———. 2016. *Evropska unija i Crna Gora*. Podgorica: EU Info Centar.

Džankić, Jelena. 2014a. "Reconstructing the Meaning of Being 'Montenegrin.'" *Slavic Review* (73) 2: 356–71.

———. 2014b. "Citizenship between the 'Image of the Nation' and the 'Image of Politics': The Case of Montenegro." *Southeast European and Black Sea Studies* (14): 43–64.

———. 2018. "Capturing Contested States: Structural Mechanisms of Power Reproduction in Bosnia and Herzegovina, Macedonia and Montenegro." *Southeastern Europe* (42) 1: 83–106.

Džankić, Jelena and Soeren Keil. 2017. "State-Sponsored Populism and the Rise of Populist Governance: The Case of Montenegro." *Journal of Balkan and Near Eastern Studies* (19) 4: 403–18.

Džankić, Jelena and Soeren Keil and Marko Kmezić. 2019. *The Europeanization of the Western Balkans: A Failure of EU Conditionality?* Cham: Palgrave Macmillan.

Dzihic, Vedran and Angela Wieser. 2008. "The Crisis of Expectations—Europeanisation as 'Acquis Démocratique' and Its Limits. The Case of Bosnia-Herzegovina and Serbia." *L'Europe en formation* (349–350): 81–98.

Elbasani, Arolda. 2008. "EU Enlargement in the Western Balkans: Strategies of Borrowing and Inventing." *Journal of Southern Europe and the Balkans* (10) 3: 193–307.

———. ed. 2013. *European Integration and Transformation in the Western Balkans: Europeanization or Business as Usual?* New York: Routledge.

———. 2019. "Untangling Europeanization, Compliance and Reform: The Missing Link of Domestic Resistance and Accountability." In *Balkanizing Europeanization: Fight against Corruption and Regional Relation in the Western Balkans*, edited by Vučković, Vladimir and Vladimir Đorđević. Berlin: Peter Lang.

Elbasani, Arolda and Senada Šelo Šabić. 2018. "Rule of Law and Democratic Accountability in the Course of EU Enlargement." *Journal of European Public Policy* (25) 9: 1317–35.

European Western Balkans. 2017. "Bechev: Russia is Playing a 'Spoiler' in Western Balkans." Accessed April 16, 2018. https://europeanwesternbalkans.com/2017/11/28/ewb-interview-bechev-russia-playing-spoiler-western-balkans/

Fabrykant, Marharyta and Vladimir Magun. 2019. "Dynamics of National Pride Attitudes in Post-Soviet Russia, 1996–2015." *Nationalities Papers* (47) 1: 20–37.

FOS Media. 2017. "Nakon zajednickog obilaska ocjenjeno: Autoput simbol prijateljstva." Accessed July 19, 2020. https://fosmedia.me/infos/ekonomija/nakon-zajednickog-obilaska-ocijenjeno-autoput-simbol-prijateljstva-cg-i-kine-foto

———. 2019. "Za prvu fazu petlje Smokovac 30.5 miliona eura." Accessed July 13, 2020. https://fosmedia.me/infos/ekonomija/za-prvu-fazu-petlje-smokovac-305-miliona-eura

Freedom House. 2017. "Nations in Transit 2017—Montenegro." Accessed August 24, 2020. https://www.ecoi.net/en/document/1428858.html

———. 2018. "Montenegro." Accessed August 6, 2020. https://freedomhouse.org/country/montenegro/freedom-world/2018

———. 2020. "Nations in Transit 2020: Dropping the Democratic Facade." Accessed August 2, 2020. https://freedomhouse.org/sites/default/files/2020–04/05062020_FH_NIT2020_vfinal.pdf

Freyburg, Tina and Solveig Richter. 2010. "National Identity Matters: The Limited Impact of EU Political Conditionality in the Western Balkans." *Journal of European Public Policy* (17) 2: 263–76.

Fukuyama, Francis. 1992. *The End of the History and the Last Man.* New York: Macmillan.

Fuše, Mišel. 2009. *Evropska unija pola veka kasnije: stanje i scenariji obnove.* Beograd: Službeni glasnik.

Gadzo, Mersiha. 2019. "Russian Spies Found Guilty of Montenegro Coup Attempt." *Aljazeera.* Accessed June 22, 2020. https://www.aljazeera.com/news/europe/2019/05/russian-spies-guilty-montenegro-coup-attempt-190509134918749.html

Galeotti, Mark. 2018. "Do the Western Balkans Face a Coming Russian Storm?" *European Council of Foreign Affairs* (April): 2–20.

Gateva, Eli. 2015. *European Union Enlargement Conditionality*. New York: Palgrave Macmillan.

Gerring, John. 2006. *Case Study Research: Principles and Practices*. Cambridge: Cambridge University Press.

Ginsberg, H. Roy and Susan E. Penksa. 2012. *The European Union in Global Security: The Politics of Impact*. Basingstoke: Palgrave Macmillan.

Grabbe, Heather. 2006. *The EU's Transformative Power—Europeanization through Conditionality in Central and Eastern Europe*. New York: Palgrave Macmillan.

Grgić, Mladen. 2017. "Chinese Infrastructural Investments in the Balkans: Political Implication of the Highway Project in Montenegro." *Territory, Politics, Governance* (7) 1: 42–60.

Grimm, Sonja and Okka Lou Mathis. 2018. "Democratization Via Aid? The European Union's Democracy Promotion in the Western Balkans 1994–2010." *European Union Politics* (19) 1: 163–84.

Hill, H. William. 2018. *No Place for Russia: European Security Institutions since 1989*. New York: Columbia University Press.

Horvath, Robert. 2014. "Putin's Preventive Counter-Revolution: Post-Soviet Authoritarianism and the Spectre of Velvet Revolution." *Europe-Asia Studies* (63) 1: 1–25.

House of Lords of the United Kingdom. 2018. "The UK and the Future of the Western Balkans." *Select Committee of International Relations*. Accessed April 17, 2018. https://publications.parliament.uk/pa/ld201719/ldselect/ldintrel/53/53.pdf

Hsiu-Fang, Hseih and Sarrah E. Shannon. 2005. *Three Approaches to Qualitative Content Analysis*. SAGE: 1279–80.

Hughes, James, Gwedolyn Sasse and Claire Gordon. 2004. *Europeanization and Regionalization in the EU's Enlargement to Central and Eastern Europe: The Myth of Conditionality*. Hampshire: Palgrave MacMillan.

Human Rights Action Montenegro (HRA). 2009. *Analiza reforme izbora sudija u Crnoj Gori 2007–2008*. Podgorica: HRA.

———. 2012. *Analiza rada Sudskog Savjeta 2008–2012*. Podgorica: HRA.

———. 2013. *Analiza rada Sudskog Savjeta 2008–2013*. Podgorica: HRA.

Human Rights Action Montenegro (HRA) and Centar za monitoring (CeMI). 2015a. *Izvještaj o realizaciji Strategije reforme pravosudja 2007–2012*. Podgorica: HRA and CeMI.

———. 2015b. *Izvještaj o realizaciji Strategije reforme pravosudja 2014–2018 u periodu 2014–2016*. Podgorica: HRA and CeMI.

Huntington, P. Samuel. 2004. "The Lonely Superpower." *Council on Foreign Relations*.

Institut Alternativa (IA) and Centar za Gradansko obrazovanje (CGO) and Centar za razvoj nevladinih organizacija (CRNVO) and Centar za monitoring (CeMI). 2018. *Crna Gora: Izmedu lidera i simulatora reformi*. Podgorica: IA and CGO and CRNVO and CeMI (March): 2–12.

International Monetary Fund (IMF). 2018. "Montenegro: 2018 Article IV Consultation-Press Release and Staff Report." Accessed May 11, 2020. https://www.imf.org/en/Publications/CR/Issues/2018/05/21/Montenegro-2018-Article-IV-Consultation-Press-Release-and-Staff-Report-45886

Jenne, K. Erin and Florian Bieber. 2014. "Situational Nationalism: Nation-building in the Balkans, Subversive Institutions and the Montenegrin Paradox." *Ethnopolitics* (13) 5: 431–60.

Juncos, E. Ana. 2018. "The European Union and the Western Balkans: Enlargement as a Security Strategy." In *EU Security Strategies: Expending the EU System of Security Governance*, edited by Economides, Spyros and James Sperling. New York: Routledge.

Kavalski, Emilian. 2019. "China in Central and Eastern Europe: The Unintended Effects of Identity Narratives." *Asia Europe Journal* (17) 4: 403–19.

Keil, Soeren. 2013. "Europeanization, State-Building and Democratization in the Western Balkans." *Nationalities Papers* (41) 3: 343–50.

———. 2018. "The Business of State Capture and Rise of Authoritarianism in Kosovo, Macedonia, Montenegro and Serbia." *Southeastern Europe* (42) 1: 59–82.

Keil, Soeren and Bernhard Stahl, ed. 2014. *The Foreign Policies of Post-Yugoslav States: From Yugoslavia to Europe*. Basingstoke, Hampshire: Palgrave MacMillan.

Keil, Soeren and Zeynep Arkan, ed. 2015. *The EU and Member States Building: European Foreign Policy in the Western Balkans*. New York: Routledge.

Kisindžer, Henri. 2015. *Svetski poredak*. Podgorica: CID.

Kmezić, Marko. 2017. *EU Rule of Law Promotion: Judiciary Reform in the Western Balkans*. London and New York: Routledge.

———. 2020. "Rule of Law and Democracy in the Western Balkans: Addressing the Gap Between Policies and Practice." *Southeast European and Black Sea Studies* (20) 1: 183–98.

Kmezić, Marko and Florian Bieber. 2017. *The Crisis of Democracy in the Western Balkans. An Autonomy of Stabilitocracy and the Limits of EU Democracy Promotion*. BiEPAG, Policy Study

Komar, Olivera and Slaven Živković. 2016. "Montenegro: A Democracy Without Alternations." *East European Politics and Societies* (30) 4: 785–04.

Kovačević, Milica. 2014. *Zakonito i transparentno koriscenje javnih resursa: jedan od preduslova za izgradnju povjerenja u izbore*. Podgorica: CDT.

Krauthammer, Charles. 1990. "The Unipolar Moment." *Foreign Affairs* (70) 1: 23–33.

Lane, David. 2007. "Post-Communist States and the European Union." *Journal of Communist Studies and Transition Politics* (23) 4: 461–77.

Laursen, Finn, ed. 2013. *EU Enlargement—Current Challenges and Strategic Choices*. Brussels: P.I.E. Peter Lang.

Lavrič, Miran and Florian Bieber. 2020. "Shift in Support for Authoritarianism and Democracy in the Western Balkans." *Problems of Post-Communism*: 1–9.

Layne, Christopher. 1993. "Why New Great Power Will Rise." *International Security* (17) 4: 5–51.

Levinsky, Steven and Lucan A. Way. 2010. *Competitive Authoritarianism: Hybrid Regimes after the Cold War*. Cambridge: Cambridge University Press.

Little, Richard. 2007. *The Balance of Power in International Relations: Metaphors, Myths, and Models*. New York: Cambridge University Press.

MANS. 2009a. *Korupcija ili EU integracije II*. Podgorica: MANS, Accessed March 3, 2018. http://www.mans.co.me/korupcija-ili-eu-integracije-2/

———. 2009b. *Studija slučaja Zavala*. Podgorica: MANS. Accessed 16 August 2020. https://www.mans.co.me/studija-slucaja-zavala/

———. 2017. *Izvještaj o sprovođenju Akcionog plana za Poglavlje 23*. Podgorica: MANS.

———. 2018. *Monitoring izvještaj: Pravođe i borba protiv korupcije*. Podgorica: MANS.

———. 2019. *Monitoring izvještaj 2: Pravođe i borba protiv korupcije*. Podgorica: MANS.

Marsh, David and Gerry Stoker, ed. 2010. *Theory and Methods in Political Science*. New York: Palgrave Macmillan.

Mauer, Leopold. 2008. "Montenegro Regional EU Integrational Leader." Accessed September 6, 2008. https://www.b92.net/eng/news/region.php?yyyy=2008&mm=09&dd=06&nav_id=53276

Mearsheimer, John. 2001. *The Tragedy of Great Power Politics*. New York: W.W. Norton & Company, Inc.

———. 2018. *The Great Delusion: Liberal Dreams and International Realities*. New Haven: Yale University Press.

Memeti, Ardit. 2014. "Rule of Law through Judicial Reform: A Key to the EU Accession of the Western Balkans." *Contemporary Southeastern Europe* (1): 58–67.

Mendelski, Martin. 2015. "The EU's Pathological Power: The Failure of External Rule of Law Promotion in South Eastern Europe." *Southeastern Europe* (39): 318–46.

Milosavljević, Slavomir and Ivan Radosavljević, ed. 2006. *Osnovi metodologije političkih nauka*. Beograd: Službeni glasnik.

Ministarstvo vanjskih poslova i evropskih integracija (MVPEI). 2013a. "Zapadnobalkanska šestorka +2." *Diplomarius broj 1*. Accessed May 5, 2018. http://www.mvp.gov.me/Diplomarius/

Miščević, Tanja. 2009. *Pridruživanje Evropskoj Uniji*. Beograd: Službeni glasnik.

Mocht'ak, Michal. 2015. "Democratization and Electoral Violence in Post-Communism. A Study of Montenegro." *Southeast European and Black Sea Studies* (15) 1: 111.

Monitor. 2015. "Vanja Ćalovic: Izvršna direktorka MANS: A: Režim je zabrinut." Accessed August 23, 2020. https://www.monitor.co.me/vanja-alovi-izvrna-direktorica-mans-a-reim-je-zabrinut/

———. 2019. "Kuda nas vodi autoput: 100 miliona izgubljeno pokraj druma." Accessed May 17, 2020. https://www.monitor.co.me/kuda-nas-vodi-autoput-100-miliona-izgubljeno-pokraj-druma/

Morrison, Kenneth. 2009. *Montenegro: A Modern History*. London, New York: I.B. Tauris.

———. 2018. *Nationalism, Identity and Statehood in Post-Yugoslav Montenegro*. London, New York: Bloomsbury.

Mujanović, Jasmin. 2018. *Hunger and Fury: The Crisis of Democracy in the Balkans*. London: Hurst and Company.

Naj, Džozef. 2004. *Paradoks američke moći: zašto jedina svetska supersila ne može sama*. Beograd: BMG.

Noutcheva, Gergana. 2009. "Fake, Partial and Imposed Compliance: The Limits of the EU's Normative Power in the Western Balkans." *Journal of European Public Policy* (16) 7: 1081.

Ofe, Klaus. 2016. *Evropa u zamci*. Beograd: Službeni glasnik.

Ostrom, Elinor. 1998. "A Behavioural Approach to the Rational Choice Theory of Collective Action." (92) 1: 1–22.

Ottaway, Marina. 2003. *Democracy Challenged: The Rise of Semi-Authoritarian Regimes*. Washington, DC: Carnegie Endowment for International Peace.

Pavlićević, Dragan. 2019. "Structural Power and the China-EU-Western Balkans Triangular Relations." *Asia Europe Journal* (17): 453–68.

Pavlović, Dušan. 2019. "When Do Neoliberal Economic Reforms Cause Democratic Decline? Evidence from the Post-Communist Southeast Europe." *Post-Communist Economies* (31) 1: 671–97.

Peral, Luis. 2009. *Global Security in Multipolar World*. Institute for Security Studies no 118.

Petrillo, Enza Roberta. 2013. "Russian Foreign Policy Towards the Balkans: Which Perspective?" *Instituto per gli studi di politica internazionale* (169) April: 1–7.

Petrovic, Milenko. 2013. *The Democratic Transition of Post-Communist Europe: In the Shadow of Communist Differences and Uneven Europeanization*. Basingstoke: Palgrave Macmillan.

Pollak, A. Mark. "Rational Choice and EU Politics." *Arena working Paper No. 12*: 32–55.

Pridham, Geoffrey. 2005. *Designing Democracy: EU Enlargement and Regime Change in Post-Communist Europe*. New York: Palgrave Macmillan.

Radeljić, Branislav, ed. 2013. *Europe and the Post-Yugoslav Space*. Surrey: Ashgate Publishing Limited.

———. 2012. *Europe and the Collapse of Yugoslavia: The Role of Non-State Actors and European Diplomacy*. London, New York: I.B. Tauris.

———. 2017a. "Assessing the Politics of Fear and Power in Contemporary Russia." *Europe-Asia Studies* (69) 8: 1310–316.

———. 2017b. "Russian's Involvement in The Kosovo Case: Defending Serbian Interests or Security Its Own Influence in Europe?" *Region: Regional Studies of Russia, Eastern Europe, and Central Asia* (6) 2: 273–300.

Radeljić, Branislav and Vladimir Đorđević. 2020. "Clientelism and the Abuse of Power in the Western Balkans." *Journal of Balkan and Near Eastern Studies*: 1–17.

Radio Slobodna Evropa. 2009. "Predizborne zloupotrebe državnih resursa." Accessed August 23, 2020. https://www.slobodnaevropa.org/a/crna_gora_izbori/1509738.html

———. 2013. "Transkripti otkrili: DPS zapošljavao kako bi dobio izbore." Accessed August 23, 2020. https://www.slobodnaevropa.org/a/transkripti-otkrili-dps-zaposljavao-kako-bi-dobio-izbore/24903362.html

———. 2015. "Slučaj 'Košljun': Šest godina za preprodaju opštinske zemlje." Accessed August 23, 2020. https://www.slobodnaevropa.org/a/slucaj-kosljun-sest-godina-za-preprodaju-opstins-zemlje/27241246.html

———. 2016. "Marovic priznao prevare i zloupotrebe, presuda za tri dana." Accessed August 23, 2020. https://www.slobodnaevropa.org/a/marovic-krivica-priznanje/27959714.html

Ramet, Sabrina. 1999. *Balkan Babel.* Boulder: Westview Press.

Renner, Stephan and Florian Trauner. 2009. "Creeping EU Membership in South-east Europe: The Dynamics of EU Rule Transfer to the Western Balkans." *Journal of European Integration* (31) 4: 449–65.

Rodrigues, Maria Joao and Eleni Xiarchogiannopoulou, ed. 2014. *The Eurozone Crisis and the Transformation of EU Governance: Internal and External Implications.* Furnham: Ashgate.

RTCG. 2014. "Rakčević: Ovakav autoput je poguban." Accessed August 23, 2020. http://www.rtcg.me/vijesti/ekonomija/73048/rakcevic-ovakav-autoput-poguban.html

———. 2018. "Crna Gora spremna za nova ulaganja." Accessed May 11, 2020. http://www.rtcg.me/vijesti/ekonomija/218424/crna-gora-spremna-za-nova-ulaganja.html

Salgado, Rosa Sanchez. 2014. *Europeanizing Civil Society: How the EU shapes Civil Society Organizations.* Basingstoke, Hampshire: Palgrave Macmillan.

Samardžić, Slobodan. 2016. *Evropska unija: sistem u krizi—sa studijom slučaja o odnosima Srbije i EU.* Sremski Karlovci, Novi Sad: Izdavačka knjižarnica Zorana Stojanovića.

Schimmelfennig, Frank, Stefan Engert and Heiko Knobel. 2006. *International Socialization in Europe: European Organization, Political Conditionality and Democratic Change.* Basingstoke: Palgrave Macmillan.

Schimmelfenning, Frank and Ulirch Sedelmeier, ed. 2005. *The Europeanization of Central and Eastern Europe.* Ithaca and London: Cornell University Press.

———. 2011. "Governance by Conditionality: EU Rule Transfer to Candidate Countries of Central and Eastern Europe." *Journal of European Public Policy* (11) 4: 661–79.

Schweiger, Christian and José Magone, ed. 2015. *The Effects of the Eurozone Sovereign Debt Crisis: Differentiated Integration between the Centre and the New Peripheries of the EU.* London, New York: Routledge.

Sedelmeier, Ulrich. 2011. "Europeanisation in New Member and Candidate States." *Living Reviews in European Governance* (6) 1: 7.

Šekularac, Ivana. 2017. "End of the Affair—Montenegro Jilts Russia by Joining NATO." *Reuters.* Accessed July 22, 2020. https://af.reuters.com/article/worldNews/idAFKBN18I0VS

Strelkov, Alexender. 2016. "The EU and Rule of Law Promotion in Western Balkans—A New Role for Candidate States' Parliaments." *East European Politics* (32) 4: 505–24.

Taydas, Zeynep and Cigdem Kentmen-Cin. 2017. "Who Is Afraid of EU Enlargement? A Multilevel Comparative Analysis." *Political Research Quarterly* (70) 3: 604–17.

Transparency International Index. 2019. "Corruption Perception Index." Accessed August 6, 2020. https://www.transparency.org/en/cpi/2019

Turcsányi, Richard Q. 2018. *Chinese Assertiveness in the South China Sea*. Cham: Springer.

TV Vijesti. 2019. "Autoput—put svile ili svilen gajtan." Accessed June 16, 2020. https://www.youtube.com/watch?v=_vRetVD0f2Q

Uljarević, Daliborka and Vladimir Vučković. 2014. "EU-28 Watch—Montenegro." *The Institute for European Politics* 10 (July): 1–7. Accessed August 2, 2020. http://eu-28watch.org/wp-content/uploads/sites/3/2015/12/EU28W10_MontenegroPDF.pdf

Vachudova, Milada Ana. 2005. *Europe Undivided: Democracy, Leverage, and Integration after Communism*. Oxford: Oxford University Press.

———. 2014. "EU Leverage and National Interest in the Balkans: The Puzzles of Enlargement Ten Years On." *Journal of Common Market Studies* (52) 1: 122–38.

Vangeli, Anastas. 2018. "Global China and Symbolic Power: The Case of 16 + 1 Cooperation." *Journal of Contemporary China* (27) 113: 674–87.

Vijesti. 2011. "DPS od ličnih donacija uknjižio 654.000 eura." Accessed August 23, 2020. http://www.vijesti.me/vijesti/dps-od-licnih-donacija-uknjizio-654000-eura-20411

———. 2013. "Audio snimak: DPS izborna strategija—jedan zaposlen, četiri glasa." Accessed August 23, 2020. https://www.vijesti.me/vijesti/politika/287286/audio-snimak-dps-izborna-strategija-jedan-zaposlen-cetiri-glasa

———. 2014. "Potpisan sporazum koji će dovesti do "konacnog početka radova" na autoput." Accessed July 17, 2020. https://www.vijesti.me/vijesti/ekonomija/245686/potpisan-sporazum-koji-ce-dovesti-do-konacnog-pocetka-radova-na-autoputu

———. 2015. "Vlada mogla da se zaštiti prilikom potpisivanja ugovora za autoput." Accessed July 23, 2020. https://www.vijesti.me/zabava/182630/vlada-mogla-da-se-zastiti-prilikom-potpisivanja-ugovora-za-autoput

———. 2018. "Kineze i domaće država častila 29 miliona eura." Accessed August 3, 2020. https://www.vijesti.me/vijesti/ekonomija/39398/kineze-i-domace-drzava-castila-29-miliona-eura

———. 2019. "Od Svetozara Marovica ni traga ni glasa." Accessed August 23, 2020. https://www.vijesti.me/vijesti/crna-hronika/409896/od-svetozara-marovica-ni-traga-ni-para

Vučković, Vladimir. 2016a. "The Europeanization of Political Parties in Montenegro." *Romanian Journal of European Affairs* (16) 3: 36–55.

Vučković, Vladimir and Boro Vučinić and Vladimir Đorđević. 2016b. "Partnership for a Secure Future: Montenegrin Road to NATO from 2006 to 2015." *The Journal of Slavic Military Studies* (9) 4: 602–25.

Vučković, Vladimir and Vladimir Đorđević, ed. 2019. *Balkanizing Europeanization: Fight against Corruption and Regional Relation in the Western Balkans*. Berlin: Peter Lang.

Weingast, Barry. 1998. "Political Institutions in Rational Choice Perspectives." In *A New Handbook of Political Science*, edited by Goodin E. Robert and Hans-Dieter Klingemann. Oxford: Oxford University Press: 167–79.

Wohlforth, William C. 2010. *Rethinking US Grand Strategy and Foreign Policy.* Seminar Series: Dartmouth College.

Wunsch, Natasha. 2018. *EU Enlargement and Civil Society in the Western Balkans: From Mobilization to Empowerment.* Cham: Palgrave Macmillan.

Zielonka, Jan. 2014. *Is the EU Doomed?* Cambridge: Polity Press.

Index

Italicized pages refer tables and pages followed by "n" refer to endnotes.

About the Author

Vladimir Vučković is a lecturer at the Department of International Relations and European Studies at the Faculty of Social Studies of Masaryk University in Brno, Czech Republic. He pursued his PhD in International Relations at Masaryk University where he specialized in Europeanization of the Western Balkans. His areas of interest span the studies of the European Union with a particular focus on EU enlargement policy and integration process and Western Balkan politics. His publications have appeared in the *Journal of Slavic Military Studies*, *Romanian Journal of European Affairs*, and *Europe-Asia Studies and Political Studies Review*, among others. He is the editor of the volume *Balkanizing Europeanization: Fight against Corruption and Regional Relations in the Western Balkans* (2019). He is the recipient of various awards and prizes including the Swedish Institute (SI) Scholarship for the Western Balkans for PhD studies (2017), Masaryk University Scholarship (2017), JoinEUscc Penta Scholarship Program (2014), Balassi Balint Scholarship Program (2013), among others.

www.ingramcontent.com/pod-product-compliance
Ingram Content Group UK Ltd.
Pitfield, Milton Keynes, MK11 3LW, UK
UKHW041841031026
15587UKWH00002B/935

9 781793 607751